The Real Wizard of Oz

The Real Wizard of Oz

THE LIFE AND TIMES OF
L. FRANK BAUM

Rebecca Loncraine

GOTHAM
BOOKS

92
Bau

GOTHAM BOOKS
Published by Penguin Group (USA) Inc.
375 Hudson Street, New York, New York 10014, U.S.A.
Penguin Group (Canada), 90 Eglinton Avenue East, Suite 700,
Toronto, Ontario M4P 2Y3, Canada
(a division of Pearson Penguin Canada Inc.);
Penguin Books Ltd, 80 Strand, London WC2R 0RL, England;
Penguin Ireland, 25 St Stephen's Green, Dublin 2, Ireland
(a division of Penguin Books Ltd);
Penguin Group (Australia), 250 Camberwell Road, Camberwell,
Victoria 3124, Australia (a division of Pearson Australia Group Pty Ltd);
Penguin Books India Pvt Ltd, 11 Community Centre,
Panchsheel Park, New Delhi—110 017, India;
Penguin Group (NZ), 67 Apollo Drive, Rosedale, North Shore 0632,
New Zealand (a division of Pearson New Zealand Ltd);
Penguin Books (South Africa) (Pty) Ltd, 24 Sturdee Avenue,
Rosebank, Johannesburg 2196, South Africa

Penguin Books Ltd, Registered Offices:
80 Strand, London WC2R 0RL, England

Published by Gotham Books, a member of Penguin Group (USA) Inc.

First printing, August 2009

1   3   5   7   9   10   8   6   4   2

Gotham Books and the skyscraper logo are trademarks of Penguin Group (USA) Inc.

LIBRARY OF CONGRESS CATALOGING-IN-PUBLICATION DATA
Loncraine, Rebecca, 1974–
The real Wizard of Oz: the life and times of L. Frank Baum / by Rebecca Loncraine.
p.   cm.
ISBN 978-1-592-40449-0 (hardcover)
1. Baum, L. Frank (Lyman Frank), 1856–1919.   2. Authors, American—20th century—Biography.
3. Storytellers—United States—Biography.   4. Baum, L. Frank (Lyman Frank),
1856–1919—Homes and haunts—United States.   5. Baum, L. Frank (Lyman Frank), 1856–1919.
Wizard of Oz.   6. Baum, L. Frank (Lyman Frank), 1856–1919—Criticism
and interpretation.   7. Children's stories, American—History and criticism.
8. Fantasy fiction, American—History and criticism.   I. Title.
PS3503. A923Z74   2009
813'.4—dc22
[B]   2009013708

Printed in the United States of America
Set in Adobe Garamond
Designed by Elke Sigal

While the author has made every effort to provide accurate telephone numbers and Internet addresses at the time of publication, neither the publisher nor the author assumes any responsibility for errors, or for changes that occur after publication. Further, the publisher does not have any control over and does not assume any responsibility for author or third-party Web sites or their content.

To Ben

Contents

Part III

CROSSING LAKE MICHIGAN, 1891 TO 1903

Part IV

LIVING BETWEEN LANDSCAPES, 1903 TO 1910

Part V

HOLLYWOOD, 1910 TO 1919

"In a utilitarian age, of all other times, it is a matter of grave importance that Fairy Tales should be respected."

—CHARLES DICKENS

"Stunt, dwarf, or destroy the imagination of a child and you have taken away its chances of success in life. Imagination transforms the commonplace into the great and creates the new out of the old."

—L. FRANK BAUM

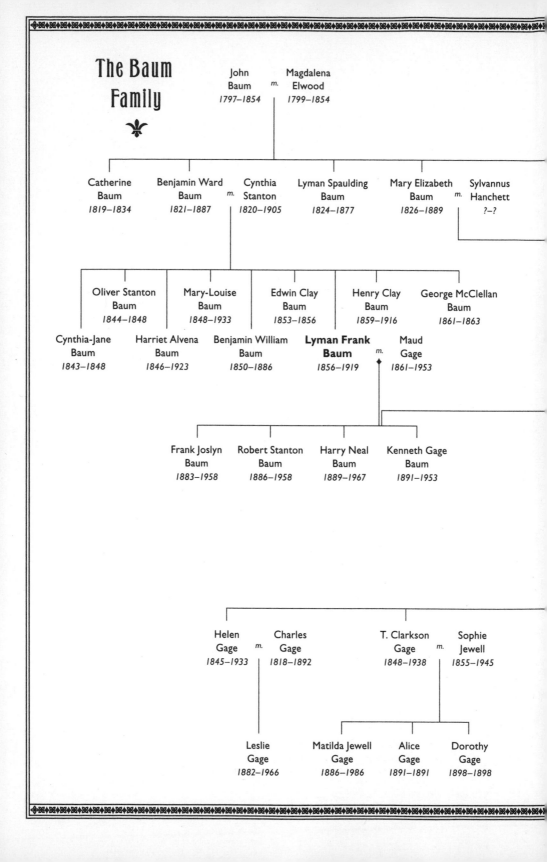

The Baum Family

❦

John Baum *1797–1854* m. Magdalena Elwood *1799–1854*

Catherine Baum *1819–1834*

Benjamin Ward Baum *1821–1887* m. Cynthia Stanton *1820–1905*

Lyman Spaulding Baum *1824–1877*

Mary Elizabeth Baum *1826–1889* m. Sylvannus Hanchett *?–?*

Oliver Stanton Baum *1844–1848*

Mary-Louise Baum *1848–1933*

Edwin Clay Baum *1853–1856*

Henry Clay Baum *1859–1916*

George McClellan Baum *1861–1863*

Cynthia-Jane Baum *1843–1848*

Harriet Alvena Baum *1846–1923*

Benjamin William Baum *1850–1886*

Lyman Frank Baum *1856–1919* m. Maud Gage *1861–1953*

Frank Joslyn Baum *1883–1958*

Robert Stanton Baum *1886–1958*

Harry Neal Baum *1889–1967*

Kenneth Gage Baum *1891–1953*

Helen Gage *1845–1933* m. Charles Gage *1818–1892*

T. Clarkson Gage *1848–1938* m. Sophie Jewell *1855–1945*

Leslie Gage *1882–1966*

Matilda Jewell Gage *1886–1986*

Alice Gage *1891–1891*

Dorothy Gage *1898–1898*

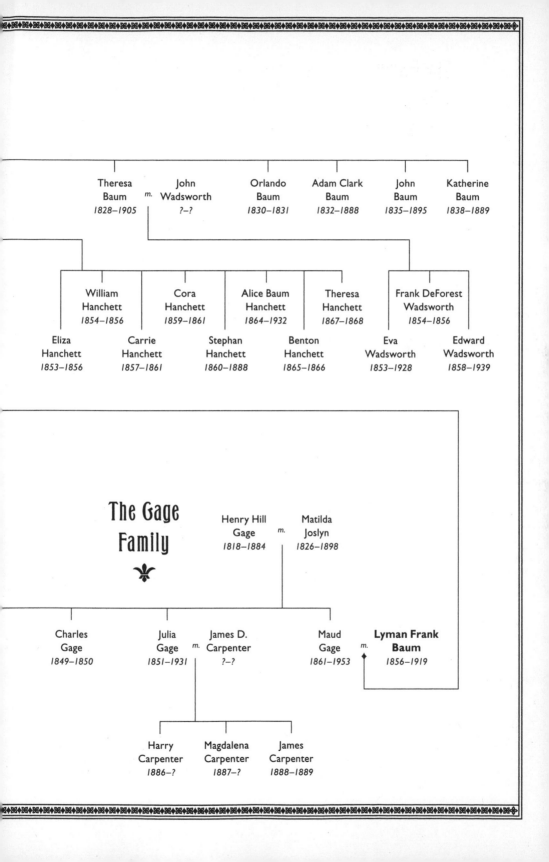

Theresa
Baum
1828–1905

m.

John
Wadsworth
?–?

Orlando
Baum
1830–1831

Adam Clark
Baum
1832–1888

John
Baum
1835–1895

Katherine
Baum
1838–1889

Eliza
Hanchett
1853–1856

William
Hanchett
1854–1856

Carrie
Hanchett
1857–1861

Cora
Hanchett
1859–1861

Stephan
Hanchett
1860–1888

Alice Baum
Hanchett
1864–1932

Benton
Hanchett
1865–1866

Theresa
Hanchett
1867–1868

Eva
Wadsworth
1853–1928

Frank DeForest
Wadsworth
1854–1856

Edward
Wadsworth
1858–1939

The Gage Family

❧

Henry Hill
Gage
1818–1884

m.

Matilda
Joslyn
1826–1898

Charles
Gage
1849–1850

Julia
Gage
1851–1931

m.

James D.
Carpenter
?–?

Maud
Gage
1861–1953

m.

**Lyman Frank
Baum**
1856–1919

Harry
Carpenter
1886–?

Magdalena
Carpenter
1887–?

James
Carpenter
1888–1889

Introduction

ON TELLING THE LIFE STORY OF A STORYTELLER

n my memory, there isn't a time before *The Wizard of Oz*. I still have my battered old copy of the book, which is illustrated with peculiar and unforgettable drawings. When I leaf through them now, as I did so often as a child, it's as though the pictures are a map or a pathway back to childhood itself. I can't remember a time before I had seen the 1939 MGM movie starring Judy Garland either. The original book and the Technicolor film are braided together in my memory, like Dorothy's long red hair. It's as though *The Wizard of Oz* has always been with me. I don't think I'm the only person who feels this way about the story.

The Wizard of Oz is so much a part of our culture that we take its existence for granted. The twisting tornado that carries Dorothy and her dog, Toto, from the arid Kansas prairie to the colorful Land of Oz, the clever brainless Scarecrow, the kind but heartless Tin Man, the brave cowardly Lion, the Wicked Witch of the West, the humbug Wizard, the yellow brick road, and the Emerald City have become iconic, highly emotive images, permanently at hand and ready to draw on at any relevant moment. This powerful story seems so old, so universal and alive, that it feels as if it must have always been there, at the bottom of our minds, rolling around like a shiny, colorful marble. It seems to have always existed, like our oldest folktales, including "Cinderella," "Snow White," "Jack and the Bean Stalk," "Bluebeard," and "Little Red Riding Hood," all stories without known originators. It's hard to imagine a time when *The Wizard of Oz* didn't exist, and it's hard to imagine that anybody ever brought the story into being; it seems authorless.

But *The Wizard of Oz* does in fact have an author. It originated in one man's mind; his name was L. Frank Baum and he lived in America between 1856 and 1919. He conjured the story out of his imagination between the spring of 1898 and fall of 1899, and it was first published as *The Wonderful Wizard of Oz* in 1900. Before Baum wrote the tale of Dorothy's journey from Kansas to Oz and back again, it didn't exist, and America had no modern fairy tale of its own.

Most people have heard of *The Wizard of Oz,* but few have heard of L. Frank Baum. This shows what a great story Baum wrote; he managed to create something that felt already ancient, weathered into such a perfect, archetypal shape that it seemed authorless from the start. But Baum's relationship with Oz also contributed to the sense that this tale had no author, because he himself didn't know where the story came from. Baum felt that he had simply *discovered* the Land of Oz rather than *invented* it. He thought he had merely channeled the story and that he was little more than the vessel in which the tale was delivered to twentieth-century America.

After he released *The Wonderful Wizard of Oz* in 1900, Baum was forced to serve the Land of Oz for the rest of his life. He became trapped inside it, forced to return there over and over again to retrieve more stories about the strange country and its remarkable inhabitants. He had created something so marvelous and universal, but also so unique and human, that it took over his life. Baum's relationship with his own imagination became increasingly peculiar, complex, and troubled after 1900: He didn't feel responsible for the many subsequent Oz stories he wrote, but they couldn't be "discovered" without him; he became trapped in the role of portal to Oz.

This book is a portrait of a man, his imagination, and his world. Researching Baum's life has made me acutely aware of the trickiness of retelling the biography of a talented storyteller. I've used all kinds of sources, including published Baum family memoirs, press reports on Baum's work, and interviews with Baum himself; all these sources are unreliable in different ways. We have to live with that. Baum's statements about himself and his writing are particularly suspect. He had a habit of making up tales about the origins of his stories to satisfy journalists; after telling these false anecdotes a few times, he might even have started to believe them himself. Baum's strength as a storyteller was born out of his inability to clearly distinguish the world of story from the world outside it. Stories, for him, were a deeper form of truth. Far from separating us from the reality of Baum's life, this labyrinthine, shadowy area brings us closer to it, to a more truthful picture of the imagination that brought Oz into being.

This portrait of Baum and his world is partly built out of an attention to the small scale, to the details of a life lived, such as the quality of light by which Baum wrote, the animal sounds that surrounded him as he wrote outdoors, the smells he grew up with, his favorite food, and the physical pains he suffered. But it's also built out of an attention to the wider, large-scale historical currents that shaped Baum. Historically, he lived through difficult and important times, through the brutal economic competition of the Gilded Age and the terrible suffering of the economic depression of the 1890s; his great story was in fact inspired by this national suffering. Baum's life was also bookended by two catastrophic wars, the American Civil War and the First World War; and he witnessed at close hand the tragic end of the wars between the U.S. government and the Native American tribes of the Great Plains. Baum saw America emerge from slavery and chaotic disunity to become a global military power.

This portrait also pays attention to the larger scale of the distinctive landscapes in which Baum lived. The book is structured chronologically, but it's broken into five geographical parts that reflect the five different landscapes Baum inhabited and moved through during his lifetime, and which had a profound influence on his imagination.

In trying to understand Baum's life and world, the contemporary reader is asked to enter an America with very different belief systems. For example, the vast majority of people living in the nineteenth century, Baum included, believed in ghosts; the spirits of the dead were living realities in this world. Many of these were the ghosts of dead children. Infant death was a widespread tragic reality visited on most families in the nineteenth century. Baum's life and the lives of all those around him were profoundly shaped by the deaths of children. We don't have to believe in ghosts to fully appreciate Baum's imagination, but we do have to accept that he and almost everybody around him did.

Baum's life spanned a period of dramatic change. His was an era of mind-boggling invention and consequent technological shock. He saw the discovery of oil in the United States and the development of the oil giants of the Gilded Age; he experienced the entrance of electricity into everyday life and the replacement of horses with oil-fueled machines. It's hard for the twenty-first-century reader to imagine how truly amazing, wonderful, frightening, and disorienting it was for someone of this era to be able to switch an electric light on and off, speak into a telephone, ride in a "horseless carriage," and, of all things, fly through the clouds. To comprehend Baum's world, we must try to suspend our familiarity with machines and electricity, and reenvision them as shocking and exciting novelties that transformed the way people understood their world, their bodies, and their minds.

Baum didn't write his great story until he was in his forties. But he couldn't have written it without everything that came before; he wrote his whole life into it. To understand how and why he wrote the story, we have to look back in detail at the years that came before, at what happened to Baum's family before he was born even, at everything that significantly shaped his mind as *The Wonderful Wizard of Oz* gestated over many years in the womb of his imagination.

The Real Wizard of Oz

"Characters, events, retrospectives shall be convey'd in gospels, trees, animals, waters, shall be convey'd, Death, the future, the invisible faith, shall all be convey'd."

—WALT WHITMAN,
"MEDIUMS," *Leaves of Grass*

"You must walk. It is a long journey, through a country that is sometimes pleasant and sometimes dark and terrible."

—L. FRANK BAUM,
The Wonderful Wizard of Oz

"The wind, in its greatest power, whirls."

—BLACK ELK,
Black Elk Speaks

Imagining October 9, 1899

 quick, cold wind swept across the vast and rippling waters of Lake Michigan, whose silver, mirrored surface reflected the fast-moving dark clouds above. The wind reached the shore, shouldered into the streets of Chicago, and picked up and whistled around the edge of a big wooden house on the corner of Humboldt Park Boulevard. It crept in through tiny cracks in the walls and through the hair-thin spaces where windowpanes met; it circled Frank Baum as he sat in his leather upholstered chair in his cluttered study. Wisps of his cigar smoke got caught up in the draft and swirled in gray and white spiraling patterns around his head before dispersing throughout the room. They pushed upstairs through the patterned rugs and pine floorboards to where Maud was asleep in her bed. The familiar smell of her husband's cigars mingled with her breath as she slept, telling her that he was still working.

By the glowing light of the kerosene lamp and the pulsating shadows it cast around the room, Baum tore a fresh piece of paper from his notebook and scribbled, "With This Pencil, I wrote the MS of The Emerald City." Then he dated it: October 9, 1899, and signed it, underlining "The Emerald City" with a strong, thick line. He knew that this moment, in the middle of his life (he was forty-three), needed to be marked; he had finally brought Dorothy home to Kansas by clicking the heels of her magic shoes together. He captured the moment by sticking what remained of the worn-down stub to the paper. This pencil would write nothing more.

Having signed his name, he returned, fully, to the room, to the golden light and the wind that shook the trees down the boulevard. He crept upstairs to bed, knowing absolutely that he had produced his best work, in his own words, his "most truthful tale." As he sank into sleep, slipping beneath the surface of the waking lake, he might have reflected on where the idea for this story had come from and where he had come from.

To find the source of Baum's famous story, which would later be retitled *The Wonderful Wizard of Oz*, it's necessary to travel east from Lake Michigan, 650 miles, crossing the St. Joseph River, moving through Indiana, Ohio, Pennsylvania, passing Lake Erie and the gigantic body of falling water at Niagara, and continuing on into the wooded valleys and lakelands of upstate New York, and finally to the shores of Oneida Lake. This was the world into which Baum was born forty-three years earlier, in 1856. This place had imprinted on him powerful memories, indentations, markings, and scars that had resurfaced in adulthood in this new tale, as though in making it up he had retold his own life story, transformed into a tale from a strange elsewhere.

Part I

IN THE PALM OF THE FINGER LAKES

1848 TO 1888

emlock, Canadice, Keuka, Seneca, Cayuga, Otisco, and Cazenovia. Sounding like a magic spell, these are the names of the Finger Lakes. The long, thin lakes spread out like the digits of an outstretched hand reaching across upstate New York. If the region above these liquid fingers is an open palm, the cities of Rochester and Syracuse are at either end of the lifeline that cuts across it. The Erie Canal, in fact, stretches between Rochester and Syracuse exactly where this imaginary lifeline creases through the geographical palm of the Finger Lakes.

In the spring of 1848, an old wooden farmhouse in the village of Hydesville, on the outskirts of Rochester, began to speak. Its language was a code of rapping, thumping, knocks, and scraping. After several sleepless nights of bravely searching the house by candlelight for the source of the persistent noises, the Fox family was exhausted. The frightened daughters, Kate, eleven, and Maggie, fourteen, were sleeping in their parents' bedroom. The sounds had become so loud that the children and their mother, Margaret, and father, John, could feel jarring vibrations coming through the floor and furniture to ripple through their bones.

On the night of March 31, the family went to bed early, hoping to catch up on some lost sleep. In the half-light, as they climbed into bed, the noises struck up once again, tapping and rapping sounds filling the house, echoing back and forth between the wooden walls. In a strange and courageous act of imitation, the two girls began to copy the odd sounds by snapping their fingers, as though they too should echo like the noises that surrounded them. Then, turning the tables, Kate suddenly challenged the "noisemaker." "Do as I do," she shouted, clapping her hands. The house, or the spirit trapped inside it, immediately responded with the same number of raps.

The rest of the family took their lead from Kate and addressed what they now assumed was a ghost. Margaret Fox asked the noisemaker to tap out the ages of her seven children. "Instantly," she said in the signed affidavit in which the details of the night's events were recorded, "each one of my children's ages was given correctly, pausing between them sufficiently long to individualize them." The youngest Fox child had died at age three, and the invisible presence left a longer pause before thumping out the final three raps. The spirit fell silent after announcing the Fox child who dwelled in the same murky region beyond life; as twilight melted into the darkness that evening, the boundary between the living and the dead became blurred.

John and Margaret Fox gathered their neighbors, and soon the house was filled with jostling bodies. They addressed the spirit, asking it to rap twice if the answer to a question was yes. One neighbor suggested establishing a code with the spirit, whereby someone slowly recited the letters of the alphabet, and the spirit rapped when it heard the letter it required. In this way, they discovered that the restless spirit was that of a thirty-one-year-old peddler who had been murdered in the house five years earlier, his throat cut with a knife and his body buried ten feet below the ground in the cellar. The spirit was also able to spell out his name, Charles B. Rosna.

Word spread that Margaret Fox's hair suddenly turned white that night, as though all the color had been sucked out of it.

The Fox girls were removed from the house. Kate was taken to their brother David's house in Auburn, Maggie to their sister Leah's in Rochester. Immediately the rapping sounds began to be heard in the two houses where the girls were staying. It became clear that this sudden outbreak of spirit activity wasn't simply the manifestation of a lone spirit trapped in the wooden house in Hydesville; it was the Fox sisters who had unleashed it. The children seemed to be mediums between the living and the dead.

On April Fool's Day, John Fox and some neighbors began digging up the cellar floor of the farmhouse in Hydesville, looking for some concrete evidence that the spirit was speaking the truth. At five feet down, they reached water and were unable to dig any farther. In the summer of 1848, the Foxes returned to the cellar to dig deeper into the ground. The five-foot hole was dug to ten feet, and there, packed in amongst the mud and grit, human teeth, bone, and hair were discovered. This unearthing didn't quite confirm the spirit's story that his whole body was buried there, but it didn't totally discredit it either. People gathered around Kate and Maggie Fox in a hall in Rochester to discuss the authenticity of the children's ability to conjure spirits and communicate with them in code. Three groups of citizens investigated the claims and all concluded that the sounds heard in dark rooms and creaking houses in the presence of the Fox sisters weren't produced by ventriloquism, machinery, or tricks. The Foxes' careers as the nineteenth century's first and most infamous spirit mediums had begun.

That summer of 1848, the border between the living and the dead seemed to have thinned in Hydesville, and fifty miles away along the Erie Canal, in a village near Syracuse, other children were edging toward that porous boundary. Cynthia and Benjamin Baum, who would become L. Frank Baum's mother and father in 1856, had four children at this time: Cynthia-Jane, age five; Oliver, four; Harriet, two; and Mary-Louise, a two-month-old baby. In early June, Cynthia-Jane came down with a fever. She began coughing and crying and her breathing became hoarse. Cynthia Baum would have frantically tried to balance nursing baby Mary-Louise with the different kind of nursing required for a very sick child. Mucus poured from Cynthia-Jane's nose, and her pulse raced.

In the mid-nineteenth century, diphtheria wasn't fully understood. It remained almost untreatable until the early twentieth century when an antitoxin was finally developed. People did know, however, that illness could be transferred between bodies in close proximity. The Baums must have tried to keep Cynthia-Jane away from the other children, but the bacteria that cause diphtheria can be spread in tiny droplets from coughs and sneezes. Sometime toward the end of June, Oliver began to show similar symptoms. The horrible rasping sound of a child with diphtheria struggling for breath was unbearable. Despite all attempts to save her, Cynthia-Jane died on June 27, 1848. The cause of death was given as "putrid throat." Cynthia-Jane's little dead body would have been washed and dressed in her best clothes, and her hair was likely washed and combed. It was common practice for corpses, even of children, to be put on display for distressed mourners to see. The small stiff body would probably have been laid out in an open coffin, small bouquets of flowers and herbs placed carefully in the pale hands and around the head.

And Oliver's condition worsened. It's almost impossible to imagine the turmoil Cynthia and Benjamin Baum must have felt in the days immediately after the death of their firstborn, as they reeled between grief for their dead daughter and desperate attempts to save Oliver. Thirteen days after Cynthia-Jane died, Oliver followed her.

During this time, diphtheria commonly struck children in ferocious waves across the population. There's evidence of an epidemic in New York State in 1848, and the Baums weren't the only family to lose children. The Lammerts, Meads, Fisks, Schoonmakers, Phillips, Taylors, and McGarrows all lost children under the age of five that summer. The distraught Baums buried their children in a small local cemetery, probably by a preacher all too familiar with the sight of grieving parents bent in pain over the graves of their infants.

These two dead children remained very important in the Baum family. Many years later, in 1877, Benjamin Baum bought a family plot in the grand Oakwood Cemetery on a hill overlooking Syracuse. Heavy stone blocks with the children's names chiseled in bold lettering were placed on the plot as memory markers if the small bodies weren't disinterred and reburied beneath them. These stone markers were the same size as those of other Baums who lived on into adulthood, whose bodies would eventually be placed beside them. There were plenty of other infant graves amid the clover and moss in the plots of Oakwood Cemetery, but they were rarely given equal status with those of other family members who lived on into old age. Cynthia-Jane and Oliver may have died in 1848, but they clearly lived on in the collective memory of the Baum family, continuing a kind of shadow life alongside their living siblings.

In mid-nineteenth-century America, at times up to forty percent of all deaths were of children under age five. The Baums had, until 1848, been lucky. All of their children had lived, and Cynthia-Jane had been nearly out of the most vulnerable age range when she was taken. Infancy was a time of acute vulnerability; like old age, early childhood was lived in intimate proximity to death.

But for the Baums and other families like them, this was an era in which the acute pain that all parents must feel at losing a child took on a new shading. In the eighteenth and early nineteenth centuries, most people had held God responsible for the high infant mortality rate. If God had freely given, so people believed, He could just as freely take away. There was nothing parents or anyone could do except bend to the mysterious will of God and seek his comfort in their grief. But by the mid-nineteenth century, advances in medicine had introduced a key element of human agency into the survival of children. Diseases were better understood and cures were being developed. People began to believe that they might be able to protect their infants. But in reality, access to sophisticated medical care still wasn't widespread enough to save children, and they continued to die.

Nevertheless, beliefs had shifted. Now that infant mortality wasn't God's will, it was believed to be the failure of doctors, of parents, and of mothers in particular to care for their children. "No one can for a moment believe," wrote the author of a popular nineteenth-century home medical guide, "that the excessive and increasing infant mortality among us, is part of the established order of nature, or the systematic arrangement of Divine Providence." Cynthia Baum clung to her Methodist religion, committing herself to a God who might bear some responsibility for the deaths of her children, or at least forgive her for failing to save them.

Many people also had to contend with old superstitions about infant mortality, brought to America by Europeans who had carried their folklore with them across the Atlantic. In the nineteenth century, many people still believed in fairies, but these creatures weren't the harmless little winged pixies we have come to think of as "fairies." They could be ugly and mean and were sometimes indistinguishable from ghosts. Some believed that infants and the unborn were vulnerable to baby-snatching fairies, which were imagined as the bitter and twisted souls of babies who had died or been stillborn, or of women who had died in childbirth.

The strange happenings in 1848 in the Fox house in Hydesville suggested that living children could communicate with the dead. Kate and Maggie Fox had discovered a talent that would shape not only the rest of their lives but the entire culture of the late nineteenth century. The sisters could communicate with the dead, and once their story spread, little girls and supernatural activity would be forever linked in the popular imagination, where ghosts and fairies had existed for generations.

Chapter 2

aum, Stanton, Hanchett, Brewster, Wadsworth, Crouse, and Stone. These are the names of some of the extended families that were tied together between lakes Onondaga and Oneida in upstate New York in the 1850s. Like a series of sailors' knots, these families were bound in different ways, through marriage, business partnerships, local politics, philanthropy, in shared diseases and medical treatment, and in religion. They were knotted in feuds as well as in friendship, and it would have taken more than a sailor's expertise to untangle them.

In October 1849, Cynthia became pregnant again. In 1850, she and Benjamin moved a day's carriage ride away from their old house to the village of Cazenovia. This was a break from a home identified with tragedy; the new baby would be born elsewhere. Cynthia's parents, her brothers, and their wives lived in New Woodstock, close to Cazenovia. This move brought Benjamin into closer contact with Cynthia's family, which was welcome after the awkward circumstances of their marriage eight years earlier. In 1842, Cynthia had chosen to marry Benjamin Baum against her father's wishes. Benjamin's intense, direct gaze and hard-set mouth were signs, like the creases on the palm of a hand, that he had a future beyond the confines of his then life as a barrel maker. Oliver Stanton, Cynthia's father, was a well-to-do farmer who wouldn't consent to his only daughter marrying such a lowly and landless man, so Cynthia abandoned her home on the farm and eloped with Benjamin. On the first Sunday after their marriage, they went to the local Methodist chapel, where Benjamin gave away his last pennies and prayed that he be offered the opportunity to make something more of himself.

By 1850, the lowly barrel maker hadn't risen all that far, but business plans were afoot and he was looking into buying land. In July 1850, in the sticky heat of summer, Cynthia gave birth to a son, whom they named Benjamin Jr.

Benjamin Baum Sr. was the eldest of a large family, which, in the following months would grow larger and tighten the complex family ties that already surrounded them. After a ferocious storm hit the area, and lightning struck a horse and a barber shop in Baldwinsville, they celebrated the marriage of Benjamin Baum's sister Mary to Silvannus Hanchett. The sprightly Mary had attended Syracuse Medical School. The announcement of her marriage in a medical journal made much of this novelty, describing Mary as an "intelligent and accomplished lady." She was one of only two women in her class, and when she graduated in 1852, she became one of the first female doctors in the United States. Mary and Silvannus set up a medical practice in the busy village of Chittenango, a few miles north of Cazenovia. Mary specialized in "all diseases peculiar to the female sex." Her parents, the Reverend John and Lany Baum, came to live with her in Chittenango.

In 1853, Benjamin Baum finalized the purchase of some land in Chittenango. Cynthia gave birth to another boy, whom they called Edwin, and she barely had time to recover before Benjamin moved his family to a modest wood-framed house on the edge of the village of Chittenango, on the cusp between the human settlement and the woods.

In the summer of 1854, the Reverend John Baum, Benjamin's father, died suddenly. This death may have turned the rest of the family's attention back to their roots and to the reverend's unique life. The Reverend John Baum was born into a farming family of prizewinning cheese makers in the Mohawk Valley in upstate New York in 1797. He married Magdalena Elwood (Lany) in 1818, and opened a general store. But in 1834, he experienced a spiritual crisis and transformation when his daughter Catherine died of tuberculosis of the bone. His devastation caused him to question his life, its meaning and direction. A week after Catherine's death, the day after her burial, John began a family record book. He wrote that he wanted the record to be kept "in memory of our well-beloved daughter Catherine whose virtues demand our highest respect of commemoration, and who is no more to be seen as she was yesterday interred in the burying ground . . . by the side of her dear brother Orlando who died about two and a half years ago—aged thirteen months and twenty six days." Now John Baum had buried two children. His fear for others led him to add, "I do hope that every member of our posterity will in early life prepare for death." Children were not safe; their souls must be directed toward God in preparation for death in childhood. This prompted questions. What was a child? What was childhood? Perhaps children were closer to God than to adults, no matter how tightly you held them. Perhaps parents shouldn't claim their children for this life too boldly; they might be taken back at any time.

John Baum's spiritual crisis, brought on by the death of his daughter, found expression in the religious revival taking place around him in upstate New York in the 1830s. The relatively settled, isolated rural communities of the area were seeking spiritual guidance, and the Methodist religion sought to provide it. An itinerant preacher could travel to those who were unable to reach a church or chapel, especially during bad weather, bringing the Lord with him on horseback. These traveling preachers became known as circuit riders. Each took on a circuit of isolated communities and would travel among them, preaching as he went. John Baum's circuit was probably the large triangle of land edged by the waters of Lake Ontario to the north and west, Oneida Lake to the south, and the Black River to the east. The Methodist preachers lived tough lives, on the move, driven forward by religious fervor. They traveled by horse (they were sometimes called saddlebag riders), with only a few belongings, the Bible, and a book of hymns. They would stop and preach anywhere they could, in a meetinghouse, a cabin, a courthouse, or even out in the open, in a clearing in the woods.

Fired up with the spirit, John Baum brought Bible stories to life in front of small crowds, who would sing hymns to work themselves into a new intimacy with God. Circuit rider revival meetings were famous for sending sinners into holy spasms and faints. The word of God was especially powerful when it hadn't been heard for a while. In a tub-thumping sermon in a shadow-dappled wood, a preacher would address the informal congregation, focusing on personal salvation and the cleansing of sins.

These preachers earned very little and were given food and shelter by the people they served. But not everybody was happy to have God's word brought back into their communities. Some felt they had escaped the fire and fury of the Lord, or thought such spirituality only stirred up more problems and questions. Best to leave well enough alone. Circuit riders were often attacked and beaten, robbed of what little they had, and turned away by people who had already turned away from God. Up until the late 1840s, few circuit riders lived beyond thirty years.

John Baum's circuit edged the Adirondack Mountains. In this northern region, the winters were extremely harsh, burying the land in deep snow and treacherous ice for months. Methodist circuit riders would brave all weathers, as suggested by the stormy-day proverb, "There's nothing out today but crows and Methodist preachers." It's hard not to imagine a crow's black feathers and a preacher's black coat flapping against the white landscape like animated shadows.

The Reverend Baum had to have been a hardy man to survive his circuit, and his eldest son revered him. Benjamin Baum was thirteen when his sister Catherine died, and he had witnessed his father's grief-stricken transformation. When, a decade after the reverend's death, Benjamin bought the family plot in Oakwood Cemetery, he not only remembered his dead children, he put up a tall stone monument at the center of the site on which he had chiseled in bold deep cuts the name of his father, REVEREND JOHN BAUM. The impressive stone monument reached up toward the oak trees that surrounded and overshadowed it.

But posterity has exposed some troublesome questions. Research has not revealed any official evidence of the Reverend Baum's status as a preacher. His name appears in no records of Methodist ministers in upstate New York in the 1840s, and his death wasn't recorded in their annual register, as was commonplace. Records may have been lost or burned in one of the numerous fires that destroyed so many wooden buildings in the age of candles and gaslight, but there's a strong possibility that John Baum appointed himself preacher and minister to God's people. Perhaps the fervor of his grief-stricken conversion led him to believe that he had a direct relationship with God that didn't require the mediation of an established Church. If he were to ride into a small village in the foothills of the Adirondacks, carrying a Bible and a blanket, claiming to be a Methodist circuit-riding minister, who would doubt him? And if he retold the stories of the Bible with conviction and power, wasn't that enough? But some more conformist voices might suggest that, no, this wasn't enough, that without the proper spiritual authority from the Methodist Church, the Reverend Baum was an impostor. We cannot know if his eldest son, Benjamin, understood that his father's revered position was rather shaky. By carving the title "Reverend" into the monument in Oakwood, Benjamin was shoring up his father's status for the future.

John Baum had died suddenly, age fifty-seven, at his daughter Mary Hanchett's house, on a warm summer evening in 1854. Such was the bond between John and his wife, Lany, that she died suddenly two days later. Their joint obituary in the local paper said that she died of apoplexy. When their surviving children buried them in the July heat after a joint funeral in Chittenango, the shock of their parents' sudden deaths must have been etched into their faces. Mary Hanchett was six months pregnant, and her sister, Theresa Wadsworth, was five months pregnant. The sisters were swollen and uncomfortable with the future as they buried the past. In October 1854, Mary gave birth to William in the house where her parents had so recently died. A month later, her sister Theresa gave birth to a boy, Frank DeForest.

The Erie Canal went straight through Chittenango; goods moved along the green watery channel at a mule's steady pace. Benjamin Baum's plan was to build a barrel factory. Raw timber could easily be brought in, and the shapely round wooden barrels sent out again. Benjamin's younger brother, Adam Baum, now a physician, married Josephine Stone in 1855; the families became more entangled and Benjamin considered going into the barrel business with the Stones.

The spirit rapping in Hydesville in 1848 had triggered a much wider discussion about ghosts and how to contact them that was preoccupying many people in the east of the country. Some believed that the Fox sisters had shown that it was possible to contact the dead. Believers banded together and called themselves spiritualists. Spirit mediums, who claimed to be able to communicate with the spirit world, began to appear everywhere; pamphlets, lectures, and books on what was now being called spiritualism proliferated. In the 1850s, the movement spread along the Erie Canal to Syracuse from Rochester, where the Fox sisters had first unleashed the dead. In 1855, a local Syracuse newspaper reported that the "new faith called spiritualism is spreading to an alarming extent." Its followers already numbered several hundred thousand. The article disapproved of the way in which the new cult was worshipped, not in official churches but in private homes, with séances often ministered by women. "Every town and hamlet has its branch agency for transacting business with the spirit world," the report went on, and it speculated about the truth of the spirit rapping, calling on all good scientists "to investigate the alleged phenomena of spiritualism," and to find out if it was "a popular delusion and deceit." The report described the new cult as a "creed which robs the grave of its dignity and fills the most mundane spheres with perturbed ghosts and chattering harlequins." Spirit mediums were unleashing disturbed ghosts into the houses of the living; the journalist didn't stop to wonder if they might be hiding there already.

Questions about the authenticity of spiritualism, its claim to direct contact with the dead, wouldn't go away. The exponential rise in the popularity of spiritualism in this period (there were two million believers by the end of the 1850s) was mirrored by equal numbers of people who saw it as a big hoax, a mass delusion, and the large numbers of spirit mediums who surfaced as an army of fakes. Frank Baum was born into a region crackling with arguments about ghosts and spirit mediums, and about authenticity and fakers.

In the height of the summer of 1855, when it was almost too hot to touch another person's skin, Cynthia became pregnant again. There were now three physicians in the family, Adam Baum and Mary and Silvannus Hanchett, to advise and watch over Cynthia. As the Baums traveled along ice-coated tracks between Chittenango, New Woodstock, Cazenovia, and Syracuse by horse-drawn sled in the frozen early months of 1856, a bundle of Baum children would have wriggled and squirmed under a layer of blankets. At extended family gatherings, children now outnumbered adults. Cynthia was heavy with child by spring, when the frozen Erie Canal began to thaw, cracking occasionally in jagged lines the shape of a lightning strike. Chittenango Falls began to rush with snowmelt; the suspended animation of winter gave way and a white world was gradually replaced by a green one, like a color photograph slowly developing in a dish of chemicals. As Cynthia approached the time of her delivery, her sister-in-law, Mary Hanchett, discovered that she herself was expecting again. That spring of 1856 was a fertile one.

But then, suddenly, as quick and unexpected as the start of a nightmare, children began to fall sick. Word traveled fast across farmland, through the woods, along the canal and dirt roads, that infants everywhere were ill. Doctors Mary and Silvannus Hanchett, who lived in the center of Chittenango, probably tried to advise and help others while they tended to their own sick children, Eliza and Willy.

For Cynthia and Benjamin Baum, the symptoms were a terrifying echo of 1848, when they had watched their daughter and son die. Diphtheria had struck again. The nightmare suddenly became all too real when, on May 13, Mary Hanchett's daughter, Eliza, died.

In the wake of this shock, Cynthia, a quarter of a mile down the road from Mary's house, went into labor. As a physician, Mary's job was to help, though perhaps it was too painful to act as midwife to her sister-in-law two days after her own child had died. In the evening of May 15, Cynthia gave birth to a boy. They called him Lyman Frank.

The child was born during a terrible crisis. As Cynthia recovered from the birth, three days later, on May 18, the terrible news reached her that her sister-in-law Theresa's boy, Frank DeForest, was dead. The children had to be kept away from their cousins. The newborn baby Lyman Frank was so vulnerable. It was hard to imagine that a child born in the middle of a ferocious diphtheria epidemic would survive. On May 24, another shock came with the news that Mary Hanchett's son, Willy, had been taken. The two physicians, who should have been able to do something, if anybody could have, were left childless.

The Baum children, Harriet, age ten; Mary-Louise, eight; Benjamin, six; and Edwin, three, must have been frightened and disoriented. The anxious expressions on their parents' faces as they checked the children's foreheads, felt their pulses, listened to their breathing with an ear to their chests, suggested that they had something to fear and that this invisible terror might be hiding inside their own bodies.

Soon after cousin Willy's death, Edwin Baum began to show symptoms. This was a ghastly repetition of 1848, as Cynthia nursed the newborn Lyman and also tended to a very sick child. Edwin died on June 15, exactly one month after Lyman Frank was born.

Children who died of diphtheria had to be buried quickly. The deadly bacteria in their bodies had to be put underground before they spread to more of the living. That spring of 1856, the numerous small cemeteries around Chittenango became horrible gothic nurseries filled with fresh little graves. A parent's mourning face would have been mirrored by other faces passed in the street. It must have been comforting to have close family members, Adam Baum and Mary and Silvannus Hanchett as physicians to advise and help Cynthia and Benjamin, but it also meant that the guilt and sorrow they felt after their children's deaths was more firmly locked inside the family.

L. Frank Baum was born into a tight-knit extended family traumatized by the sudden deaths of so many infants. His parents and aunts and uncles must have lived with an aching part of their hearts turned toward those children who were no longer with them. Baum grew up amongst shadow siblings and shadow cousins, and this would have a founding influence on the development of his imagination.

In those frightening first weeks after his birth, it was as though Lyman Frank had passed his brother Edwin in a dimly lit corridor suspended somewhere between life and death. As the newborn Lyman Frank held on to life, Edwin was losing his grip on it. The newborn baby survived the epidemic, but his parents surely realized that he had been very close to having barely lived at all. This sense of being in between, of existing in an indeterminate place between the living and the dead, would mark the child for life. It would become, perhaps, the place where Lyman Frank felt most at home.

Chapter 3

f it's true, as they say, that smell is the sense most strongly connected to memory, then one of L. Frank Baum's earliest sensory memories was almost certainly the acrid stench of rotten eggs. Chittenango was famous for its sulfur springs. People would come from miles around to stay at the hotel or the little shacks near the spring, and bathe in the smelly water. The sulfurous air was thought to be good for you, especially if you breathed it in deeply. The smell was particularly strong after rainfall, when earthy water would surface and mingle with the air. The Baums lived a mile or so from the spring; the strange, underground smell would have drifted over the house in the damp air after a rainstorm. In January 1857, a local astrologist predicted that the sulfur springs hotel would soon burn to the ground. Visitors to the spring were terrified, packed their bags and slept with their clothes on, so they could flee in a moment if fire did break out. The rumor spread across Chittenango, but the sulfuric air didn't erupt into fire that winter.

The child known as "Frankie" (never Lyman) spent the first five years of his life in a simple two-story wooden house built of tree trunks pegged together; the bark hadn't been stripped off so the prehistory of the walls as living trees was visible. The staircase had thirteen steps, and the house was surrounded by thirteen springs that supplied it with water. This wooden house would have creaked and groaned in the heat of summer and in the icy chill of minus-twenty winter winds. Wooden houses, more than brick and stone ones, can seem to be alive, expanding and contracting, breathing against the elements.

Chittenango was a bustling rural village with about one thousand inhabitants, five miles from Oneida Lake, sometimes called the thumb of the Finger Lakes. Several roads from different directions converged there, and the Erie Canal ran through the village. Farmers from all around brought produce to be shipped by canal southeast to New York City. Main Street was a wide slash cut through trees. The village was self-sufficient, with two hotels, three churches, and several businesses, including numerous general stores, four blacksmiths, boot stores, a tannery, and a wool mill. Most of the year, Main Street was mud or dust, rutted with wagon wheel tracks and horses' hoofprints. But during the long winters, the village could be under as much as twelve feet of snow from October until May, and the leafless trees that lined the street looked like upended bare black broomsticks.

The name "Baum" means "wood" in German, which suggested that Frankie's European ancestors had had professions entangled with trees and wood. Now his father's demanding business depended on wood to make barrels. In the fall of 1857, the barrel factory, which would make "fine barrels and butter firkins," opened for business. The wooden caskets were designed for alcohol and dairy products, the mainstay of the adult diet. Fat plus fiery whiskey would get a man through the winter.

Business was tough from the start, and Benjamin Baum was unlucky. In 1857 an economic crisis ripped through the eastern economy, and many rural banks went bust. Financing the business proved tough, and he struggled to pay the sawmills that provided timber for the barrels. Angry letters flew between Benjamin and his business associates. It "is now the darkest time," he wrote to one sawmill owner. "I think things will brighten by and by, as soon as spring," he added, as though the economic situation were part of the seasonal cycle. Benjamin was forced to take out more loans, one from the Chittenango bank and another from Cynthia's brother, William Stanton. Family and business were further interwoven. This was the start of a financial instability that would dog Frankie's childhood.

The Baum's small wooden house near the barrel factory was full of adults and children jostling for room. And there would soon be another baby; in the summer of 1858, Cynthia became pregnant again. To add to the crowd, there were two Irish servants living with the Baums, Peter McGraff and Mary O'Keith. Recent immigrants from Ireland often found their way north from New York City to upstate New York along the Erie Canal.

In the snow-locked winter of 1859, Aunt Mary Hanchett gave birth

again, to cousin Cora, and then Cynthia had a boy, Henry Clay Baum. At
three, Frankie's status as the youngest was broken with the birth of a brother
who would become his closest childhood friend.

In June, the bank foreclosed on Benjamin's loan; the barrel business was
in deep crisis. Anxieties about money and about how they would cope must
have seeped into the atmosphere at the Baum home.

In those days, fire made life possible in the frozen months. It was the
source of warmth, cooking, washing, and light. Fire was life, but it could also
destroy. If only the person who had wrongly predicted the sulfur springs fire
could have seen the future of the Bethel building, the important meetinghouse in Chittenango. Fire consumed the wooden building, reducing it to a
pile of smoldering, smoking, broken timbers and ash. Then in a separate
incident, the Baum's barrel warehouse caught fire, destroying 750 butter
firkins. The "fire was the work of an incendiary, without a doubt," wrote
Benjamin in a letter, his fury and exasperation leaping off the page. Benjamin's brothers-in-law, John Stone and Silvannus Hanchett, took control of
the barrel factory, and Benjamin began to look elsewhere for opportunities.
The new direction he needed had recently been discovered in a hole in the
ground in Pennsylvania. In 1859, a man named Drake found oil in Titus-
ville. Drake's simple drill was pumping crude oil up into an old tin bath.
News of the discovery traveled like wildfire across the Northeast. "Baum has
gone to PA. Has the oil fever," wrote John Stone in 1860. "Hope he makes
a fortune." Before Benjamin left for the Pennsylvania oil fields, he was forced
to secure another loan on his property. He was now deep in debt.

Four-year-old Frankie wouldn't have been directly concerned with these
problems, even though his family's money worries must have intruded into
his little world. His life was the house, his siblings, and his cousins. He
shared a bed with his two brothers; they all must have squabbled but at least
they didn't have to face the night's darkness alone.

Baum was adamant that he had loved stories as a child. "I can remember
my eyes have always grown big at tales of the marvelous," he wrote much
later in 1900. "I demanded fairy stories when I was a youngster," he told a
journalist in 1904. In these early years, before he could read, some of these
stories surely came from his mother's Bible. Perhaps the Irish servant Mary
O'Keith told him Celtic tales of goblins and magic stones. Some of the most

influential stories he was told, and later read for himself, were the tales of the Brothers Grimm and Hans Christian Andersen.

Jacob and Wilhelm Grimm first published their two collected editions of *Household Tales* in 1812 and 1815. These spectacled scholars had spent many years traveling Europe, collecting old oral folktales from "the lips of the people." By the 1850s, cheap editions of the Grimms' tales were readily available in English and were hugely popular. The Grimms saw these old stories as organic things, like plants and flowers. The brothers believed that by gathering oral folktales and writing them down for the first time, they were somehow preserving the stories of giants and lost orphans, evil stepmothers, witches, forests, and frightening wolves like summer fruits in pickling jars.

Hans Christian Andersen was the Danish author of several collections of fairy tales published since the 1840s and soon translated into English. Some of Andersen's tales were based on old Scandinavian folk stories and others he invented from scratch. In his tales the supernatural enters the ordinary world; the fantastic coexists with the everyday. Humans, objects, and plants are all given an animated inner life.

It was now, in these first five years of his life, that Baum was introduced to the tales of the Grimms and Andersen. Like many children, he first heard these stories at the very time when memories were beginning to form. His mother, Mary O'Keith, or his father, aunts, and uncles may have read them to him. These tales had so thoroughly absorbed the popular imagination by the 1850s and '60s that adults may have known some of the stories by heart, and whispered them to the children, adapting them here and there along the way. Baum certainly grew up with a highly developed sense of oral storytelling.

From the Brothers Grimm, there was the story of "Hansel and Gretel," the children who get lost in the woods and are lured by a gingerbread house into a witch's lair. There was also the sinister "Almond Tree," whose unpredictable magic powers caused havoc. There were odd little people called elves that visited a poor cobbler in the night to help him make shoes but then ran away when the cobbler was kind to them. The Grimm tales were filled with fear, peopled with unreliable parents, wicked stepmothers, untrustworthy kings, evil imps, hungry wolves, child-eating ogres and witches, and tricksy elves.

From Anderson, there was "The Fir Tree," in which an animated, talking tree yearns for adventure, to escape its sedentary home in the northern forest. The only way the fir tree can travel is to be cut down and turned into a Christmas tree. In "The Snow Man," another frustrated animated creature watches the boys skating, gliding up and down on the creaking ice, and wants desperately to join them, but he is stuck, rooted to the spot. He falls in love with the glowing fire he can see through the frosted windows of the farmhouse, and he melts when the sun comes out. In Andersen's "The Galoshes of Fortune," a pair of magic time-traveling shoes has "the property that every one who puts them on is at once transplanted to the time and place in which he likes best—every wish in reference to time, place, and circumstance, is at once fulfilled."

Baum's later deep anxiety about the role of fear in children's stories was ignited by his early exposure to the frightening tales of the Grimms and Andersen.

Running alongside Baum's world in the wooden house on the edge of Chittenango was the world of fairy tales, an elsewhere of castles, forests, and kings, of talking fish, giants, and dragons. This other place might have seemed on occasion to protrude into the visible world around him, so that the boundary between the two worlds became muddied. It wouldn't have been difficult to imagine, for instance, little elves creeping into one of the four boot makers' shops in Chittenango, to nail together leather strips from the local tannery to make magic boots. The boundary between animals and people wasn't always clearly maintained; Chittenango was having particular problems at this time with stray animals wandering the streets as though the village was theirs. And adults were always talking to their horses, which were at the heart of life, essential for pulling carriages, coaches, and sleighs.

In fairy tales, everything is alive. Animals talk, as do objects such as a mirror, a broom, a bottle, or a bucket. Magic flows through ordinary objects, such as a tin trunk, a carpet, or a spinning wheel. The law of fairy tales matches the child's view of the world; young children can't always clearly distinguish between what is alive and what isn't. They find it easy to breathe life into their inanimate toys. But the old rules of fairy tales, whereby one thing can transform into another (a frog into a prince, a witch into a house with chicken's legs) and a life force moves through and inhabits objects, also matched the new laws of spiritualist activity now at work in upstate New

York. At séances, spirits entered the most ordinary of things and made them speak; another term for a séance, for instance, was "table-talking." Invisible forces would seem to lift tables and chairs into the air and play musical instruments, and voices would emerge out of walls.

The popular tales of Tom Thumb found in both the Grimms and Andersen fitted a child's scale. Tom Thumb is a tiny, perfectly formed child, a plucky one whose small size doesn't prevent him from having adventures. His stature gives him access to the world in miniature. He rides behind a horse's ear, whispering directions into it; he hides in a mouse hole and in an empty snail shell. He creeps through a window left ajar, to hide and listen to adult conversation. For a child, the world beyond is large and cumbersome: An individual step must be scaled like a boulder, a chair is out of reach, adults' shoes are more familiar than their faces, dogs loom large, and a horse is a towering giant. Tales of Tom Thumb made children feel less small.

When Frankie was a child, a real live Tom Thumb regularly came to town, blurring any distinction between old folktales and the visible world around him. Charles Sherwood Stratton, born in 1838, had stopped growing before he was a year old. P. T. Barnum, the notorious showman, circus promoter, and manager of Barnum's American Museum in New York, discovered Stratton and showcased the tiny person in his "museum" on Broadway (where the Fox sisters' talents as "ghost-talkers" were also on display). Stratton went on tour with Barnum's traveling shows as General Tom Thumb, a "perfect man in miniature." Syracuse was an important stop in Barnum's annual itinerary.

The world of folktales protruded into the material world in other ways too. Renwick Castle stood on a hill overlooking Syracuse. This imposing gothic mansion featured turrets and towers, stone gargoyles, and ornate fountains. A grinning cat's face was carved into the huge wooden front door. The castle was grand and spooky enough for any Bluebeard or Rapunzel.

The world depicted in the Old World's folktales might have seemed more familiar to the Baums than the very different world of the Haudenosaunee Native Americans, otherwise known as the Six Nations of the Iroquois, who were an ancient, important, and controversial presence in the region Baum was born in. The local Syracuse newspapers were filled with news from the Onondaga Reservation and of relations among the Six Nations.

But a local elderly Native American woman known as Aunt Dinah, re-nowned for her powers, was very much like a figure from the Grimm and Andersen tales. She lived on the Onondaga Reservation, south of the city, and was said to be over one hundred years old. Her hair was white, her toothless mouth sucked in her cheeks, her hands were gnarled and twisted, and her sunken eyes seemed to look inward, to another place. She was one of the wise old women who in stories seem to pull on the strings of destiny. The faraway world of stories and Frankie's immediate world were all tangled up together, like twisted brambles.

The Baums' finances were becoming increasingly complex. In January 1860, a loan from Cynthia's brother, William Stanton, remained unpaid. William signed the loan over to Cynthia. Married women had been granted the legal right in New York State to own property in 1840, and husbands began to use their wives' new legal right by turning their property over to them. This ensured that husbands' finances would be safely removed from other business dealings. Now Benjamin owed his wife thousands of dollars, and she legally owned the barrel factory. Fortunately, Benjamin's business interests in the new oil industry were developing well, and in 1861 the Baums left Chittenango and the failing barrel factory, and moved to the rapidly growing city of Syracuse.

They left the small rural village in the wake of a new grief. Mary Hanch-ett's four-year-old daughter, Carrie, had died. A few months later, Mary's two-year-old daughter, Cora, also died. Frankie's cousins would have seemed to him to be there one minute and gone the next, who knew where.

When the Baums left Chittenango by horse-drawn cart, five-year-old Frankie left behind a place where both memory and stories had begun. We can't know what particular features were fixed at the bottom of his memory, but the vague impressions might have been of the stench of sulfur and the fear of fire. Since the house was close to Chittenango Falls, the sound of cascading layers of icy water, tumbling over cold gray steps of stone, was there in the background.

In the long cold winters, the dark green waters of the Erie Canal froze into thick, deep ice, and the shallow Oneida Lake froze too. Everybody learned to skate. Frankie would have taken his first steps onto the ice early, encouraged no doubt by his older siblings, to test out this indeterminate territory between land and liquid. These very early years, lived between lakes

Onondaga and Oneida, must have established Baum's lifelong desire to be near (and later to write next to) large bodies of water.

Much larger forces beyond the young child's small world began to press in upon it. Deep tensions over the future of the United States and the infamous institution of slavery had been building for decades. The abolitionist North was growing increasingly furious at the continued existence of slavery. This frustration had been made worse by the 1850 Fugitive Slave Law, which forced free-state Northerners to help recover escaped slaves. Many abolitionists refused to comply with the law, and continued to aid escaped slaves traveling to Canada via a loose network of helpers known as the Underground Railroad. In 1851, locals in Syracuse formed a committee to thwart the law. Most famously, they rescued William Henry, a barrel maker, who was arrested as an escaped slave. A large crowd gathered around the building in which he was being held, rammed in the door, and rescued the man. He was hidden for several days in a butcher's home before being taken across Lake Ontario into Canada. Frankie's younger brother, Henry Clay Baum, may have been named after the moderate antislavery statesman Henry Clay.

The future of slavery was now more important than ever, as the expanded territories of the West joined the Union. The North was concerned about the economic effects of the possible expansion of slavery into newly acquired territories in the West. Some people envisaged with horror the possibility of slavery spreading beyond southern plantations to slave-manned western mines and farms. The economic as well as the moral progress of the whole nation now depended on whether slavery was to expand into the new territories or be eradicated altogether. This thorny issue cut to the heart of the principles of the United States. What united the individual states? Who had the right to decide on their future? What shape was democracy to take? Who had rights? Who was free?

In December 1860, South Carolina seceded from the Union. In February 1861, six more southern states followed and formed the Confederate States of America, with their own president, Jefferson Davis. The Republican Abraham Lincoln had just been elected president of the United States. When he took office in March 1861, his only goal was to save the Union. On his way to Washington, DC, to take up the presidency, his train stopped briefly in Syracuse, a city that was a stronghold of Union support and abolitionist fervor.

Disunion had begun. War became inevitable when in mid-April, Confederate forces fired on a Union base at Fort Sumter in Charleston Harbor. Lincoln took immediate action and called for volunteers to build an army to defend the Union.

In the spring of 1861, both sides were gathering large armies. The future of the collective states would have to be decided through war. When five-year-old Frank Baum left the wooded seclusion of Chittenango for the noisy streets of Syracuse, he left a cozy, intimate network of extended families for a competitive, commercial city where life was being shaped by oil and by war.

Chapter 4

ynthia gave birth to a boy in December 1861 and named him George McClellan Baum after the Union Army military hero. General McClellan was in charge of the Union Army of the Potomac, a substantial force marshaled in the hope of making the war short and decisive. The rebel Southern states would have to be brought back under federal power.

It was soon after George was born that the Baums moved into their new house in central Syracuse at number one Rust Street. The property was in Cynthia's name, to keep the house from the uncertainty and instability of Benjamin's business dealings. Built of brick instead of wood, the impressive mansion had numerous large windows that looked out onto a flat, grassy yard planted with young trees.

Syracuse was built on the edge of Onondaga Lake, a watery expanse that was the source of the city's growth. Salt, in an era before refrigeration, was essential for preserving meat and fish, and it was Syracuse's main product. Salt pans, in which water was evaporated by the heat of the sun, lined the lake. Horses and mules pulled cartloads of white crystals to the railroad and the canal, where the salt was sent East. Flying south from the lake, across the salt pans toward the city, a bird would have seen several church towers and buildings made of white limestone with patches of deep-red brick, so the buildings that housed the city's striving investors seemed to blush.

Syracuse was a colorful city in other ways too. The boats that traveled the Erie Canal were brightly painted to attract the attention of new immigrants arriving in New York City and looking to travel northwest in search of work. Some boats were red; others were blue, yellow, or pink. Many Irish immigrants stopped off at Syracuse and found jobs at the saltworks; German immigrants found work in the city's many breweries, producing another staple of the nineteenth century.

The canal was a central feature of life in Syracuse, as it had been in Chittenango. It reached right into Clinton Square, the city's center. Each winter, in November, the canal was drained of water; otherwise the water would freeze, expand, and burst the canal walls. Boats were then "mudlarked," sunk to sit on the canal's empty, muddy bottom. But enough water was left in the Clinton Square section of the canal to allow it to freeze into a skating rink. Throughout the winter, adults and children strapped skates made of wood and sharp iron runners over their flat shoes, to slip, slide, and race across the ice. The red-and-white buildings that circled Clinton Square would spin and whirl about them.

All year round, the streets of Syracuse were flooded with noises: cartwheels rolling over cobbles, horse hooves clopping, men shouting, and the tinkle of bells that chimed each time a shop door was opened. The city's many general stores were filled with goods made locally, such as Lee and Green's Ginger Ale, Rock Spring Brewery beer, and Young's biscuits. Locally concocted medicines included an antimosquito balm called Wood's Improved Lollacapop. This was a stimulating world full of bright colors and the smell of camphor.

In July 1862, New York State issued a weak draft law that made all men between the ages of twenty and thirty-five, and unmarried men between thirty-five and forty-five, liable for military service. The only way a man in one of these categories could get out of service would be to find someone else to sign up in his stead, or pay three hundred dollars. The war came closer to Frankie when, in August 1862, his uncle Adam Clarke Baum, a physician, enrolled as an assistant surgeon with the New York 50th Engineers Federal Army. Adam joined in Albany. His unit would soon head south to Virginia, to build roads, bridges, and pontoons to help the Union army's progress toward the Confederate capital at Richmond.

As a married man over thirty-five (he was now forty-one), Benjamin Baum wasn't required to serve military duty. Debts from the barrel factory were still hanging over him, but in the fall of 1861, he had opened a new business with his brother Lyman and brother-in-law John Wadsworth. With oil from Pennsylvania, they started manufacturing kerosene for lighting. The business had, wrote a Syracuse newspaper, "sprung up among us as quickly and magically as the genii, and is working wonders." Kerosene-fueled oil lamps began to replace candle lighting. The oil of ancient buried forests would light the late nineteenth century, replacing candles made from animal products: beeswax, tallow, and whale oil. "We can predict for the company," the article went on, "a broad field for their operation and a golden harvest." The new kerosene light was in fact golden; its constant, gentle glow created undulating shadows that flickered and leapt far less than those of candlelight. Books were becoming increasingly affordable, and the glow of kerosene lighting extended reading time in the dark evenings of winter.

In later years, after gas and then electricity had fully illuminated the night, Baum would often prefer to turn all the lights off and set up an old kerosene lamp to read and eat by. This light would glow, for Baum, with associations of his father's success as well as with nostalgia for childhood and stories.

The winter of 1862 was bloody and gruesome. Armies on both sides lost thousands of soldiers in battles and to disease. At the Battle of Antietam in Maryland, the Union forces led by McClellan lost twelve thousand men. The Confederate States Army, led by General Lee lost almost as many. Lincoln began to see the horrific bloodbath that was engulfing the nation as God's punishment for the sin of slavery. He read into the violence and bloodshed God's instruction that slavery must be abolished for good, and he took a giant step toward the abolition of slavery when in September of that year he announced the Emancipation Proclamation, which would take effect on New Year's Day, 1863. His hand shook uncontrollably as he signed it. News of the proclamation spread fast across the nation. The South wouldn't only be returned to federal rule; its economic reliance on slavery would also be forcefully ended.

It now looked as though the social and moral cause of the war would be achieved, but the violence only escalated. The year 1863 was pivotal. Battles and deaths continued, and North and South alike suffered terribly from war weariness. The numbers of volunteers in the North declined. In March, the federal government enacted a conscription law, which meant that all men aged between eighteen and thirty-five had to fight for a minimum of three years, unless they could afford three hundred dollars (roughly two times a soldier's annual pay) to get out of it. This was followed by violent anticonscription riots in New York City, during which an orphanage for black children was burned to the ground. The North was holding to its position, but deep fractures had opened up. The Battle of Gettysburg in Pennsylvania in July was one of the bloodiest of the war, with forty thousand casualties in two days. General Lee finally ordered a retreat. It began to look as though the North had the advantage.

P. T. Barnum took the nation's attention away from the war very briefly in 1863, when he announced the marriage of Tom Thumb, now twenty-five years old and eleven inches tall, to Mercy Lavinia Warren Bump, twenty-two years old and thirty-two inches tall. The couple had a lavish wedding, and the press was filled with the news. "The Loving Lilliputians" was the headline in *The New York Times*.

Adam Baum wrote from battlefields in the South to his wife, Josephine, as often as he could. In July 1863, he wrote saying that he hoped "the war will soon be ended." He tried to reassure her that he was well, but he admitted that he missed home terribly and wanted news. "You are now probably at home enjoying the felicity of loved ones. . . . I think of home often and really wish I was free . . . But such is not my good fortune," he wrote. "Good bye and God bless and keep you for tomorrow," he signed off, adding, "much love to all." Adam's letters to his wife are written in an intimate but also practical, informative style that suggests he expected her to read them aloud to family and friends, as was commonplace. The letters may have been read to Cynthia and Benjamin Baum.

Back in Syracuse, Benjamin's business was expanding. He and a group of investors owned land and wells in Pennsylvania, and they established the Commonwealth Oil Company. Benjamin was also looking into investing in a new project out west. Investors were hoping to dig up more precious minerals from inside the earth in the form of silver. The Keystone Silver Mining Company was set up to invest in mines and mills in Nevada (Mark Twain was already out there trying to make a fortune from Nevada silver). This was a risky investment; nobody really knew if large amounts of silver were buried there. As a young child, Frankie probably overheard his father discussing the complex financial web he was spinning, including talk of drilling, mining, silver mines, and oil wells. His later fascination with underground tunnels, caves, and mines may have begun here.

The winter of 1863 brought terrible news from the battlefield, and death came again to the Baum home in November when one-and-a-half-year-old George McClellan died. It was as though the child named after a central figure in the war had become truly caught up in it. The death was announced in the Syracuse newspaper, which also stated that the funeral would be held at the house on Rust Street.

Frankie was now seven years old. He hadn't been alive when his siblings Cynthia-Jane and Oliver had died, and he had only been one month old when Edwin had died, but he definitely knew all about these deaths. However, George's little body, washed, dressed, and laid out in an open coffin for the wake, was likely the first corpse he ever saw. How shocking it must have been to see his baby brother, who had so recently been there to play with and tease, suddenly cold and still, ashen and stiff, with a pale face and closed eyes.

Cynthia had now buried four children, including her first and her last born.

The long, icy, grief-stricken winter of 1863–1864 dragged on. In May 1864, Adam Baum wrote to Josephine from camp after a "long thunderstorm," which "has done us a world of good." "It has helped our wounded very much as the great suffering on the field of battle after being wounded is for water," he explained. He also sent her a lock of his hair folded inside the letter. "I enclose a lock of my hair," he wrote, "I had it cut yesterday and thought I could send a lock of it so you can see how old I am getting." He underlined the word "old." His hair had turned gray and brittle through the strain of war. At the time it was common to keep the hair of loved ones as a memento, but hair was also associated with death. In the popular, somewhat macabre craft of hair wreaths, strands of dead loved ones' hair were wound around thin wire and then bent, twisted, and turned into elaborate flower shapes. Adam's lock was a memento for his wife, but perhaps it was also a way of acknowledging that he might be killed. If he were, his body was unlikely to be found, identified, and sent home for burial. At least his wife would have a small piece of him to bury or to weave into a wreath.

Later that month, one night when Cynthia lay awake in bed, she heard slippered feet padding quietly downstairs. She could see the edge of a light passing through the house, from the kitchen to the dining room and into the hall. She went downstairs to investigate, and discovered a strange man with a light in one hand and an armful of her clothes in the other. Alarmed, she woke Benjamin, who, bleary-eyed, grabbed his revolver. He rushed downstairs to see the burglar climbing out of a window. He fired at him and missed; another shot hit the window before the intruder disappeared into the thick darkness. Cynthia and Benjamin caught a glimpse of him in front of the house, illuminated by his light, but they couldn't make out the features of his face.

The burglary took place two days before Frankie's eighth birthday. He was no doubt asleep at the time but would have been woken by the gunfire and hullabaloo. The following morning, when the family searched the house, they found a wire pick in the door lock and a candle under the window that had the bullet hole in it. This unnerving incident of intrusion and sudden outburst of violence stuck in Frankie's memory, like a sharp knife. Years later he wrote a short story called "The Loveridge Burglary," in which a diamond is stolen; the story was loosely based on his early experience but treats a house burglary comically. Baum would later use humor in his stories to discharge the power of what frightened him.

News reached the Baums in May of battles in Virginia in which Adam was involved. General Grant took his Union forces south into the thick woods of Virginia, where they confronted General Lee's army in a series of horrendous, bloody, and indecisive battles: the battles of the Wilderness, Spotsylvania, and Cold Harbor. Union casualties were fifty-five thousand and Confederate forty thousand. Adam cared for the wounded at Cold Harbor, one of the worst battles of the war. It took place at a key crossroads, ten miles from Richmond, where several roads led down to the Confederate capital. Thick fog and swampy ground impeded Union progress.

In his letter to Josephine after the battle, Adam tried to reassure her that all was well, but he explained that "the booming of the guns and the whistling of the shells are anything but pleasant, I assure you." He tried not to complain, but the horror seeped through between the lines.

Lee's forces were decimated, but so too were Grant's. In the aftermath of the battle, Grant became known as the "fumbling butcher." Northern morale slumped. But then, in September 1864, Union General Sherman took Atlanta, Georgia, a crucial city in the Confederacy. Northern morale surged and the country reelected Lincoln as president in a landslide victory in November. Sherman headed south and took Savannah by the end of the year. Union victory now looked certain. The North had many advantages over the South that would help them triumph, such as a bigger population, industrialization (the railroad), and wealth. On a small scale, for instance, for many people, decent footwear was still a luxury, but the North had recently mastered the mass manufacture of boots and shoes. Unlike many of the Southern soldiers, who were often barefoot, Northern forces were rarely without boots. This was a considerable advantage in both the swampy South and the freezing winters. One of Benjamin Baum's business associates in Syracuse was Elijah Fenton, one of the first men to mass-manufacture boots.

Sherman's devastating progress through the South continued. Grant prepared to face Lee's weakened forces in Virginia. The Confederate forces were now in rags, barefoot and starving. Lee's desperate remaining forces were trapped between Union armies. On April 9, 1865, Lee met Grant at Appomattox Courthouse, at a rural crossroads in the Virginia forest, and surrendered. Over six hundred thousand men had died. Slavery was abolished. Reconstruction would have to begin, and now the scars would surface.

Adam Baum left the army and returned home. He brought with him tales of horrible violence and unimaginable suffering. In a letter written to his wife from camp, he had admitted that sometimes the battlefield was "terrible to think of, and much worse to look on." New York State had provided more Union soldiers than any other. Twelve thousand men from Onondaga County alone had served. An area of Oakwood Cemetery in Syracuse was dedicated to them. After the war, those who had survived returned, many of them physically as well as mentally maimed. Many of these veterans were amputees. The Civil War was one of the first conflicts to use amputation on a large scale. The ammunition used in the Civil War, the rifle bullet called the minié ball in particular, created devastating wounds; the discovery in the 1840s of effective pain relief with ether and chloroform enabled the wounded to withstand amputation.

Surgeons were issued wooden boxes containing a terrifying collection of tools designed to perform amputation on different bones and joints. A fine-tooth saw, a miniature cleaver, scalpels, and clamps were neatly arranged in a handy portable instrument kit lined with soft baize. Whiskey and morphine were issued as well, to help patients (and possibly surgeons) cope in the agonizing days after an operation. Brave surgeons, who had often received only basic training in field hospitals at the edges of battlefields, performed gruesome operations. Amputations were performed on thirty thousand Union soldiers. People expressed their horror at what they saw as the unacceptably high number of men who lost limbs, but the truth was that courageous surgeons had stemmed the death rate by preventing gangrene.

In photographs of Civil War veterans from Syracuse, many men with missing limbs are visible. A jacket arm or trouser leg hangs limp. People whom the Baums knew before the war would have been recognizable but changed. Many men walked with a limp, with the aid of a stick, and concealed prosthetic legs and arms beneath their clothes. Some, having lost their right arms, were forced to learn to write with their left hands. Others had to remain seated in church while everyone else stood; young men were helped up steps by old women.

One veteran, Henry A. Barnum (no relation to P. T. Barnum), became widely known in Syracuse in the years following the war, and young Frank Baum was sure to have seen him. The veteran had been shot through his side, and the bullet's passage through him remained open. He displayed it as a curiosity, pushing a long stick all the way through his flesh, following the line of the original wound, as though he were made of dough and didn't bleed or break. To display one's injuries so was peculiar, distasteful perhaps; it was reenacting what was supposed to become a hidden, painful memory. It forced those who hadn't been there to see what had been done in the name of freedom. Adam Baum had witnessed bodies broken and battered by war, and he may have saved men by performing terrifying acts of barely medicated butchery.

One of the most peculiar aftershocks of amputation was the widespread experience of what was known as "phantom limb syndrome." Between fifty and eighty percent of amputees experience phantom limb pains. Amputees feel sensations in the missing limb, such as itching, coldness, tingling, or burning. Some feel an absent arm, hand, or leg twitch, gesture, or even touch a familiar texture. Damage to severed nerves and their wiring in the brain creates the very real illusion that the missing limb is still attached to the body. The limb thus becomes a phantom, a ghostly body part that haunts its former body.

Phantom pain was a strange mirror of the grief felt by those who had lost family members and children. Baby George McClellan Baum had become a phantom sibling of sorts, along with Frankie's other dead siblings and cousins. The high infant mortality rate, combined with the huge losses during the Civil War, created a society forced to live with haunting, phantom pains of many kinds. It's hardly surprising that the popularity of spirit mediums continued to soar after the Civil War. In those days, not a week went by in Syracuse without a medium or spirit rapper of some sort offering their services in one of the many lecture halls, meeting houses, or theaters in the city. The Reverend Uriah Clark passed through town, giving lectures from his popular book *A Plain Guide to Spiritualism*. The Eddy mediums of America produced spirit manifestations at séances. Admission was fifty cents.

The war years had shaped people and life in profound ways. Frankie was five when the war began and nine when it ended; these were crucial years of play and imagination, when the tragic losses of the war as well as the euphoria in upstate New York at the Yankee victory surely filtered into the child's world. Baum's main playmate throughout his childhood was his younger brother, Henry, known as Harry. Mid-nineteenth-century toys were usually homemade, constructed out of bits of wood, cloth, or discarded cotton reels. Children had to use their imaginations to bring wonky, throwaway bits of junk to life. Other common toys were clay and glass marbles in various rich colors—cobalt blue, bright red, mottled green—used in games of Spans and Snops or Bost-About. Waitt and Bond's Totem Marbles came in a smart wooden box with a painting of a native chief on the lid. Jacks was played with a ball and five jacks, often the vertebrae of small animals. Children made spinning tops and whirligigs. Thaumatropes were also popular. Invented in 1825 and meaning "wonder turner," a thaumatrope created a simple optical illusion using a circular card with, for example, a man painted on one side and a horse on the other; string was attached to each side of the card and when the circle was spun around fast, the images on the two sides would blend, so that the man would appear to ride the horse.

When the veterans returned, many with missing or prosthetic limbs, this seemed to connect to the world of stories. In the Brothers Grimm tale "The Girl Without Hands," for instance, a poor man accidentally promises his daughter to the devil, who then forces him to cut off her hands. A king takes pity on the girl and has silver hands made for her to fit onto the end of the dreadful stumps at her wrists. But then, at the end of the story, the young woman's piety and perseverance are rewarded, and she grows a new pair of hands, discarding her prosthetic silver ones. Perhaps the missing parts of the veterans would regrow? Was it possible? Or maybe Frankie imagined that his father's Nevada mine would produce silver to make replacement limbs for the veterans. Baum was growing up in a world where the human body could be broken into pieces and reassembled from inanimate matter. But such transformations had been taking place in folktales for hundreds of years.

About this time, Samuel Larned was traveling the Erie Canal with a boatload of waxworks. He would display his numerous, costumed wax figures on a series of pedestals in rooms and halls in towns and villages along the canal. Visitors could see a life-size, three-dimensional pirate Captain Kidd up close or English kings and queens, including King Henry VIII and his six wives; they could stare at George Washington, at Thomas Jefferson and various Revolutionary War heroes. It was an odd mixture of monarchs, rebels, and politicians. The wax models had a peculiar sheen, like real skin, and they almost seemed to breathe, to be alive. The nineteenth-century fascination with life-size wax models stemmed from the ability of the wax to embody lifelike qualities and yet appear corpselike at the same time. The wax figures were a visual echo of the disturbing memories of laid-out corpses that most people had witnessed from a young age.

In April 1865, President Lincoln, hero of the reunited country, was suddenly ripped from the visible world to become a national ghost. He had been suffering terribly under the strain of the war (magnified by the pain of losing his son in 1862). He had been plagued by dreams of his own death for months. He and his wife, Mary, decided to take a break by attending the theater on Friday, April 14. *Our American Cousin*, a comic farce, would offer a brief respite. As Lincoln, seated next to his wife, watched the play from a box, actor and Confederate sympathizer John Wilkes Booth crept into the theater and up the stairs. At ten o'clock, just as the central character in the play uttered his funniest lines, Booth burst into the box and shot Lincoln in the back of the head. The last thing Lincoln heard before he passed out was the rippling sound of laughter.

The president died the following morning. The news was shocking. His millions of supporters went into mourning. His body was transported from Washington, DC, to Illinois for burial. His coffin was placed in a glass-sided carriage pulled by a magnificent steam train. As it traveled north, people lined the railroad to see it pass. The funeral train passed through Syracuse on the evening of April 26. In the cold darkness, Lincoln's grieving support-ers turned out with lamps. Some dipped brooms in kerosene oil (manufac-tured by the Baums perhaps) and lit the oil to create flaming torches. People stood on both sides of the track for miles with burning brooms and lamps held aloft, as the glass-sided carriage passed by. The glowing torchlight was reflected in the glass, and people peering through could just make out, through the dispersing steam from the train's engine, a coffin with many wreaths of flowers crowded around it.

The president was dead. The nation would have to be reborn.

Chapter 5

enjamin Baum accidentally shot his wife, Cynthia, on a hot Sunday morning in the summer of 1866. They were setting off in their horse-drawn carriage from New Woodstock to Cazenovia, when Benjamin's loaded revolver dropped from his coat pocket, the heavy metal hitting the ground and causing the gun to fire. The bullet passed through Cynthia's left leg (probably the calf). Benjamin, in a state of shock no doubt, drove Cynthia, bleeding and in pain, to Cazenovia, where two doctors were summoned. A man shooting his wife accidentally merited a mention in the Syracuse newspaper, and Benjamin's near-fatal error was publicized throughout the city.

That same summer, Frankie's aunt Mary Hanchett, the physician from Chittenango, lost another child, Benton, age one, who now became another shadow cousin. This was the fifth infant Mary had lost. Only three of the eight children she had given birth to were still alive. Such tragedy was unusual even in this era of very high infant mortality. Poor Mary Hanchett, a pioneering woman doctor, who nursed other people's children, lost most of her own. Alice, now two, would be the only one of Mary's nine children to live into old age.

Outside the Baum family, the name "Alice" had taken on a wide new significance with the publication of a new children's story in 1864. A child named Alice falls down a rabbit hole into a bizarre world full of talking animals, peculiar games and riddles, and vicious monarchs from a pack of cards. Lewis Carroll's *Alice's Adventures in Wonderland* was an immediate hit. Here was a strange new fairy tale, starring a girl child hero, whose independent spirit and self-composure help her navigate Wonderland, to make it back up to the tedious world of school lessons and being told what to do by grown-ups.

Benjamin was now president of the Syracuse Second National Bank; he had offices in New York City, was speculating on the stock market, and owned land. In 1866 the Baums bought land just outside of Syracuse. The several-acre estate was bought in Cynthia's name from gentlemen who had used the land to grow orchards of fruit trees, including pears, apples, and plums. The grounds were also planted with hundreds of rosebushes. This was an ideal spot for a Baum estate, a luscious patch well suited for demonstrating Benjamin's success. It's unknown whether or not there was a house already on the grounds. If not, the Baums had one built over the next two years.

Now twelve years old, Baum could read by himself. He loved to read Charles Dickens (whose occasional pen name was Boz), as well as the Grimms, Andersen, and John Bunyan's *The Pilgrim's Progress*. In 1868, Dickens was touring the United States, giving readings from his work; in the cold and snowy March, he came to Syracuse. He read on Saturday night, March 9, at the Weiting Opera House. Tickets were two dollars. At eight o'clock, Dickens, dressed in finery, with diamond rings on his fingers and red and white flowers in his breast buttonhole, stood behind a table draped in a maroon cloth and read from *A Christmas Carol* and *The Pickwick Papers*. Bright gas lamps illuminated his animated face as he became the characters from his stories. Dickens, famously, didn't simply read his work aloud, he performed it, drawing on his skills as an actor. "It would have been impossible," read an article in the *Syracuse Standard*, "for Dickens to have been so successful as a novelist if he had not been an actor in early life." Dickens's popular readings showed how effective oral storytelling could be.

We don't know if Baum attended the reading, but the news of Dickens's visit was everywhere, and he would have known about it at the time or subsequently; the great author's visit was one of the city's proudest moments. The local newspapers ran detailed reports on Dickens's performance. "Here is a single magician," read one, "whose hand raises spirits that lead to such happy transformations."

But for Dickens, the most memorable part of his visit to Syracuse was the food; on March 9, he wrote in his diary simply that he had "supped on a tough old nightmare called buffalo."

In 1868, Cynthia sold the house on Rust Street and the family moved to Rose Lawn, which she named after the rosebushes that grew all over the grounds. Cynthia was now forty-eight years old. Her dark hair was graying above her ears and her body had thickened after giving birth to eight children. Her pointed nose reached down toward her thin mouth. Benjamin was forty-seven; his generous beard and bushy moustache seemed to elongate and exaggerate the thinness of his face and body. Frank's generation was also advancing. His older sister, Harriet, had been married at the house on Rust Street in 1866; she had a child in 1867.

Baum explored Rose Lawn, the grounds and the house. The walls of the three-story wooden mansion were papered in dark patterned wallpaper. The fashion was for leaf and plant prints; these stylized patterns would appear to undulate in the moving flames of gas, kerosene, and candlelight, as though blown by a breeze. Some of the furniture was made out of dark and deeply patterned walnut. The grain of this unusual wood swirled in loops and ornate knots, in rich, organic shapes, ideal for finding faces in. Baum enjoyed roaming the house and grounds by himself, hunting out private hiding places in the dark mansion cluttered with furniture, mirrors, rugs, and ornaments, in the style of the day.

Baum read stories and played games with his brother Harry. The house had many generous bay windows looking out onto the garden. Broad wooden porches ran along each side of the house, creating a threshold between the house and the garden, and were one of Baum's favorite places to read.

The interiors of popular books mirrored the insides of rooms of the time, creating a sense of continuum between the outside world and the world of stories. The inside leaves of many editions had marbled, swirling paper, much like the wallpaper in many well-to-do homes like Rose Lawn. The elaborately decorated first letters that began each new story were like the ornate brass locks that adorned most front doors.

Outside the house were rosebushes and fruit trees, and no doubt, seasonally, swarms of insects came to feast on nectar. The house had no running water, and the bathroom was an outhouse, the door of which was hidden in foliage. How creepy nighttime visits must sometimes have been (when the chamber pot under the bed wouldn't do); a person would have to lift the foliage out of the way by kerosene or candlelight.

Beyond the garden, Baum would have seen the Plank Road curving north. Hundreds of years prior, the route of the Plank Road had been the Native American Thousand Island Trail weaving from Pennsylvania to Canada. Next it had become a worn dirt track, rutted by wagon wheels and horses, then the Salt Road, built of logs that sank into the mud. The sixteen-mile toll road, built in 1846, was the first plank road in America. It was made with eight-foot-long hemlock planks, laid side by side to form a wide wooden road. It was designed to accommodate the flow of goods, including wagonloads of salt to and from Syracuse. However, the planks became worn, cracked, and rutted from the extreme weather and use, and the old planks frequently had to be replaced. Fresh hemlock is a light yellowish color; when new planks were laid, the famous Plank Road would have curved, like a yellow band, through the countryside north of Rose Lawn.

Benjamin's position as a well-to-do man of business demanded that he look to his boy's education. He decided to send Frank to a military academy in Peekskill, southeast down the Hudson River. A professional portrait photographer took a photo of Baum in his new Peekskill uniform. He stood self-consciously in the tight-fitting dark blue wool uniform (based on that of the Union army), gripping his regulation cap in one hand.

In the fall of 1868, Frank Baum, now age twelve, traveled southeast by rail or by boat down into the Hudson Valley, through the forests and boggy marshlands, to Peekskill. The small town edged the Hudson and reached up a hill to look back down into the purplish waters of the river.

Numerous ironworks and charcoal factories puffed billowing smoke out along the waterfront to mingle with steam from trains. The main product of the town was cast-iron stoves, potbellied or square stoves and heaters. Some stood on feet in the shape of lion's claws, and their air vents, handles, and knobs gave them faces. It would have been easy to imagine these objects coming to life, walking about awkwardly on their iron animal feet.

The military academy was located on Oak Hill, overlooking the Hudson. A magnificent oak tree crowned the hill and stood proudly in front of the school building. The Old Oak, as it was known, was the school's mascot, symbolizing the values the academy hoped to instill in its pupils. Be firm as an oak, cadets were told. But the tree gathered other stories around it too. It had another name, the Hanging Tree. In 1777, during the Revolutionary War at a camp on Oak Hill, a soldier named Daniel Strang was found to be a spy for the British and was court-martialed. He was hanged from the tree and buried beneath it. Some said his distressed soul haunted the site, circling the big old oak, rustling its leaves. Daniel Strang's skeleton would be dug up from under the tree in the early 1900s and reburied elsewhere.

The education offered at Peekskill was progressive, varied, and "modern" for its time. The fact that the Baums chose to send Frank to Peekskill suggests that they took education seriously and wanted their son to have a contemporary outlook on the world. The school also emphasized the need for vocational, commercial education, which would have appealed to the business-minded Benjamin. Boys were taught bookkeeping, commercial correspondence, law, and economics, as well as Latin, Greek, literature, mythology, French, and German. Students also studied botany, chemistry, geometry, geography, history, map drawing, figure drawing, and oil painting. And boys were taken on geological field trips to local quarries and copper mines.

"No act of immorality or special impropriety will be suffered to pass unnoticed," read the school's prospectus, written a few years after Baum left the school. The academy was determined to instill in pupils a "sense of religious and moral obligation," to teach them "the elements of physical and moral manhood." In the aftermath of the Civil War, the school's military character was reinvigorated. Pupils were taught infantry and artillery tactics, and they performed regular marching drills in the spacious parade ground in front of the Old Oak. The hundred or so pupils were always directed, occupied, told what to do and when and for how long. They had to wear their school uniforms at all times, so that a boy from the academy could be instantly recognized, even if he were strolling into town during a brief respite from school activities. On such rare occasions, boys might make a trip to Paul Wessell's and Sons Bakery, where they could buy fresh cakes, careful not to drop crumbs or cream down their dark blue wool coats, which were clasped tightly across their chests with rows of shiny brass buttons.

Brick roads were common throughout the Hudson Valley, and one of the roads that wound down to the docks through Peekskill was made of bricks that had a distinctive yellowish hue. Many of these bricks were first brought over from Europe in Dutch ships in the 1700s as ballast, and were then reused to build sturdy roads. Later, local brickmakers, such as James M. Porter, manufactured yellowish limestone bricks for further road building.

Baum didn't like Peekskill Military Academy. His temperament wasn't suited to it. He found the teachers cruel, the discipline arbitrary. His lifelong dislike of military and educational institutions, which later surfaced strongly in his stories, was fueled by his experience at the school. Peekskill had a list of Things Forbidden, which included, "visiting a Billiard Saloon or place where tobacco or liquors are sold. To have in possession or use tobacco, cards, firearms or weapons. To contract debt or borrow money." Baum would enthusiastically embrace all these activities later in life.

One of the reasons he found the discipline so unacceptable may have been connected to the fact that he was left-handed, a southpaw, as they say in boxing and baseball. Baum's left-handedness wouldn't have become visible until he entered formal education and began to write in the company of scrutinizing teachers. People don't tend to notice or care if someone opens a door or picks up a tool with his left hand, but teachers always notice a left-handed writer. The history of prejudice against left-handed writing goes back centuries. In the nineteenth century, left-handedness was seen as much more than simply an awkward way of writing that resulted in smudges; it was considered a sign of moral deviance, of disobedience, a sinister weakness and evidence that a child was "backward." In nineteenth-century schools, left-handed children were often forced to write with their right hands. They were made to sit on their left hands, and their left hands were slapped with rulers or canes. A torturous invention with a leather strap and a buckle was designed to tie the left arm firmly behind a pupil's back.

It wouldn't have been in his writing only that Baum's difference and so-called deviance was visible. Peekskill prided itself on games and military drill. While marching in sequence holding a gun, boys had to follow in synchronized patterns; in baseball, southpaws are highly noticeable. Being left-handed didn't simply make a pupil feel awkward in the classroom and on the playing field. Tools, games, guns, and machinery were all designed for use by right-handers. The left-handed person lived in a world in which everything was designed for the opposite hand, a reverse world through the looking glass.

It's a sign of Baum's determination and independence that he continued to write with his left hand into adulthood, because many pupils in the nineteenth century buckled under the pressure and tried to write with their right, resulting in illegible handwriting.

When the academic year came to an end in June, Peekskill cadets celebrated by forming a circle and tossing their caps into the air. Baum was relieved to return home to Rose Lawn, where life was so much more flexible. His parents weren't strict disciplinarians, as long as he went to church on Sundays. And there was an endless supply of Cynthia's delicious cottage cheese, which was one of Baum's favorite things to eat. The house was lively. Evenings were spent visiting friends and family or hosting them, playing cards, backgammon, checkers, or chess. Baum learned to play some simple tunes on the piano and he had a good singing voice. Sometimes they arranged a room with a few lamps to make shadow shapes. Hands and fingers were interlocked and twisted in front of a light, to throw animated shapes of a barking dog, a flying goose or a hook-nosed witch; the shadows danced over the already moving wallpaper patterns. At home, Baum was given space to explore his imagination, to daydream, to fully enter the stories he was so avidly reading.

Fairy tales again entered Baum's local environment, to blur the lines between stories and the world around him, when in the fall of 1869, a petrified giant was found buried on a farm on the outskirts of Syracuse. Two farmhands discovered the twelve-foot stone man while digging a well on Stub Newell's farm outside the village of Cardiff. They initially thought they had come across an ancient Native American grave. One of the farmhands' spade hit something solid with a clunk, and a gray stone face with an enigmatic smile emerged from the mud. The giant stone body was naked, as though the ground had given birth to it. It had one hand placed demurely over its crotch; its wide rib cage and giant leg bones were prominent, as though its skin had sunken, dried and hardened over its outsize skeleton.

News of the strange discovery erupted across the state. "Go where you will in this city, and the surrounding country," read the *Syracuse Standard*, "everybody is talking about it." Baum would soon have found out about the extraordinary discovery. People began to travel to Newell's farm, braving the rocky, bumpy tracks locked in treacherous ice. The farmer erected a tent around the uncovered giant and charged visitors fifty cents to pass through and look down into the enormous muddy pit where the blank-eyed stone face of the giant stared back.

Arguments about the origins of the giant raged. An Onondaga woman declared that it was the petrified body of a gigantic Native American prophet. No, it was a statue, said others, carved by a Jesuit priest in the 1600s to impress the local tribes. Another popular theory was that it was the petrified body of a man from thousands of years ago, when, according to the Bible, "there were giants in the earth."

A group of local businessmen brought "His Giantship" to Syracuse to be displayed in a storefront so that more money could be made. Crowds flocked to see him. The giant brought hundreds of visitors to Syracuse by train; this was good for local business. Benjamin Baum was among a group of businessmen who argued that the giant should stay in Syracuse for as long as possible.

The giant and the stories surrounding him had been dug up from inside the earth, like a huge potato. It was as though the famous old English folktale "Jack the Giant-Killer" had come to life in Baum's own backyard. In this story, brave Jack kills the violent, murdering giant, Cormoran, by digging a pit outside the giant's home and concealing it with sticks and leaves. The giant charges out of his hovel and falls into the pit; Jack kills him with an ax and then fills the pit with earth. It was as though Cormoran had been discovered where he fell.

Experts traveled to Syracuse to see the stone man, now known as the Cardiff Giant. But the debate about its origins was stopped short when a tobacconist named George Hull announced that he was responsible for it: It was a grand hoax. After an argument with a Methodist preacher about how he should understand the Bible, Hull had been incensed. The reverend had insisted that the Bible should be taken literally. What nonsense, Hull had thought. Were we to believe that giants were really in the earth as the book of Genesis says? Hull convinced some artisans in Iowa to make a rough carving of a statue, which, he said, was later to be made into a reverential statue of Abraham Lincoln. Hull, at great cost to himself, arranged with the Cardiff farmer to have the great hulk of stone, now weathered by acid buried and rediscovered a year later.

Articles proliferated with the revelation of the hoax. "A Crazy . . . Stone Cutter Worked in Secret Behind a Curtain," screamed one headline. But the public didn't seem to care. The exposure of the hoax only intrigued them more; they came in hordes to see the fake. P. T. Barnum became interested. He offered thousands of dollars for it, saying he wanted to travel the country to show "Old Hoaxey" to the curious public. But the Syracuse men refused the offer. Barnum was furious, so he had a plaster replica of the Cardiff Giant made, and took that on the road instead. His fake of a fake proved popular too.

Baum would no doubt have seen the giant during the Christmas break from Peekskill. It clearly stuck in his imagination and would reappear later in his writing.

At an extravagant New Year's party in the city's main square, twenty thousand people celebrated the year 1870 with a grand feast of flaming barbequed meats followed by two hundred plum puddings. Afterward, Baum reluctantly returned to Peekskill. While the furor over the revelations of the giant's origins rolled on, Baum was marching up and down, feeling awkward and miserable in his dark blue military uniform. He later explained, "I complained to my father about the brutal treatment I felt I was receiving at the school." Baum told his father that "the teachers were heartless, callous and continually indulging in petty nagging." He complained that the masters were "quick to slap a boy in the face, or forcibly use a cane or ruler to punish any student who violated in the slightest way any of the strict and often unreasonable rules." The masters of Peekskill were, he said, "about as human as a school of fish."

The matter came to a head when, sometime before June 1870, Baum was punished for not concentrating in class and he collapsed. This was one of many episodes of dizziness and chest pains that Baum would periodically suffer throughout his life at times of stress. It might have been that he had a weak heart, possibly as a result of contracting rheumatic fever as a young child. This incident was certainly brought on by stress, as his very body rebelled against life at Peekskill.

That episode was the end of it. Baum's father agreed that he should leave. The Hanging Tree stood firm and silent as Baum departed. The ghost of Daniel Strang may have watched as Baum disappeared down the hill toward the Hudson River, the ribbon of water that led back home.

Chapter 6

aum returned to the comfort of rural family life at Rose Lawn, but his vivid imagination found things to fear there. A wild scarecrow chased him through the darker regions of his mind in recurring nightmares. A misshapen, awkward straw man, so familiar in the fields around Rose Lawn, would climb down from its pole and run after him through the fields, with its arms flailing about. At the last moment, just before it caught up with him, the scarecrow would collapse into a harmless inanimate heap of yellow straw and old clothes. Baum's love of stories broadened his imagination, but this also made room for fear. Years later he explained that "one thing I never liked . . . was the introduction of witches and goblins into the story. I didn't like the little dwarves in the woods bobbing up with their horrors."

A mile and a half from Rose Lawn was a seventy-acre woods where such horrors might lurk. Now fifteen, Baum could roam alone, with his brother Harry or with friends. Many extended members of the Baum family lived locally, including various uncles who had properties on the edge of these woods. There were Amanzo, Artemas, and Granville Baum, and there was Great-Uncle Isaac Baum, a farmer and an agent for a lightning rod company. Isaac distributed metal rods that called to the lightning, distracting the devilish electricity and channeling it down into the ground.

Baum enjoyed the outdoors and must have explored these local woods with Harry and other boys, playing among the unusually tall black, red, and white oak, the maple, black cherry, beech, and yellow birch trees. At ground level, a boy would push through musty ferns, wary of insects and poison ivy. This was an ancient forest; the ground had never been cleared or plowed by settlers. Each new sapling grew out of a ground rutted and mulched with rotting trunks of fallen trees; it was at once a cemetery and a nursery. Many years later, Baum imagined a woodland and trees with "their roots intertwining below the earth and their branches intertwining above it." In the summer heat, the forest was dappled with shade, and the canopy became a lush green ocean overhead, so that a boy running through the cool woods might feel as though he were moving under water. In winter, the tall leafless oaks, maples, and beeches formed an imposing giant skeleton that spiraled across the landscape.

There was also a prominent oak grove close by, where trees towered above open fields. In among the densely packed oaks was a clear, still pond that reflected the trees that stared down into it. Years later, Baum revealed his knowledge of forests in his description of a woods with "bushy foliage that roofed the entire forest, save where the sunbeams found a path through which to touch the ground in little spots and to cast weird and curious shadows over the mosses, the lichens and the drifts of dried leaves." A boy could never feel alone in a woods. There were birds, drilling woodpeckers, squirrels, deer, and rabbits, and other creatures real or imagined. The sounds of snapping twigs, flitting birds, and rustling undergrowth could stir an active imagination.

The Plank Road weaved north by the edge of this forest and Baum must have often passed alongside while traveling in a horse-drawn buggy. In summer, the trees would reach out from the woods and bend down over the road.

Baum went with Harry and other local boys on camping trips to Oneida Lake, where they'd take a small boat across the lake to Frenchman's Island, named after a French aristocrat who fled there with his family to hide from creditors in the 1790s.

At home, Baum was growing up surrounded by animals. The heavy traffic on the Plank Road echoed with the sound of hooves trotting on hemlock, of horses, cattle, sheep, and oxen. His father was making good money from his interests in the oil fields. He had extended his property and owned two farms adjacent to Rose Lawn. Benjamin expressed his ambition through his land; nothing but the best was good enough. He built a magnificent barn with a clay floor and running spring water, to house Thoroughbred horses. The homes of many local people weren't as luxurious as this grand stable; some called it Baum's Folly. People paid to have their horses stabled there in the winters. Benjamin was one of the first people to import a herd of Jersey cows to America from England. These brown cows produced unusually thick, creamy milk that could be churned into bright yellow butter and rich cottage cheese. Benjamin's Jersey bull, called the Duke of Hartford, was rented out as a sire.

On a trip into Syracuse with his father in 1870, Baum saw a printing press in a store window. He told his father about it, who then kindly bought him a child's printing press as a birthday gift. Toy printing presses were becoming popular, driven by the new craze for children's amateur journalism. The idea of childhood was changing. Reform movements that aimed to end child labor were making progress, and universal education was on the agenda. Schooling would become compulsory for all six- to fourteen-year-olds in New York State in 1874. Childhood was emerging as a distinct and elongated period of life. Not long before, children had been considered small adults who, after brief years of dependency, were to enter employment and take up adult roles as soon as possible. Now children were to be educated, and between lessons, they inhabited a world apart from adults, defined by play. But what was play? It wasn't clear. Sometimes child's play emerged as a version of adult life in miniature, in which children mimicked grown-ups. A market for commercial toys grew in the mid-nineteenth century, and companies manufactured small versions of adult products, replacing the old homemade toys of the past with such things as tiny armies made of tin, little farmhouses with matching livestock, horse-drawn carriages, and steam trains. The child's printing press, including ink and paper, was another such toy.

Frank and Harry set to work, and in the fall of 1870, they began printing the *Rose Lawn Home Journal*. It included short stories, history, puzzles, riddles, jokes, and poems. The journal reveals Baum's early fondness for wordplay and silly puns, and for scary stories, but it also reveals that he and Harry were deeply curious about the world, intrigued by its nature on any scale. They printed stories by established writers, such as Washington Irving, and various members of the Baum family contributed items. Sister Mary-Louise wrote a poem for the journal and a "Rose Lawn Alphabet," in which each letter stands for someone or something in the Baum family. Under the letters *E* and *G*, the dead siblings Edwin and George are remembered; "G for Georgie," it reads, "our brother in Heaven, Who was taken away."

Benjamin Baum wrote a "History of the Oil Industry," which he called the "new production of the God of Nature." Advertisements for local businesses appeared alongside the stories and articles, to mimic the business angle of a commercial paper.

The title, *Rose Lawn Home Journal*, was printed in a font designed to look like tree branches that had been chopped up and arranged into the shapes of letters. The font was lumpy, knotted, and grainy, suggesting that words were organic. This touched on the idea that stories were themselves organic, living things from inside the human imagination.

The Baum boys printed several issues of the journal in 1870 and 1871, arranging the individual metal letters in reverse mirror writing, then coating them in ink to press against carefully laid-down paper. One issue contained a story about a haunted house and a mysterious stranger believed to be a witch. Baum contributed a riddle that drew on his early fascination with scarecrows:

> *My FIRST expresses much alarm*
> *Or sense of some approaching harm.*
> *My SECOND's heard at early morn;*
> *Or seen amid the new sown corn*
> *Unless my WHOLE in strange array*
> *Frightens th' intruding thief away.*

Baum also wrote a spooky epitaph that read, "Shall we die? We shall die all, all die shall we, die we shall," the point being that it reads the same forward or backward, destroying any sense of right and left. The summer issue of 1871 included a strange article, "Three Curious Needles," that explores a variety of scales from the miniature to the gigantic. One needle is as fine as hair. Another is a sewing needle with scenes from the life of Queen Victoria painted on it that required a magnifying glass to see. And, finally, there is Cleopatra's Needle, a huge obelisk covered in hieroglyphics.

A scientific report notes that all living things are able to maintain their temperature in extremes of hot and cold; "the temperature of birds is not that of the atmosphere, nor of fishes that of the sea," it reads. "The sap of trees," it goes on, "remains unfrozen when the temperature is many degrees below the freezing point of water." The common thread among humans, animals, and plants is called the "vital power." The report offers a democratic vision of what it is to be alive; trees exist on a continuum with animals and humans.

Baum was clearly fascinated by the grand hoax of the Cardiff Giant, unearthed only fourteen miles from Rose Lawn. For one issue of the journal, he wrote a long poem on the true origins of His Giantship. The poem imagines the giant aboard Noah's Ark, which is made "of hickory bark." The stubborn giant jumps overboard to prove that the waters of the flood are shallow; he drowns and "went down to the bottom and stuck in the mud." But the poem also says that perhaps "someone had made it to get up a sell." In this light and silly poem, Baum spun a story around a profitable fake.

Creating the journal involved composition and editing but also the physical craft of setting type, applying ink, and rolling paper through the press without creating smudges. Baum loved it all, from the thrill of arranging his own words into shapes on the page to the dark smell of the sticky ink.

A few days after the Baum boys rolled their July 1871 issue of the *Rose Lawn Home Journal* off the foot-pedal press, a powerful tornado ripped through the area. The sky grew dark in the middle of the day. It was one of the most fearful storms ever witnessed in central New York. The flashes of twisted, silver lightning were followed by cracking eruptions of thunder, and then a "tornado swept through and over the city." Two men were struck by lightning and killed; the roof of a schoolhouse was ripped off; another house was "lifted from its foundation and carried a distance of several feet." A small child was blown into Limestone Creek and drowned.

Trees across Syracuse and its outlying villages were uprooted. A very tall, ancient pine tree that stood on an old Native American burial ground on the edge of Onondaga Lake was blown over. Sturdy old fruit trees were felled. It "was a terrible storm," reads the newspaper, "and will not soon be forgotten."

Two months later, the people of Syracuse looked up into the sky for very different reasons. Since the 1700s, daredevils had been ascending into the unpredictable elements in gas-fueled hot air balloons. The art of aeronautics, as it was called, had been highly developed by the 1840s, and aeronauts demonstrated their skills at reading the winds in towns across America.

There had even been a Balloon Corps in the Union Army of the Potomac during the Civil War. Aeronauts could observe enemy battle positions from the skies. Balloons sailed overhead during several bloody battles; through binoculars, shocked balloonists looked down on the horrors below.

By the 1870s, showman aeronauts were demonstrating their bravery for crowds of stunned onlookers. It had become possible to make fairly straightforward balloons from stitched cloth coated in a mix of glue, alum, salt, and whiting. The sky antics became increasingly impressive. Some strapped a trapeze below the basket, and aeronaut-acrobats would swing beneath their flying balloons, turning and twizzling against the sky. Other aeronauts leapt from their ascending balloons to parachute down to cheering crowds. In September 1871, as high, fast gusts billowed across Clinton Square at the center of Syracuse, a local aeronaut, "Professor" C. C. Coe, attempted to rise into the air in his balloon, called the *New World*. It was to have been a race with other balloons, but the wind put Coe's competition off. They were firmly grounded, yet Coe was determined to make a flight. Crowds of expectant people encircled the giant balloon as it was inflated in the square like a giant lung. By the time it was inflated, the balloon had become the size of a small cloud. A crowd of onlookers filled the square; others stood on the rooftops, peering down on a sea of hats. When the *New World* rose into the air, spectators stared in fright as the basket crashed into telegraph wires and became entangled in them; the balloon finally managed to break free and rise over the wires, only to collide with a block of buildings near Warren Street. But at last the beast began to ascend, swaying to and fro up above the trees and rooftops.

At two miles high, the balloon, heading east, was buffeted south, and Coe and his passengers looked down as farmland, winding rivers, woods, houses, and livestock passed by below. The balloon finally landed safely in Oneida.

Later that month, P. T. Barnum returned to Syracuse for the first time in many years. Financial problems had dogged him for some time and he hadn't been touring since the 1860s. Now he was back with a bigger, better, and more astonishing show. His grand extravaganza, which he called his Grand Traveling Museum, Menagerie, Caravan & Hippodrome, appeared each year in Syracuse for the next decade. For a few days every summer or fall, the city would be transformed by the arrival of "The Greatest Show on Earth." This was more than a circus, although it included circus animals and acrobats.

It was a pageant and a carnival. Caravans of ornate wagons passed through the city, each float representing a different story. There were Sinbad, Bluebeard, and a miniature chariot filled with little people from Lilliput, the land of miniature people in *Gulliver's Travels*. The sides of these dazzling floats were decorated with scenes from the Bible or from history; some included mirrors so that stunned passers-by could see their own distorted faces grinning back at them from amid a scene out of an old fairy tale or Biblical miracle story.

A few weeks before the arrival by train of Barnum's show, an advance guard of promoters would turn up in a gaudily painted wagon to distribute flyers. The *Syracuse Journal* noted that, on one handbill for Barnum's forthcoming show, the "picture of the great showman's face looks like a great big full moon." These handbills aroused people's curiosity with grandiose claims. Barnum promised that for fifty cents they could witness "A Hundred Thousand Rare, Novel and Interesting Curiosities," including marine monsters and an "Equestrian and Hippodramatic Exposition," with two thousand men on horseback, who would perform great feats of horsemanship in three enormous circus rings, viewed simultaneously in an amphitheater. There was "nothing like it ever known on earth" the handbills screamed; it was "the largest and most attractive combination of exhibitions ever known and remains absolutely without a parallel in the history of the world." The three-mile procession, which formed just one part of the pageant, included a herd of elephants, several marching bands, camels, reindeer, elk, gymnasts, jugglers, giants, dwarves, Fiji cannibals, Comanche warriors and chiefs, and what were described as "comic automaton clowns." Barnum claimed that his "collection is greater than even that of the famous builder of the Ark," Noah himself. This was a clashing cacophony, a wild kaleidoscope of animals, people, and strange new machines. Barnum's extraordinary, over-the-top claims for his shows were impossible to ignore, even if, in truth, many of his exhibits weren't quite as authentic as he made out.

Thousands came to Syracuse from the outlying towns and villages to witness Barnum's "mammoth exposition"; they would be shadowed by an army of pickpockets.

Baum was imagining the exotic on a much smaller scale, through his new enthusiasm for stamps. In many U.S. states and foreign countries, postal networks and stamps were a novel invention. Highly skilled artists were creating crafted miniature engravings of elaborate scenes, which were then reproduced en masse. Through his interest in stamps, Baum learned about foreign lands, their currencies, and their heads of state or monarchs, whose faces often appeared on the stamps. We don't know exactly which ones Baum collected, but stamps were available from France, Holland, Cuba, Sweden, Mexico, Java, Japan, Mauritius, Austria, Persia, and Jamaica. American stamps were often decorated with strange, miniature scenes that drew on local legends or national myths and symbols, and each seemed to tell a story. One stamp of the time showed two grizzly bears rearing up on their back legs, like circus bears; another portrayed a bearded angel flying through the air. Another showed a gigantic, long-legged postmaster leaping over the rooftops of a city. One outrageous New York City stamp featured a naked woman standing upright on a bareback pony that leapt through the sky, with steam snorting from its nostrils. This was an exotic sight worthy of Barnum.

At age sixteen, Baum was already ambitious. He developed another amateur journal dedicated to his new interest. *The Stamp Collector*, printed in 1872 and 1873, contained collectors' news, puns, jokes, and reviews of other amateur journals. Written in what the journal called "boy style," a new note of self-assurance leaps from its pages. Baum's interest in stamps revealed his love of things in miniature. Perhaps his printing skills had developed his eye for small details.

Baum was busy. He and Harry were now attending the Syracuse Classical School and on top of his lessons and printing, he was writing stories and poems. In addition to the Grimm and Andersen tales, he read Dickens, Shakespeare, Thackeray, and Charles Reade, whose historical novel, *The Cloister and the Hearth,* he particularly liked. The novel was a richly detailed account set in 1500s Europe. Reade saw himself as a dramatist, and he wrote his fiction with a playwright's eye to staging and dialogue. Baum was working on a novel; he showed his older sister, Harriet, who showed it to their father and encouraged him to keep writing. In 1873, Baum acquired a new, superior press and began doing printing jobs for local businesses. He was so pleased with the new press that he wrote to the company. "In less than ten minutes," he stated, "I had it in perfect working order . . . I never expected to find a press to please me so well." Baum knew many amateur journalists and he discussed launching a new literary journal; he dealt and collected stamps and produced a *Stamp Dealers Directory*. His family encouraged his literary interests but also encouraged him to focus his attention on business. Although his father and family supported his eclectic enthusiasms, they also believed he should direct this dynamism, inherited from Benjamin no doubt, toward clear product and profit rather than to the pure creative pleasure of writing a good story.

In 1873, an economic crisis erupted. The New York Stock Exchange went into a panic due to the collapse of banks that had been overlending to railroad companies. The exchange closed for the first time in its history, for ten days. The crisis sparked a chain reaction of bankruptcies, including Benjamin's Second National Bank. Railroad companies across the country went bust and many people lost their jobs. The years of post–Civil War economic expansion, which Benjamin had been a part of, came abruptly to an end. The economy slipped into a depression that would last for many years. Benjamin's financial losses were a burden that began to affect his health. There was no money for Frank's schooling, and he ended his formal education, at age seventeen, without any real qualifications.

Mortgages and loans were looming, and Baum's beloved Rose Lawn was at risk. In May 1874, two weeks after Baum's eighteenth birthday, Rose Lawn went up for sale. Baum's childhood home was disappearing along with his childhood. The "elegant country residence of B. W. Baum, Esq., well known as Rose Lawn," read the advertisement, "is now offered for sale on very easy terms, or in exchange for property in the city." The announcement added, "This place needs no description from us, as most of our citizens have passed it many times on the pleasant and popular drive on the Plank Road north of our city." To be forced to sell the great estate was a public humiliation for the Baums. But the property didn't sell. It was in limbo; it still belonged to the Baums but they couldn't afford to keep it. They had to sell it as soon as they could.

Putting Rose Lawn up for sale was the culmination of a tension that ran through Baum's childhood between ambition, dynamism, wealth, status, and privilege on the one hand, and creditors, debt, and impending bankruptcy on the other. Beneath wealth and success there always lurked profound, unpredictable insecurity for Baum's family, and this would shape Frank's volatile attitude toward money in the future.

His schooling over, Baum began working for the family. He started work in central Syracuse at Baum, Neal and Co., as a clerk for the family dry goods store, as older brother Benjamin Jr. had done before him. The store was run by his sister, Harriet, and her husband, and it was on Clinton Street in a building rented from the Yates family, who owned Renwick Castle. Baum boarded at the Remington House, now exiled from his childhood home and its hiding places, the oak groves and fruit orchards that had nurtured his imagination in comfort and in fear.

In his employment, Baum was following an established path, not one of his own making. His ambition was growing but lacked direction. The men in his family were in business, farming, or medicine; none of these fields drew him. He was like the restless boy in the old folktale "Jack and His Golden Snuff-Box," who lives in a "great forest" with his father and mother, but whose love of reading stories has made him long to leave the forest to look for adventure. "I see nothing at all here but great trees around me," cries Jack, "and if I stay here, maybe I shall go mad before I see anything."

Benjamin Baum's brother Lyman (Frank Baum's uncle) died in 1877, age fifty-four. Now Benjamin's health was clearly in decline, and his attention turned toward his own death. He purchased the family plot in the grand Oakwood Cemetery. The plot was close to the section for Civil War soldiers, where rows and rows of white stones bearing the names and dates of men all under the age of forty glinted in the sunlight. Opened in 1859, Oakwood was part of the garden cemetery movement in America. The country's growing cities needed suitable burial grounds. The cemetery was a beautifully landscaped park full of old oak and beech trees. Winding paths weaved around undulating slopes, topped with grand stone monuments, gothic mausoleums built by the successful men of Syracuse, the salt manufacturers, wholesale grocers, canal boat haulers, bankers, and railroad investors. Benjamin Baum would be among them. Oakwood had been meticulously landscaped out of sixty acres of dense oak forest that had been thinned out, leaving only the sturdiest trees standing, some of which were over three hundred years old. But the knotty root systems of fallen trees still wound through the ground, and gravediggers were forced to cut through them.

Lyman was buried in the Baum plot. Benjamin had the stone monument to his father, the Reverend John Baum, placed at the center of the site, and memory markers for each of his four dead children, Cynthia-Jane, Oliver, Edwin, and George, were placed in a row beside it. Their bodies may have been disinterred from small local cemeteries and reburied in Oakwood, brought together with their uncle and grandparents.

If so, the process must have disinterred the infants in the family memory as well, and affirmed the ghostly presence of Baum's shadow siblings. Benjamin had chosen the spot where he and Cynthia would be buried. Frank, now twenty-one, came of age in the same year his father established the family grave site. Baum's entrance into adulthood was shadowed by the curious knowledge of where he assumed he would be buried.

Chapter 7

ome time in 1878, a man climbed onto the roof of the Weiting Opera House in Clinton Square in central Syracuse
and placed a small, glass-domed object there. A long wire
attached to it trailed along the roof and down the side of
the building, along the sidewalk, and into a store adjacent
to the theater. Here it was attached to a large metal drum
called a dynamo. That evening the dynamo began to whir and the light on
the roof was switched on. This was the first electric light to appear in Syracuse. A powerful yet invisible force sent crisp, white arrows out into the
night, banishing the darkness, startling dilated pupils that shrank in fright.
Later that year, the city's first telephone was demonstrated inside the Weiting
Opera House. A packed house listened to music coming out of a speaker on
stage, being played by an orchestra in Auburn, twenty-five miles away. How
could the complex woven sounds of many instruments travel so quickly
from Auburn to be heard here in Syracuse? This was surely a form of magic.
New and disorienting technologies were extending the human senses and
collapsing time and space. Humans were being dismembered, the voice
separated from the body and sent down tubes, along wires, to make inanimate machines speak. It's no accident that both these demonstrations of new
technologies took place in a theater. Science had become theatrical.

In the 1870s, Syracuse was an industrial city, but it also had a lively
theatrical scene. There were several opera houses, the Weiting, the Grand,
the Bastable, and numerous halls and meeting rooms where performances of
many kinds took place. The daily newspaper described coming attractions
as the "emotional and the spectacular." There were vaudeville acts in which

stereotypes in funny hats slapped one another and sang songs; there were melodramas, comic operas, and concerts. In the icy cold, dark winters, theaters offered cheap warmth and light. A play called *Without a Home* featured "dog actors" Romeo, Zip, Hero, and Leo. Beyond theaters, there were other forms of entertainment, such as winter ice-skating shows that included Jessie Darling, "The Roller Queen," and William Drown as Humpty Dumpty. There were literary readings and lectures; Henry H. Ragan, for instance, took audiences on an illustrated tour of Italy. Small circuses, though no competition for Barnum's annual show, passed through town, bringing colorful acrobats, caged beasts, and foolish, pranking clowns. And nightly, spirit mediums and clairvoyants offered their services in public séances across the city. These were, some might say, highly stylized theatrical performances starring the dead.

Miss Teenie advertised her skills as a "baby medium." She appeared at the Weiting Opera House, where she demonstrated "the facts of spirit power in full gas light." During her séances, apparently, she would rise into the air and float above her chair, as the pale moon-shaped faces of babies circled her. Disembodied hands would appear bearing flowers, which were handed to people in the audience. A piano would float on stage and play by itself.

And Tom Thumb rejoined Barnum's Annual Extravaganza. The famous little man was now billed as "General Tom Thumb and Wife," Mercy Lavinia, "the Smallest Married Mites on Earth." They were accompanied by Chang the Chinese Giant, "Not the Ogre of Fairy Tales, but Gentleman, Scholar and Linguist—the Tallest Man in the World." Chang's giant presence emphasized Tom and Mercy's tiny stature.

Syracuse was on the route of national touring companies and famous performers like Sarah Bernhardt and Jenny Lind. Local amateur groups put on shows too, allowing audiences to witness familiar faces from the store, the bank, or the local church transformed by makeup that melted and ran under hot gaslight.

The humdrum world of the dry goods business didn't fully occupy or excite Baum. Farming seemed to be the only other option, but that didn't appeal either. Baum saw Uncle Adam Baum and Aunt Kate, his father's sister, in various amateur dramatics. They were both leading lights in the active amateur theater world of Syracuse. Acting might give Baum a chance to try being someone else.

As the first pulse of electricity illuminated the light on the roof of the Weiting Opera House, Baum was leaping into the dark unknown. In 1878, he left the dry goods store and traveled south to New York City. He passed Peekskill, with a shiver perhaps, and watched as the green Hudson Valley gave way to the bony ridged back of Manhattan Island. Baum may have visited New York City with his father as a boy, but now he was alone. The city was in the process of making itself; the Brooklyn Bridge was under construction. Its main pillars were built and a tangle of thick wires and iron poles jutted out across the big brown river into open space. The bridge would open five years later in 1883. The era of the skyscraper hadn't yet arrived, but the crowded streets were still overshadowed by five- and ten-story buildings. The sky between them was crosshatched with telegraph wires and clotheslines. Horse-drawn carts and carriages forced their way through crowded streets. Voices shouting in many different tongues mingled with the smells of horse manure, boiling ears of corn, and roasting nuts. Steam-driven El trains clanked and rattled overhead, cutting out more sunlight. The city was home to thousands of newly arrived Italians, Irish, Germans, Poles, Hungarians, and Russians. The Statue of Liberty hadn't yet arrived; most people didn't feel free. Many were locked into a life of poor sanitation and poverty.

The city was so unlike upstate New York. There were no wild or farm animals here, only horses buckled into harnesses, caged chickens in the market, and rats and insects that scuttled beneath the floorboards. There was no open countryside either, only the recently opened Central Park, a wholly landscaped green space with many small man-made lakes.

Two rivers encircled Manhattan, drawing a clear boundary around a city so teeming with multilayered life as to seem without borders. A young man from upstate who didn't quite know who he was could easily get lost here. This was a form of liberty. Baum was free to build a new, ambitious self, like the vast bridge being assembled over the East River.

Now twenty-two, Baum was tall and slim, with clear gray eyes and a strong nose that pointed down to a great, bushy moustache that curled upward at each end. He explored New York, looking the part of the man-about-town in a velvet coat, smoking fat cigars that he could hardly afford. He secured a role in Albert M. Palmer's theater company, based in Union

Square on the corner of Fourteenth Street and Broadway. In the center of Union Square, statues of Lincoln and Washington stared down at restaurants serving food from the Old World—Hungarian, Italian, French, Russian, and Polish cuisine. Baum loved strong coffee, cold meats for breakfast, and cheese of any kind.

Palmer trained young actors and put them on stage. Baum appeared in *The Banker's Daughter* by Bronson Howard. He performed under the stage name "Louis F. Baum."

The Banker's Daughter was a popular success. Its themes tapped into the troubled economic situation of the time and into those undernotes that had shaped Baum's life. The play was a tale of financial intrigue, a story of threatened bankruptcy and the effects of this on family life and romance. Baum found himself a success in a drama about the very things he was trying to escape.

He supplemented his meager acting income by writing articles for the *New-York Tribune*. Once in New York, Baum's interests in theater, stories, and printing intersected with popular journalism. The dailies were filled with stories about the theatrical life of the city, both on and off the stage. Theatricality spread beyond the theaters onto the streets, as people in the fashionable parts of town, including Union Square, strutted about. The women wore long, dark dresses, lace collars and cuffs, pearl-buttoned jackets, pointed ankle boots laced as tightly as their corsets, and big hats weighed down with drooping ostrich feathers dyed in many bright colors. The men dressed in long, dark coats over suits and soft, dark beaver skin or silk hats.

Baum's acting career in New York didn't expand fast enough, however, and soon he left the city for Bradford, Pennsylvania, a small oil town, where he worked on a weekly journal for a while, drawing on his old days at the pedal printing press. He spread his energy and enthusiasm across a variety of interests, lacking any real direction or focus. He was living between Bradford and Syracuse, staying with family and appearing in various amateur performances with Aunt Kate. With his father and brothers, Baum set up an organization for the breeding of rare fancy fowls, which was fashionable at the time. B. W. Baum & Sons won several prizes for their fine-feathered hens and cocks. Baum helped found a poultry association, wrote articles on the detailed and quirky practices for breeding and showing birds, and founded and edited a specialist journal, *The Poultry Record*, for The Syracuse Fancier's Club. His obsessive eye for detail filled his numerous articles on the subject. For instance, in preparing birds for exhibition, Baum recommended rubbing their scaly legs with Stoddard's Poultry Ointment daily, "beginning at least two weeks before the show." Three weeks before a show, Baum asserted, a bird's "ear-lobes should be washed each day with sweet milk applied with a sponge." His favorite breed was the Hamburg, with their bright, gilded, iridescent feathers. "The Hamburg fancier," he wrote, "may be pardoned for his unbounded enthusiasm." He liked their "aristocratic and dressed-up appearance"; they strutted about in regal finery, like pompous little monarchs.

At Christmastime in 1879, Baum returned to Syracuse and was pulled back into his childhood when he appeared in an amateur production with family members and others. The December production, a pantomime of sorts, was in aid of the Church of the Messiah, a Unitarian church in the city. For one dollar, guests were given a meal and a ticket to the show, *A Mother Goose Entertainment*. Mother Goose, the folk nursery storyteller, introduced old tales, which were then acted out with music and song. Cynthia Baum played Mother Goose, and Frank, though twenty-three, played her son, Jack, the generic cheeky hero of many tales and rhymes, including "Jack and the Beanstalk" and "Jack the Giant Killer." Friends played other folk characters, such as Mother Hubbard, the Big Bad Wolf, and the Man in the Moon. How odd it must have been to return home from his big-city experiences on the New York stage to reenact stories from his childhood.

In March 1880, Rose Lawn was put up for sale again. The "magnificent farm of B. W. Baum" was to be sold at auction due to "mortgage foreclosure." The notice went on: "Somebody will get a splendid barn, and we predict, very cheap." In a bizarre turn of events, Frank Baum bought the house and gardens for $3,500 at the auction. We don't know if Baum possessed such a large sum of money or whether, in the family tradition, he took out a loan to buy the property. The rest of the farmland and the big barn were sold to the influential Crouse family. Baum now owned his childhood home and the 3.75 acres of fruit trees and rosebushes that surrounded it, like the veins around a heart. By holding on to the house and grounds, the seat and hiding place of his imagination, he could perhaps keep a grip on his childhood too.

Benjamin Baum acknowledged his son's modest acting success and his determination to pursue a career in the theater, but he simultaneously moved to discourage him from acting. Benjamin had opened a string of opera houses in the small oil towns where he had business interests. In 1880, he asked his son to manage them. Thus began a new era in Frank's life. For the next three and a half years, he lived on the road, traveling between Syracuse and the small oil towns of New York and Pennsylvania. These were boomtowns of several thousand inhabitants. Most consisted of a few houses along a makeshift main street, with a store or two, a church, a meeting house, a school, a saloon, and an opera house. Each boasted a view of an oil pump tower. The village of Bolivar, New York, for example, grew up around oil works in which Benjamin had invested. He established the Cynthia Oil Works there, which produced oil to burn for lighting on ships. The township grew from a population of 160 to 4,500 in no time. Houses were hastily put up, made of rough hemlock banged together and covered inside with muslin. The town itself was like a flimsy stage set.

Hardworking people needed entertainment, especially in the dark winter evenings, but Baum found it difficult to lure touring companies because many of the towns were isolated and impossible to access in winter. He realized that if he was to keep the little opera houses busy, he would have to produce his own plays, as well as manage the houses.

Baum established a theater company and went on tour performing Shakespearean plays, which he had read and loved since he was a teenager. Many of these theaters were very basic. The company arrived in one small town to discover that the playhouse had no stage. A makeshift stage was put together by laying planks across rows of sawhorses, and Baum's company set about performing *Hamlet* on the wobbly wooden planks. The glowing, gaslit faces of the audience looked on as the ghost of Hamlet's father, played by an actor under a ruffled sheet, tripped and fell into a gap between the planks. The audience erupted into laughter at this unexpected slapstick moment, and the company (with Baum playing Hamlet) was forced to replay the scene many times for their amusement. It was as if a séance had been transformed into a clown show. The aging actor who played the ghost was furious and left the company shortly afterward.

The prospect of empty opera houses with nothing but the breeze and dust passing through them gave Baum a perfect space in which to begin writing. He knew what the boomtown audiences wanted. He set about writing musical melodramas.

The winter of 1881 was a turning point. Baum was traveling between oil towns (he had just opened a new opera house in Richburg, New York), writing plays, and gathering together a touring theater troupe. He returned to Syracuse for a family Christmas party. There, in the warm atmosphere of jellied fruits, mulled wine, and the scent of orange and cinnamon pomanders, he met Maud Gage, a tall, self-willed, and independent young woman with unusually smooth, soft skin. "You'll love Maud," he was told. On meeting her, Baum remarked, cheekily, "Consider yourself loved, Miss Gage." Rather then responding by demurely lowering her eyes, as would have become a nice young lady, Maud looked directly into Baum's face, reached out her hand to his, and said, "Thank you, Mr. Baum. That's a promise. Please see that you stick to it."

There must have been flirtations, at least, in the transient and exotic theater world in New York. But if there were other romances in Baum's life prior to meeting Maud, we know nothing of them; history remains firmly shut here. Over the icy weeks that followed, Baum took every opportunity he could to borrow his father's bay mare and black buggy and travel the ten miles across the wintry landscape, passing the leafless trees along frozen ice-packed roads, to the village of Fayetteville, where Maud lived with her parents. They talked and sang songs at the piano.

As his affection for Maud progressed, so did his writing. In February 1882, Baum registered the copyright of three new plays, all beginning with the letter "M": *The Maid of Arran, The Mackrummies,* and *Matches.* Baum was taking his writing seriously and was about to have his first success, but it would be etched with a trail of fire. The wooden gaslit theaters filled with yards of hanging curtains were tinderboxes. In the spring, his new opera house in Richburg burned to the ground.

The Maid of Arran opened in Gilmour, Pennsylvania, where it was mildly successful. It was good to have the opportunity to try out the new play in front of a small audience, before it moved in May to Syracuse. On May 15, 1882, his twenty-sixth birthday, Baum appeared in *The Maid of Arran* at the Grand Opera House in Syracuse, playing to an audience of friends and family. Baum had adapted the play from the popular novel

A Princess of Thule, by William Black. It was a story of love and social pressure, set on the remote isle of Arran and in London society.

The play featured a ruined castle, like the Renwick Castle recently up for rent, the owner having fallen on hard times. Donning a blond wig, a cap, tight trousers, and leather spats, "Louis F. Baum" played Hugh Holcomb, the romantic lead, a "fair haired stranger." At the beginning of the story, he is an ambitious painter who falls in love with a local Arran woman while visiting the isle to paint the ruined castle. He marries her and takes her with him back to London society, where he turns into a terrible snob and a callous husband before learning the error of his ways. He finally returns to Arran with his wife to live in rural seclusion among simple country folk, in the shadow of the ruined castle, which stirs his artistic imagination. The dry and stilted dialogue was interspersed with seven songs, also written by Baum, worked out on an old piano, no doubt.

Maud was in the audience; she enjoyed Baum's pleasant baritone voice accompanied by a full orchestra. But the review the following day was far from glowing. "Mr. Baum presented his part very quietly and handsomely," read the paper, but others were criticized for overacting. It must have hurt to receive lukewarm reviews at home.

In June, his play *Matches* opened in a small oil town. The musical comedy was broken into three acts: "Brimstone," "Ignition," and "Fire!" True to the title, a fire broke out during the debut performance. The theater was evacuated while the fire was put out, and the play went on again the following night. Baum played the lead, Jack Hazard, a fortune hunter on the make. "Mr. Baum is to be congratulated," read the notice in the *Oil Echo* the following day. "Mr. Baum has a fine presence," it went on, "a handsome countenance and . . . an ease and grace in his stage movements." He "showed himself a complete master of the role."

The troupe packed up their costumes and stage set and headed off to play *The Maid of Arran* on a fast-paced tour of the East and Midwest, traveling many miles by train and horse-drawn carriage in the summer heat. This rapidly expanded Baum's sense of the country, new geographies generating material for new imaginative landscapes. First they headed south to play in Brooklyn for a week, before moving back upstate to Auburn and Rochester. Then they traveled north across Lake Ontario into Canada, to Toronto and Brantford, Ontario, and west to Milwaukee, crossing

Lake Michigan to Grand Rapids, then south over the Wabash River to Indianapolis. After that, the tour's next stop was Chicago. This was Baum's first glimpse of the city that would later play an important role in his life and writing. Chicago was in the process of being rebuilt after the devastating great fire of 1871 and Baum was struck by the city of ruins. It was hardly a city at all, more a burned-out shadow in search of a structure to cling to.

Baum was managing the touring company and playing the lead role. His obsessive attention to detail meant that everything had to be perfect. Uncle John Baum joined him to help manage the finances, but the pressure began to manifest through Frank's body, in dizzy spells and chest pains.

As time passed, the reviews improved. The actors settled into their roles, polished their performances, and rubbed off the rough edges of the plot. Most notices point to Baum's understated performance, his "quiet intensity," "manly dignity and tenderness." The reviews also highly praised the play's innovative use of mechanical scenic effects. Act Four was set aboard a ship that rocked across the ocean, traveling from London to Arran. Designed and engineered by Baum, the mechanical scene was "one of the finest and most elaborate pieces of stage-mechanism ever presented to the public." It was, remarked one notice, "a triumph of mechanical art." As with his first publications made on the toy pedal press, Baum's creative output was often intertwined with practical, skillful manipulation of machinery. There could never have been a *Rose Lawn Home Journal* without a detailed understanding of the workings of the press. Baum liked to tie his storytelling to ingenious new devices.

Amid his busy schedule of touring, performing, and managing the opera houses in the oil fields, Baum's interest in Maud Gage was growing. In the fall of 1882, his dizzy spells and chest pains continued. In addition to the strains of his work, he may have been nervous because he intended to ask Maud to marry him. She had many other suitors; what if she refused? But when Baum looked in the mirror, tweaking his moustache so it curled up evenly at each end, he saw a handsome, fashionable, well-groomed young man. Maud accepted. She told her mother, Matilda Joslyn Gage, who objected. Matilda didn't want her youngest child, her favorite, to marry an actor with no security. Maud was acting rashly, she insisted. Mirroring her mother's strong-willed and independent spirit, Maud told her mother that she would marry Frank whether her mother liked it or not. Matilda relented, seeing that there was nothing she could do. She had brought her daughter up to know her own mind and heart. This was the result.

In November 1882, 148 electric lights were strung up in the streets of Syracuse and switched on. The city appeared anew. After the sun went down, people saw one another's faces clearly as they passed in the street. The shadows that followed them had crisp edges, unlike the wobbly, warped ones cast by gaslight. In the same month, Frank and Maud were married in a simple ceremony at the Gage home in Fayetteville. In the large front room of the grand, white, pillared house, where generous windows ushered in streams of daylight, a large stuffed owl looked on as the couple exchanged their vows in the presence of family and friends. The Reverend Hawley, a local Baptist minister, presided. Frank's parents and sisters were present, as were Mary Hanchett and her daughter, Alice. But his younger brother, Harry, was not on the list of witnesses; he may have been away at medical school in Michigan. Maud, tall and slim, wore a long, fitted white dress with layers of ruffles descending like a waterfall. A lace collar and round earrings framed her face. Her soft, pale cheeks were set off by her dark brown hair and strong dark eyebrows. Baum wore a tall black silk hat and a smart, full-length woolen coat over a dark suit. A local newspaper announced the marriage and reported that, unconventionally, the couple's vows were identical; Maud didn't promise to obey her husband. This marriage marked the beginning of an all-consuming love that sustained Baum and grew more powerful with time.

On the surface, the union looked like a standard rite of passage. Maud was a local girl, a sensible match. The marriage looked conventional to the casual eye, like a sturdy wooden blanket chest, but in truth, it was more like an elaborate jewelry box filled with hidden drawers and priceless charms. Baum's marriage would eventually offer him a way out of the more confining aspects of his background.

The Gages didn't share the values of the Baums. Maud had been brought up, the youngest of four children, in an unconventional household that encouraged intellect, outspokenness, and the questioning of convention. Maud hadn't been baptized. Her father, Henry, was a successful businessman and her mother, Matilda, was an intellectual, a political radical and activist. She was one of the founding figures in the American women's suffrage movement, along with Elizabeth Cady Stanton and Susan B. Anthony. The issue of whether women should have the right to vote had been discussed across the world since the French Revolution in 1789, but the American movement had really geared into action in 1848, at the first women's rights convention held in Seneca Falls, New York. After two days of debate, sixty-eight women and thirty-two men signed a "Declaration of Sentiments," which set the agenda by calling for voting rights for women. The two main campaigning organizations were both formed in 1869, the National Woman Suffrage Association (NWSA) based in New York, and the American Woman Suffrage Association (AWSA), based in Boston. In 1869, Wyoming Territory granted women the vote. But since then, no states or other territories in the West (which weren't officially states yet) had followed suit. Wyoming women remained the only American women who could vote, and they could do so only within that territory.

After 1848, campaigners for women's suffrage met annually at conventions to discuss their strategy. Since the 1850s, Matilda had been an important vocal thinker in the movement; she was a published author and gifted speaker at conventions across the country. Her cellar and attic, so they said, had been stops on the Underground Railroad in the abolitionist years before the Civil War. She was also interested in the history and customs of the local tribes of Native Americans. She had many friends from the Onondaga Nation who would come to the house to visit and talk. The discussions that took place in the Gage household were not simply about commenting on the social, political, and spiritual conditions in America, they were focused on how to change them, were fired by a vision of a different, better world. This environment pushed Baum out of his familiar world and into the intellectual unknown.

Maud was one of the first women to attend Cornell University, where she studied literature. Baum hadn't even finished high school, but the Gage family, in their way, provided him with a college education. He had found an intellectual companion as well as a wife, and a close-knit family in which books, ideas, dreams, and stories were taken seriously, beyond their business utility. Matilda didn't approve of the marriage and she must have seemed an obstacle at first. But, unknown to Baum, he had found in her a vital ally and a fairy godmother of sorts.

Baum had grown up in an ambitious atmosphere of business investment and negotiation, oil prospecting and medicine, and his mother's staunch Methodism. He had broadened his world by entering the theater. The Gages opened his mind in new ways and took him in intellectual and spiritual directions he couldn't have imagined. He absorbed this new atmosphere like the blotting paper that was laid over his fresh, inky signature on his marriage certificate.

Chapter 8

rank and Maud spent their honeymoon at the "fashionable watering" resort of Saratoga Springs. The small town of gaslit piazzas and grand hotels was surrounded by lakes and the health-giving sulfur springs Crystal, Empire, Congress, Eureka, Geyser, Glacier, Star, Seltzer, and High Rock. Saratoga Lake was famous for its tranquility: The Mohawks believed that this stillness was sacred and that if a voice was uttered on its waters, the speaker's canoe would sink instantly.

The newlyweds may have stayed at the Grand Hotel, or at least visited it. Covering seven acres and six floors, the Grand was the largest hotel in the world. It was decked out with lavish marble pillars and colonnades and had a dome-ceilinged ballroom, where crystal chandeliers hung like heavy costume jewelry. On the grounds of the hotel were "illuminated colored lights, presenting a fairy-like scene of bewildering beauty." Maud dressed fashionably in straw hats, long, tight skirts, and high-heeled boots. Visitors could indulge in fine food (freshly caught trout was a specialty), dance, drink, and listen to concerts. A daytime visit to one of the springs, to drink the mineral water and soak in the sulfur steam, was said to restore health, undoing the effects of the night before. In fact, Saratoga Springs was advertised as one of the few places where people could come "for pleasure—living fast and indulging" and yet "return to their homes in better health . . . than when they came." This must have appealed to Baum after months of exhausting touring, dizzy spells, and chest pains.

When the honeymoon ended, the couple soon rejoined the *Maid of Arran* company and set off on tour. The theater troupe traveled west through a trail of small towns, spending one or two nights in each. They passed through Kalamazoo, Michigan; Elkhart and South Bend, Indiana; and Lawrence, Kansas. Traveling so far and for so long by train was a relatively new experience; some people experienced it as flying above the ground or as burrowing through it. Trains rocked travelers into a hypnotic mechanical rhythm that was accompanied by clanking iron and a high-pitched echoing whistle; it was at once industrial and magical.

Maud wrote to her brother, Clarkson, from Omaha. "I like the life very much," she said. "I am very, very happy," she added, underlining both *verys*. "Now as I look back at that day [of her wedding], my joy is perfect." Omaha would feature in Baum's writing in years ahead, as the hometown of the Wizard of Oz.

Four days later, the show played in Topeka, Kansas. "I don't think much of Kansas as a state," wrote Maud to her brother. Topeka also would resurface years later in Baum's stories, as the town closest to Dorothy's farm. Something about these towns must have lodged, like dust or lost pins, at the back of Baum's mind. "The trains in the west," wrote Maud to her brother, "stop at the many small stations and are very slow." Maud and Baum had time to contemplate the flat, open landscapes of Kansas and Nebraska as they traveled slowly by train across them, looking out of windows at enormous skies that overwhelmed small isolated farms, dusty herds of cattle, and vast expanses of arable crops.

By day they moved through the flat, dusty, dry plains of the rural Midwest; by night they took audiences to the exotic and remote isle of Arran.

From Kansas they traveled to Sioux City, Dakota Territory. "I never in my life saw such a wild rough place as Sioux City," wrote Maud to Clarkson. "I saw cowboys and all such and was glad to get away from there." Clarkson had moved out West to the new town of Aberdeen in Dakota Territory. Maud didn't refrain from expressing her feelings: "I don't know how you can like the west. I wouldn't much like to live here. Perhaps I might like Chicago better." Maud went on to assert confidently that "Frank will eventually settle in Chicago or New York." She couldn't have been more wrong or known how deeply intertwined her life would become with the "rough" West she so disliked.

Maud was tiring of touring, of cheap, musty hotels and the constant traveling, but she was also happy. "I would advise you to marry at once," she told her bachelor brother, "and then you will know what it is to enjoy life. Get some nice girl and try my advice. You won't regret it." Maud was certainly enjoying married life, and there were obviously no problems in the marital bed. This was the nearest a middle-class young lady of the late nineteenth century could get to admitting, especially to a man, that she enjoyed sex.

They pushed back East, playing in St. Louis, Missouri; Detroit, Michigan; Columbus, Ohio; and Toronto, Ontario. A few days after they left Toronto, the Royal Opera House, where they had played, burned to the ground.

From here they reentered New York State, and spent February 1883 traveling in freezing temperatures through the towns of central New York and southern Canada; the thick theatrical makeup must have almost frozen onto the actors' faces. They played in Syracuse at the Weiting on Valentine's Day. "A Great Success," screamed the review headline the following day, and of Baum's performance, the notice said that he "was forcible and dramatic to a remarkable degree." Despite the heavy touring schedule, there were financial problems. In early March 1883, the company came to a standstill. Many of the actors refused to continue unless their back salaries were paid. Baum's uncle John Baum was helping manage the company's finances, not very successfully, it seems.

In the same month, Maud became pregnant.

Baum reorganized the company and employed a new leading man. *The Maid of Arran* continued on without him and Maud, traveling south to play in Brooklyn, where thirteen members of the company narrowly escaped being burned alive when their hotel, the Ansonia, erupted into flame.

In the summer of 1883, Baum reexamined his life. He was back in Syracuse. The previous year of ceaseless touring must have passed before his mind, like the landscapes he had seen out of train carriage windows. He folded his memories up into a scrapbook, along with his clippings and reviews. With a child on the way, Baum became the responsible husband and looked for new ways to become a settled breadwinner. His health began to dog him again that summer. The strain of finding himself back in Syracuse with mounting responsibilities and difficulties with money was like a heavy stone on his chest.

In the fall of 1883, the couple moved into a rented house on Shonnard Street in Syracuse, where, in December, Maud gave birth to a son, Frank Joslyn.

In the very same month, Baum sold Rose Lawn, which had been in his possession since 1880, to his mother, Cynthia, for $1. He therefore took a loss of $3,499 on his investment. But his purchase of his idyllic childhood home had never been financially motivated. It may have been a necessity arranged by Benjamin and Cynthia to protect their own holdings. At the very moment his son was born, Baum gave up his childhood home and passed it back to his mother to do with as she saw fit.

Baum's life on the stage receded. He reduced his acting ambitions to local amateur dramatics. He wrote new plays when he could find the time, but they didn't progress beyond outlines and drafts. He was now back in the network of his extended family and he started a business with his older brother, Benjamin Jr., who had trained as a chemist. They opened a store on Water Street in Syracuse, selling all different kinds of oils. Some were derived from animals, such as sperm oil from whales, animal fat, and neat's-foot oil, made from the boiled hooves and leg bones of cattle. Then, with Benjamin Jr.'s skill, they developed Baum's Castorine, a "Great Lubricator," "the best axle oil in use!" "It will not gum or chill," announced one newspaper advertisement. This oil was used to keep machinery and tools working, including carriage wheels and sewing machines. It was also burned for illumination onboard ships.

A raging fire broke out in the opera house in Gilmour, Pennsylvania, while Baum's company was performing *The Maid of Arran* there. All the props and costumes were burned and destroyed. There wasn't enough money to replace them. This fire made explicit that Baum's theater days were over. The company disbanded. Baum's artistic ambitions seemed to have gone up in smoke along with the elaborate mechanical ship and moving seascape that he had designed and built for the production.

Baum was working hard as the superintendent and salesman for Baum's Castorine, traveling with samples of lubricating oil that swilled about in cans. Uncle Adam Baum soon joined the company as manager. Adam hadn't been himself since he had served as a surgeon in the Civil War. His mind was partly broken. Frank now spent a great deal of time with his uncle, and, between business discussions, over lunch or at evening drinks, Adam probably shared some of his war stories, reminding Frank of the terrible things that had happened to men's bodies during the war, which he had only vaguely witnessed as a child.

Raw biology and physical vulnerability dominated Baum's life for the next few years. In October 1885, a frightened runaway horse bolted down Turtle Street, pulling Benjamin Baum Sr. and a farm boy, John Burkey, behind it in a small buggy. They were both thrown to the ground. Benjamin cracked his head, which then oozed with blood on the stony road. The boy wasn't badly hurt. Doctors were called and took Benjamin to Rose Lawn for treatment, but the head injury would cause permanent damage. His bruised body soon began to heal, but his mind and general health declined. The Baums consulted widely; they looked into specialist doctors in Germany.

Meanwhile, Maud became pregnant again and in the spring of 1886, she gave birth at home to another boy, Robert Stanton. The labor was unusually long, painful, and difficult. Soon after the birth, Maud developed peritonitis, a dangerous internal infection, which, in the days before antibiotics, killed many. Maud couldn't leave her bed; a tube was inserted into her side to drain off liquid and pus. Baum had to take charge of Frank Jr. He must have been terrified that Maud would die.

Two weeks later, unexpectedly, Benjamin Jr., Frank's elder brother, died. He was thirty-six years old and apparently died at Rose Lawn. This was shocking news. He was buried in the Baum plot in Oakwood. Harry, recently graduated from medical school and back in Syracuse, was now Baum's only living brother; the other four were dead.

On May 1, 1886, Baum moved his family to another rented house, closer to his sisters so they could help care for Maud and the children. They moved to the oddly numbered 43½ Holland Street. Maud was in bed for six months fighting the peritonitis. Her husband and others worried frantically for her. They knew that death was near, circling Maud. "I have so much on hand," Baum wrote to Maud's brother, Clarkson, "with Maud's sickness, business and moving combined."

He was also writing to congratulate Clarkson on the birth of a daughter (Clarkson had taken Maud's advice and married, a woman named Sophie Jewell). "We have a 'fine jinks' of a baby at our house by the name of Matilda Jewell Gage," Clarkson wrote to him. Baum joked about the benefits and freedom accorded boys more so than girls. He also told Clarkson what he had in store: "You can awaken a dozen or two times each night and soothe your daughter. You can trot her all your evenings upon your knee to remove the blizzards that accumulate. . . . [Y]ou can walk the floor with her over your shoulder, and have a friend point out to you when you reach the store a stream of milky substance down the back of your coat." It was a tiring business, he concluded, one fraught with troubles, but, he added, the smiling faces of children "will brighten our lives for years to come, and make us thank God heartily that they have arrived at all." Baum knew from his own childhood how vulnerable infants were. With Maud ill, Baum spent a great deal of time with three-year-old Frank Jr. and with newborn Rob, building strong, intimate bonds not typical of nineteenth-century fathers. Frank Jr.'s first memory of his father was of waking up, at age three, from a terrible nightmare to see Baum by the light of the kerosene lamp in the hall, rushing to comfort him in one of the white, billowing full-length nightshirts he wore his whole life.

Baum often sang the eerie lullaby to Frank that went "Bye, Baby Bunting, Papa's gone a-hunting, just to get a rabbit skin, to wrap his Baby Bunting in." From this, the child was known as Bunny or Bunting.

Benjamin Baum Sr. died on Valentine's Day 1887. His obituary in the *Syracuse Courier* was rife with errors, but it correctly noted that he had had nine children, five of whom were dead. One of his living children was referred to as "Louis F. Baum"; Frank's stage name had crept off the stage to become his public name in Syracuse, where he had gained a reputation as an actor rather than as a salesman for Baum's Castorine.

Benjamin was buried in Oakwood, next to his son, Benjamin Jr., whose grave was still a fresh mound. Widowed Cynthia sold Rose Lawn soon after her husband's death and moved in with her youngest, Harry, who had opened a medical practice in Syracuse. She sold Rose Lawn to the powerful local Crouse family. This must have galled both Frank and Maud. The Gages had been involved in an unpleasant legal battle with the Crouses when Maud was a child. The Gage children had found a wounded crow and fed and looked after it until it grew into a friendly, wild pet. The bird flew about squawking and flapping. Bob Crouse, their paranoid and powerful neighbor, became convinced that the crow was calling his name in jest. He became incensed and shot the bird. This turned into a local feud. The Gages took Bob Crouse to court; after much wrangling, they lost. But this case contributed to the eventual introduction of a new law that protected wild birds from harm if they were kept as pets.

The death of his father and the sale of Rose Lawn marked the beginning of a downward spiral in Baum's fortunes in Syracuse. The oil business wasn't going well, and Baum wasn't wildly interested in it anyway. His theatrical and artistic ambitions had shrunk to the occasional amateur production. His only publication aside from small journals and newspapers was *The Book of the Hamburgs*, a collection of his writings on fancy chickens.

Maud was recovering very slowly (it would take her two years to heal fully); the boys were doing well. She and the children spent much time in Fayetteville with Matilda, especially while Baum slogged it out on the sales circuit, dragging cans of lubricant around with him. He now got on well with Matilda; he joked and pranked with the whole Gage family, whose house he called Hotel La Femme in a funny menu he wrote for a Sunday lunch. For July Fourth celebrations at the house in Fayetteville, he brought large boxes of fireworks that erupted into bright sparks and sulfur smoke over the flower beds and vegetable patch in the well-tended garden.

In the summer of 1887, Helen Lesley Gage, Maud's sister, wrote an article for the *Syracuse Weekly Express* called "The Dakota Cyclone." Helen, like their brother Clarkson and sister Julia, had moved out West to Aberdeen, Dakota Territory, several years earlier. Julia and her husband, Harry (known as Frank) Carpenter, had moved onto a homestead in Edgeley in 1882, to live on an isolated farm on the open prairie. After visiting her sister in Edgeley during a storm, Helen described how "lightning in a storm is grand, and the storm clouds are always changing; glowing with beauty, a pile of feathery cumulus can change to a terrifying mass of black nimbus, carrying death and destruction with it." She "witnessed two dark vaporous looking clouds . . . from one of which depended a long pointed end looking somewhat like a funnel. . . . It rolled on down into the valley, throwing up a cloud of earth as it grazed the newly ploughed ground." The spinning funnel zigzagged across the road toward a farmhouse, whose inhabitants ran for the storm cellar. As the tornado passed over the house, "boards began to fly against the sides, the house creaked and groaned." It was then suddenly torn from its foundations, "carried a little above the ground to the southeast, where it struck the earth and was lifted over two or three feet north and set down at an angle of forty-five degrees."

Shortly after Helen Gage published this account of a western storm and tornado in a Syracuse newspaper, Baum began to formulate a plan for his escape from the woodlands and lakes of central New York, where his business was faltering and his ambitions were being crushed. In prairie Native American belief, a vision quest was often initiated by powerful lightning and a spinning tornado. Helen Gage's account of the tornado was a sign of sorts; Baum was about to begin a quest of his own, which would take him out West to the land of violent storms.

Part II

THE GREAT PLAINS

1888 TO 1891

Chapter 9

In 1888, Baum bought a human-head-size box with a big glass eye at one end. This was the new Kodak, the first-ever amateur portable camera. Newly released onto the market, this revolutionary device made the technology of photography (first developed in the 1830s) available to nonprofessionals. Until now, anyone interested in taking their own photographs had to wield large cameras and awkward tripods. Most people went to professional photographers if they wanted portraits. With the Kodak, the ability to capture images in light was liberated from experts and put into the hands of anyone with twenty-five dollars to spare. "You Press the Button, . . . We Do the Rest" was the slogan that advertised the Kodak. The box was sent to the purchaser preloaded with enough film for a hundred pictures. Once the film was used, the amateur photographer sent the whole thing back to the company in Rochester, New York, where the images were developed, the camera was reloaded with film, and both were sent back to the owner. The novel device was highly portable since it didn't require a tripod. In the manual that came with it, detailed drawings of disembodied hands demonstrated how to take a photograph and wind the film, and they looked much like the drawings in manuals for magicians, where similarly free-floating hands demonstrated card and coin tricks. Ever enthusiastic for novel technologies that blended science with what seemed to be magic, Baum bought a Kodak as soon as it came onto the market, spending twenty-five dollars he could barely afford. He soon learned how to develop his own photographs; this was another form of printing, in pictures rather than in words. He soon equipped a darkroom, where he brought out grainy images of the world around him with toxic mixtures of chemical potions.

"I've got an idea into my head," admitted Baum in a letter to his brother-in-law, Clarkson Gage, in July 1888. A month earlier, he had taken a detour from a sales trip to Minneapolis to visit Clarkson and his sisters-in-law, Helen and Julia, in Aberdeen, Dakota Territory. It had been a surprise visit. He arrived in Aberdeen by train with his Kodak on June 15 and stayed around five days, capturing many photographs during his stay. He would have passed through Illinois en route, which in June 1888 was experiencing the cicada hatch across the region, the seventeen-year cycle when millions of grubs surface out of the earth in one mass emergence and hatch into flying insects that together create an intense, overwhelming, deafening buzz. At train stations across the state, people pinned the insects to posts and threw knives at them. Baum had passed through Dakota Territory in 1882 in a quick visit to Sioux City on tour with *The Maid of Arran*, but this was his first trip onto the northern Great Plains, where the new town of Aberdeen had so recently sprung up on the flat land, under the big sky. Baum's novel interest in the new art of photography caught the attention of a local newspaper. "Mr. Baum," reported the *Aberdeen Daily News*, "was proficient in the art," of "the fascinating pursuit, amateur photography," and "during his stay in the city secured a number of fine negatives of Dakota land and cloudscapes." When he pointed the glass eye of his box and clicked the brass button, the land and sky were captured as a memory written in light; "photography," after all, means light-writing. The deep startling blues of the sky would have dominated his view as he looked through the lens, but these colors couldn't be caught as the film was black-and-white. Instead, the images were like extremely detailed pencil sketches. George Eastman, Kodak's inventor, said he wanted to make amateur photography "as convenient as the pencil." Photography was to become an important interest for Baum, a noncommercial form of technological creativity that trained his eye to notice details.

Aberdeen had grown into a town of four thousand inhabitants at the juncture of several railroads; people called it the Hub City. The town had begun as a few shacks along the railroad just seven years earlier, in 1881 (only four years after the first settlers had arrived in the area in 1877). Geologically, the town was situated on the bottom of a prehistoric lake, which is why the prairie in this region was totally flat for miles, unlike the undulating plains farther south. Now the vast dome of the sky, instead of water, covered the ground. It's no surprise that Baum turned his attention and the mechanical eye of his camera to the sky to capture cloudscapes. This was the land of Big Skies. Some Dakota people said it felt as though the sky had swallowed the land; it was in a sense a skyscape. In photographing the sky and its epic drama of shape-shifting cloudscapes, Baum was in effect photographing pure light, emptiness, and potential. The plains looked to the newcomer, wrote Willa Cather, not like "a country at all, but the material out of which countries are made."

The history of the area could be heard in the layered sounds that filled Aberdeen. Beneath new sounds, such as the whistling of steam trains, the buzzing of the recently erected electric streetlamps, and the ringing of bells in the telephone exchange, were older sounds like the rushing of wind through the grass, the chirruping of meadowlarks, and the humming of insects. Baum couldn't capture these with his camera.

This place was totally different from central New York and the East. There were few trees, which was good for agricultural settlement because there were no woods to clear and stumps to pull. But easterners and Europeans were used to seeing trees that shaped the landscape. The land lacked a sense of scale without them. The open western prairie was so shocking to the droves of newcomers that arrived from the end of the Civil War that they called up images of a moonscape when trying to describe it.

When Baum returned to Syracuse after that first visit to Aberdeen in 1888, he took with him images, in his mind as well as in his camera, of a wide-open space, a vast, uninterrupted sky, an endless stretch of short, waving grassland, and amid this, a new town in its infancy. He saw a space into which he could project his ambition.

In his July letter to Clarkson, Baum acknowledged his frustration. "I find since my arrival home that there is very little prospect of my being able to arrange my business here in a satisfactory manner for the future." Of the Baum's Castorine company he wrote, "I can see no future in it to warrant my wasting any more years of my life." One of his problems was his business partner, Uncle Adam Baum. There were rumors of gambling and debts, but Baum simply said that he found it impossible to instill "business qualifications into my partner, to enable him to rise to the occasion." Baum admitted that this and serious competition had discouraged him. The space of the prairies had gone to his head; "since coming home I realize how crowded the east is," he wrote. The open landscape he had caught on film was calling to him. "In your country there is opportunity to be somebody," he wrote. "I feel as though Aberdeen is destined one day to be a good city, and it may be a metropolis," he added. Yes, Baum admitted, he did have what they called the "western fever," as though his plan was a kind of madness he had caught out there, something that had taken hold of his mind and body and made both shiver.

The town of Aberdeen was in its infancy, he said, and what it really needed was a variety store, a "bazaar selling fancy goods." He could sell all manner of luxury items, start a camera club, and provide some eastern luxuries to the hardworking folk on the prairie. He would move out to Dakota Territory in the fall and open the store in time for Christmas.

That summer, his last in central New York before leaving for Dakota, Baum took a series of photographs with his new Kodak. He took pictures of his parlor at 43½ Holland Street. In his photograph of the uninhabited room, Baum tried to capture the multipatterned wallpaper, the glass dome of the kerosene lamp, the piano, and the numerous framed prints hanging on the walls. This was a novel way of gathering memories; you could abandon a home, but the layout of the rooms you no longer inhabited would stay with you in photographs, which brought vivid details back in a way memory alone never could. He also took many pictures of the Gage house in Fayetteville. He caught a shot of the house out front. Then he turned and captured the tree-lined street sloping downhill toward the river. People stood outside their homes and stared at him as he brandished his strange little box. He snapped the garden to the side of the house; the flower beds and neat lawn paths winding between them would be an alien sight in the open grasslands of the Dakota prairie. He went inside the house and captured more images of the uninhabited rooms. He was leaving this old house, its reassuring pillars and quirks, such as the upstairs windowpane where, during a stay with Matilda on suffrage business, Susan B. Anthony had scored her signature into the glass with a diamond ring.

Baum also photographed Maud, his two boys, and other family members. In professional portrait photographs of the era, people often look severe and formal. This was in part a result of having to sit absolutely still for quite some time while the photographer opened the aperture to let in enough light to capture the stiff images of his clients. In contrast, the amateur Kodak enabled images to be taken instantly, and as a result, the pictures of Maud and the boys are informal, relaxed, and intimate. Baum took photographs of friends and his extended family, people he was leaving behind, and captured their faces in images that wouldn't age with them.

In the fall of 1888, after several farewell parties, the Baum family left Syracuse and traveled west by train, their furniture and belongings packed up in crates. They stopped off in Chicago, where Baum ordered items for his new variety store from wholesalers. After traveling for a week, they arrived in Aberdeen on September 20, at twilight. What did they see when they stepped down from the train, as the steam sailed upward to mingle with the clouds, and the reality of their decision was laid out before them? Their new home came in the shape of a dusty, wide street packed with wooden and brick buildings, two banks, several hotels and drugstores, and numerous other business, including Clarkson's general store. There wasn't a single tree along the flat expanse of Main Street. The uninterrupted sky reared up between the buildings. On their way into Aberdeen, they would have crossed the James River and looked down upon it as the one vital feature of the landscape that made this vast, flat, dry place livable. Clarkson was there to meet the travel-weary group. They drove back by horse and buggy to the brand-new Gage home in the newly platted district of West Hill. Not long ago, this area had been flat grassland where only coyotes, antelopes, prairie dogs, snakes, and grasshoppers had lived.

Baum had arranged to rent a store on Main Street from Helen and Charles Gage. They had moved to Aberdeen in 1887 and put up the building, and they lived in the apartment above it. Clarkson and two friends from Fayetteville ran the town's main general store a few blocks away. Beard, Gage and Beard (known by local children as "Bird Cage and Beard") sold all essential items. Rolls of patterned cloth (including gingham) were piled in the front of the store. The ceiling hung with brass lights; behind the counter, shelves reached up to the two-story ceiling and were stacked with necessities. Jim, the store dog, roamed around sniffing at customers.

Once the goods had arrived from Chicago, Baum wrote advertisements for local newspapers, announcing that Baum's Bazaar would open on Monday, October 1. The promotions promised "a magnificent and complete assortment" of household goods and luxuries for adults and children. Customers would be able to buy such fancy goods as glassware, Japanese baskets, table lamps, vases, tea sets, goblets, finger bowls, foot warmers, silver call bells, knife rests, piano lamps, ornate mirrors, gold pens, sugar tongs, gold toothpicks, silver paperweights, barometers, manicure sets, candlesticks, and cloth flowers. In other words, all those eastern niceties that, Baum imagined, the homesteaders out on the prairie must be yearning for. He also provided them (and himself) with high-quality cigars. And for children, who until then had likely played with homemade toys, pets, and imaginary friends lost in the prairie grass, there was every toy imaginable, including dolls, Chinese lanterns, bicycles, tricycles, music boxes, hobby horses, toy clocks, popguns, tin trains, magnetic toys, and soldier sets. Baum promised that every "lady attending the opening day will be presented with a box of Gunther's Candies."

"Peruse, Ponder, Purchase," called one advertisement. The store was an Aladdin's cave of ornate, multicolored, exuberant luxuries packed from floor to ceiling. It was a modest-looking wooden building from the outside, but inside, it was full to the brim with what Baum saw as people's unfulfilled desires. The Oriental goods, fancy items, and up-to-date fashions would enable the people of Aberdeen to live a refined lifestyle featuring sugar tongs, finger bowls, gold toothpicks, silverware, and ornate mirrors that would reflect back rooms cluttered with clear evidence that the West had been won, that this life out here on the Great Plains was working.

From the town's birth in 1881, many of those who had traveled west to build Aberdeen were from central New York; some were from Syracuse. Beyond Maud's siblings, Baum already had many connections with Aberdeen people. Since the 1862 Homestead Act, people had flooded onto the land in the outlying plains around Aberdeen; by 1888, all the land had been claimed. Julia Carpenter, Maud's sister, still lived out in Edgeley, fifty miles north of Aberdeen, on a remote homestead with her husband, Frank, and their two children, Harry and Magdalena. Other settlers in the town and surrounding farms were German, Scandinavian, and Russian. Many of the easterners who had started new lives in Aberdeen were well-educated professionals; the town boasted many lawyers, bankers, and doctors. Several households had pianos, which sent tinkling, genteel music out into the wide-open prairie, to be lost on the wind that never stopped blowing because there were no trees to act as windbreaks.

The people of Aberdeen were ambitious and had brought to the town as much modern technology as they could. Water was drawn from an artesian well, which had a terrible taste until you got used to it, and many people added sugar, ginger, or vinegar to make it more drinkable. There was also a modern sewage system, and the first telephone exchange had opened in 1886. The town had many hotels (including one with an ice cream freezer), an opera house (although it was rather run-down, Baum noticed), several schools, and well-established churches. Dressmakers charged seventy-five cents per day to work at a client's house, and a milliner ensured that the women of Aberdeen dressed in the latest fashions gleaned from the pages of eastern magazines. Walking along Main Street in summer, women would hold on to their lavish new hats to prevent the hot prairie wind from blowing them away.

A woman named Elizabeth Edgegoose ran a steam laundry to bleach and starch the town's bed linen. She also opened a fifty-foot glass greenhouse for growing flowers. She grew heliotropes, fuchsias, carnations, roses, and houseplants from seeds sent west in packages from eastern suppliers. These flowers were very different from the wild prairie flowers that bloomed every spring amid the grasslands, the sage, yucca, prairie cactus, buffalo berry, and junipers, which the easterners of Aberdeen had no taste for. Grown under Mrs. Edgegoose's glass, the red, yellow, and pink flowers and the dark green leaves of aspidistra plants were a surprise to see in homes on the flat prairie, where no such things grew naturally. Baum sold fresh flowers in the Bazaar, which must have come from the Edgegoose greenhouse; they were extremely popular with people who missed flowers that spoke of gentler climates where trees and vegetation were abundant, where the emptiness didn't press upon you so.

The town was full of optimistic and ambitious settlers who promoted their new town and encouraged others to join them, in pamphlets that called Aberdeen "the new trade and railway center of the northwest." "Six years ago," read an 1887 booklet, "this wonderful young city was founded upon the prairie marked by the fresh imprint of the buffalo's hoof. . . . Her future is certain. Aberdeen is a town fixed by fate for a Big City, and she cannot help it." The early and mid-1880s had been prosperous because the crops in the outlying farms had been plentiful and wheat prices good.

But in January 1888, five months before Baum's first visit to Aberdeen, a catastrophic blizzard had hit the area, the worst in living memory. It became known as the Children's Blizzard because so many schoolchildren died in it. In midmorning of January 12, without warning, the temperature across Dakota Territory plummeted by eighteen degrees in less than three minutes, the wind began to roar, and tiny dust particles of ice blew across the prairie. Snow as fine as flour blew in through keyholes and under doors, filling the ground floors of homes and schools. There was zero visibility outdoors, so many people became disorientated and lost; one farmer lost his way in the space between his house and his barn and froze to death. Five hundred people died in the blizzard, many of them children who froze because they were trapped in schoolhouses or traveling on their way to school when the blizzard struck. In the spring of 1888, just before Baum arrived in Aberdeen with his Kodak camera, the snow had melted to reveal the dead bodies of missing adults, children, and livestock.

The number of farms in Dakota Territory had increased fivefold in the eight years before the infamous blizzard. The population had quadrupled; this devastating freak weather shocked them all. The climate on the plains was extreme and unpredictable, but now people turned to look at the enormous sky with redoubled mistrust and fear. The blizzard suggested that this unfamiliar landscape and its wild weather harbored forces the settlers couldn't understand or control.

Baum's Bazaar opened to roaring trade in October 1888. One thousand people visited the store on its opening day. In one advertisement, Baum explained that he had bought a "poetry grinder" that pumped out rhymes to celebrate the store, advertising "good real Japanese" and lamps that "can't fail to please," "bric-a-brac so rare" and "flowers so fresh and fair." This was a quirky way to attract customers, and showed that Baum understood the importance of marketing and promotion.

One week after the store opened, Aberdeen was visited by a group of Native American chiefs traveling east by train en route to Washington, DC, to meet the president. They stopped in Aberdeen for food. The group of fourteen men was heading to Washington to discuss treaties and land rights in regard to the Standing Rock Agency, which would soon become the

Standing Rock Reservation in northern Dakota Territory. John Grass, a Blackfoot Sioux chief, was outspoken in his condemnation of the U.S. government's offer of fifty cents per acre to purchase tribal lands. He was accompanied by the nationally famous Hunkpapa Sioux, Sitting Bull. The group would rendezvous with fifty more chiefs in Minneapolis and then travel together as a large delegation to Washington to discuss the complex web of treaties in which they were trapped. The numerous plains tribes were being forced onto reservations after years of violence, intertribal wrangling, and badly managed, confused U.S. government policies.

Crowds of Aberdeen people thronged to see them, curious to stare at the native people they had learned to admire and fear. The profound ambivalence in settlers' attitudes was clearly expressed the following day in the *Aberdeen Republican*, which described Sitting Bull, John Grass, Big Head, Mad Bear, Thunderhawk, High Eagle, and Bear's Rib as "the heroes and sages of the great nation." The scene was a "strange and picturesque sight," a band of "original proprietors" surrounded "by crowds of curious white men, themselves wandering strangers in a city built upon the very plains upon which many of them have pursued and struck down the buffalo, deer and antelope." This was a clear admission that the native peoples had been there in Aberdeen, on the land where the town was built, first. Baum may well have joined the crowds of onlookers. A week after his business had opened and his new life on the prairie had begun, this visit reminded him that the plains and their dominating skies might look wide open, uninhabited, like an ocean of wilderness and potential, but in fact the land had been occupied before and had a long human history attached to it.

Native peoples were highly visible here. Drifting Goose, a local Sioux chief, was on good terms with the white settlers of Aberdeen and was often seen in town. Clarkson was extremely interested in the history of the area, including its pre-settler days. He kept a large scrapbook he filled with clippings from newspapers and magazines about the history of the region; he was historian of the town's Old Settlers Association. He knew many stories about Drifting Goose and about the removal of native peoples from the area during the construction of the railroad.

The settlers ideally wanted to see the open plains as a blank canvas onto which they could project their dreams for the future. But if they looked carefully, they saw that the landscape wasn't a blank canvas at all but filled with native history and stories. Five miles north of Aberdeen, for instance, was Paha Waken, or Spirit Mound, a hill said to be inhabited by tiny people eighteen inches tall with large heads, who would attack anyone who dared to climb the mound. South of Aberdeen there were more landscape features with layers of stories attached to them. In the highly contested region of the forested Black Hills, there was a cave system known to the Lakota as Wash Niya (the Breathing Place). Strong winds and rolling fog billowed out of the cave, so it became a giant exhaling mouth. Native lore said that out of the cave the First Man had emerged from the Underworld; hordes of tiny buffalo the size of ants had climbed out too, which had then grown large and fat on the grasslands. Discovered by a white traveler in 1881, the cave was taken over and managed as a popular tourist site known as the Wind Cave. Inspired perhaps by the Cardiff Giant, an enormous petrified man was "found" in the opening of the cave in 1892, guarding its secrets and stories.

Northwest of the Black Hills, just over the border into Wyoming, was a huge stone hill known as Bear Lodge Butte. In Native American terms, seven sisters and their brother had been playing when the boy was transformed into a monster bear that chased his sisters. The girls ran and reached a giant tree stump that called to them to climb on top to safety. Once on top of the stump, it began to grow and reached upward away from the bear, which clawed at it, leaving deep rakes in the side of the stump. From here the sisters ascended into the sky to form the constellation Pleiades. The giant rock was named Devils Tower by a white explorer in 1876, and it soon became a popular tourist attraction. These contested geological sites, surrounded by varied tales, would emerge in different forms later in Baum's own stories.

The profound ambiguity felt by many of the settlers of Aberdeen toward plains tribe peoples, whom they revered, feared, looked down upon, admired, and loathed, didn't prevent them from being fascinated by these local landscape legends, where stories buried in the earth gave the land a human significance beyond attempts to build a modern town on top of it or plow it into productive agricultural fields. Baum and other settlers had believed they could build a future from scratch out in the wilderness, but once they learned more about the prairie on which they had staked a claim, they realized that this was a highly contested landscape, brought to them through conflict with tribes and decades of violence. The myth of the West as an open space ripe for civilizing clashed with a different story, one of intertribal conflict, confused diplomatic relations between the U.S. government and the tribes, and a trail of broken treaties. In the decades after the Civil War, when millions of people had moved onto the plains, violence between the U.S. military and tribes had escalated; there had been over one thousand military engagements between them in this period. In this borderless landscape, an epic struggle between cultures and peoples was taking place. Beneath the optimism and entrepreneurial energy that was building Aberdeen, there lurked a rhizome of complex fears, guilt and racism, and the threat of violence. Baum had entered a region and staked his future on a ground bloodied and traumatized by conflict between opposing groups, who competed not only over the land and its natural resources but over what the land itself meant. Baum began to drink in this volatile cocktail along with the brackish water from Aberdeen's artesian well.

The Bazaar was doing so well that Baum opened a branch store fifty miles east of Aberdeen in Webster. He put in orders for Christmas season stock and advertised his store as Santa Claus's headquarters. But news soon arrived that all his stock had gone down with the *Susquehanna*, sunk in Lake Huron. The Chinese lanterns, glassware, music boxes, hobby horses, and wax dolls had sunk to the bottom of the lake, to be stared at by disconcerted fish and be slowly interwoven with reeds. Baum had to hurriedly reorder. In the bitter cold and deep snow of winter on the plains, icicles would form on men's moustaches, people often had to dig tunnels through the snow rather than clear it, and front doors could be buried, forcing people to use upstairs windows as main entrances until the snow melted. Many feared a repeat of the January 1888 Children's Blizzard. Christmas was a welcome holiday. Baum's new stock arrived and tinkling sleigh bells, Christmas trees, now quite a sight on the treeless plains, and brightly colored gifts lifted moods in the harsh winter. The Christmas trade was buoyant, and on December 24, Baum sold goods amounting to $230. He was a dapper storekeeper, pacing about the Bazaar among the dolls, silverware, lamps, and mirrors in his tailor-made suits and shiny patent leather shoes, examining his fob watch tucked into his waistcoat pocket, and slicing off the ends of his cigars with the silver cigar clipper he kept attached to the other end of the gold chain.

News of change arrived from Syracuse at the end of 1888. Uncle Adam was dead; there was rumor of suicide. The Civil War surgeon had survived the war but had struggled during the years of his own and the nation's reconstruction. Sadly, Baum's niece, eleven-year-old Mary-Louise, was also dead. We don't know how or why she died. A photograph that Baum had taken of Mary-Louise with Frank Jr. before he left Syracuse now took on renewed significance. This was most likely the first and only image of the girl, a sad, grainy, monochrome snapshot taken in the year she died, and it must have kept her memory unusually vivid. Her face could be remembered in detail now, in ways the faces of other children who had died but hadn't been captured in light never could. Mary-Louise and Adam were buried in the Oakwood Cemetery on either side of the central monument to the Revered John Baum.

There was more strange news from the East. The *New York World* published a story signed by the Rochester medium Maggie Fox, now in middle age, in which she said her spiritualist gift was a hoax. "Spiritualism is a fraud and a deception," she wrote. She said she had produced the noises and rappings by cracking her double-jointed toes. She stood in her stockinged feet on a pine platform in front of an audience of two thousand in a hall in New York City and demonstrated how she could pop and crack her toe joints. A girl had seemed to conjure spirits; now a woman, she claimed that her ability to perform occult magic had been a trick created by her mischievous clicking feet.

Chapter 10

rank and Maud launched into the social whirl of Aberdeen, trumping neighbors and winning tricks in long evenings of card games like whist and euchre. Cards worn rough at the edges and made waxy from hands were passed from palm to palm, shuffled and reshuffled. The women of Aberdeen would knit in groups, with needles made from polished turkey quills, and gossip at innumerable teas, children's birthday parties, and church meetings. Social gatherings were reported in the local papers as an official form of gossip, and Maud Baum's name often appeared on the guest lists. She joined in but years later admitted to her niece, Matilda, that she found the small social network frustrating. She didn't like people "who were always maintaining a standard, afraid to try anything new." Unlike most women, Maud proudly wore elaborately decorated hats to lunches. Maud's personalized book labels read "It matters not what others think of me, it is what I think of myself." Beneath this was a drawing of an Asian figure that looked much like a samurai warrior.

The Baums joined in the amateur theatricals sponsored by the Episcopal church. This was the only Christian church the Baums were ever affiliated with during their marriage, and Baum's resistance to it was initially suppressed by his enthusiasm for its theater productions. In plays, he could call up some of his old life on the stage. There were other entertainments too. Local musicians played at musical evenings, and Clarkson stood in front of his house on clear dark nights and gave talks about the constellations and geology, two of his particular interests.

The Baums held séances at their home, especially if Maud's mother,

Matilda Gage, a spiritualist enthusiast, was staying with them. Mediums and clairvoyants visited the Baums to sit in a circle and call up the dead (one medium seems to have been called Genie Van Loon). The table would tip and occasionally they heard a knock, confirming the existence of some spiritual presence.

Baum was reading the works of Madame Blavatsky, the founder of the Theosophical movement, which heightened his interest in invisible realms and the spirit world. She founded the movement in New York in 1875, and her great Theosophical treatise, *Isis Unveiled*, was published in 1878; Matilda Gage, the intellectual engine of the family, had joined the Rochester Theosophical Society in 1885. She sent her theosophist books and pamphlets to her children, and the family formed a reading group to discuss the books in letters and in person when they met. Maud and possibly Frank read *Isis Unveiled* in the summer of 1888, as well as works on Buddhism. In the two volumes of *Isis Unveiled*, subtitled *A Master-Key to the Mysteries of Ancient and Modern Science and Theology*, Blavatsky compared religions and catalogued the outrages done in the name of Christianity in medieval witch burnings, noting particularly the persecution of children and teenage girls as witches. The aim of Theosophy was, according to Blavatsky, to unite science and theology through Hinduism and Buddhism, and "to show true souls how they may lift aside the curtain, and, in brightness of that Night made Day, look with undazzled gaze upon the Unveiled Truth." She discussed the occult qualities of minerals and plants, and outlined her belief in the hidden reality of Elementals, unchanging immortal spirits perceptible only to the inner eye of the clairvoyant. Electricity was a form of natural magic; the astral soul could leave the body and move about on a higher plane before returning to the physical body. If Baum didn't take all the tenets of Theosophy literally, the imagery of hidden spheres, Elementals, astral traveling, and the occult powers of nature became potent influences on his imagination.

Baum's other reading out on the prairie took his mind in different directions. Edward Bellamy took him into the future, and Andrew Lang took him back to folktales of prehistory. Bellamy's 1888 novel, *Looking Backward*, was a sensation, selling over a million copies to become the bestselling book since Harriet Beecher Stowe's *Uncle Tom's Cabin*. It was as much a manifesto as a story. A man falls into a hypnotic sleep in 1887 in Boston and awakens in the year 2000 to find a society transformed into a utopia, in part through the use of elaborate forms of advanced technology.

The Blue Fairy Book, Andrew Lang's first edited collection of classic folktales, came out in 1889, and was a bestseller. The book included old tales from France, Norway, Germany, and England. Terrifying Bluebeard, little Tom Thumb, Jack the Giant Killer, Red Riding Hood, and Sleeping Beauty all came back to Baum now, in a fashionable new collection aimed at both children and adults. "The Terrible Head" featured a magic cap of darkness and "shoes of swiftness" that enabled anyone who wore them to "fly as fleet as a bird or a thought." Baum read these old tales to his two boys, now six and three, experiencing his old love of fairy tales again but now blended with the anxieties that many parents feel about reading odd and frightening stories to their children before bed; what kinds of nightmares might these tales provoke?

Blavatsky, Bellamy, and Lang were a potent mix for Baum's mind. Out on the open prairie, so recently settled and without an established Christian history, it was possible to think new thoughts. It must have been eerie to read about hidden Elementals, futuristic utopias, and ancient fairy-tale woods cursed by witches out on his porch overlooking the flat plains. The wide-open skies and the sparsely populated land made space for these ideas to develop; there was nothing on the horizon to hold them back.

The spring of 1889 was unusually dry. The people of Aberdeen wanted the luxury goods available at Baum's Bazaar, but they couldn't always afford them. Baum started selling on credit, and once he'd given credit to one person, he had to extend it to another. The list of credit accounts grew. Despite the increasing fear of drought, Baum remained hopeful. His Easter advertising campaign was full of optimism. "Aberdeen stands upon the threshold of the grandest era in her history," he wrote. "About her are millions of acres covered with tender, ambitious shoots, of infant grain," he went on, animating the crops with the same ambition that fueled the people of the town. He predicted "peace and plenty in our midst." "The sun of Aberdeen is rising," he called, "its powerful and all-reaching beams shall shed its glory all over the length and breadth of the continent, and draw the wandering eyes of all nations to our beautiful hub." Baum's response to the whispers about fear of drought and economic problems was to shout all the louder that all would be well, that the crops wouldn't fail.

In a further attempt to boost the town, Baum and a group of young Aberdeen businessmen established a local professional baseball team, the Hub City Nine. "Nothing creates enthusiasm like baseball," wrote the *Aberdeen Daily News*. Baum was elected the club's first secretary; he threw himself into the task of establishing and promoting the team, turning precious energy away from the Bazaar. But he hoped the new venture would be good for both the town and his store; Baum's Bazaar would provide the uniforms and equipment for the team. Money from local businesses was raised to fund the venture, and a grandstand to seat five hundred people was built for the games. While the Hub City Nine was getting under way, Baum had yet another idea for promoting the store. An Ice Cream Boudoir, costing one thousand dollars, was installed in Baum's Bazaar. The soaring heat gave people an appetite for ice cream. Baum offered exotic flavors like bisque, caramel, tutti-frutti, and blood orange. A carved red-granite soda fountain with silver draft tubes was placed in the center of the store, dispensing sweet, fizzy sodas to accompany fruity ices. This was an enormous extravagance in the face of mounting concerns about a possible drought.

Baum could never concentrate on one thing at a time; his ambition-driven multiple interests skittered through his mind, pushing him in many different directions at once. He found an opportunity to use his camera and to write an article for *Harper's Monthly* about life on the prairie in a Russian community north of Aberdeen, near Julia Carpenter's homestead in Edgeley. In July 1889, he set off by horse and buggy, along dusty roads scored across the flat plains to Edgeley, where he stayed for several days. He attended a Russian wedding and observed the four-and-a-half-hour ceremony, the wedding chants and wailing hymns. "Wagon after wagon arrived," wrote Baum in his subsequent article, "laden with whole families." There wasn't sufficient room for everyone inside, so many people sat on the ground in the open prairie, bringing their Russian Orthodox religion out into the open air. During this visit, Baum witnessed struggling immigrant homesteaders up close, and as he slept in the remote Carpenter homestead in Edgeley, the wind rattled the house.

The Carpenters had moved out there in 1882, dragging wagonloads of timber from the railroad to build their small house. Homesteading in this remote place was a tough life, and it didn't suit Julia or her husband. Frank

Carpenter would leave Julia alone with her two children to go away on business for days at a time. She would confide her loneliness to her diary, writing, "This is awful country . . . and I want to live East." "Alone all day and night again . . . dreadfully, dreadfully forlorn. Can't stand being alone so much," she wrote. One infant had died and was buried out on the prairie; this linked her painfully to the ground she wanted to abandon. At night out there, people listened to the wind and the wolves howling. "The howl of a wolf," said one prairie farmwife, "is the cry of a child from the grave." Another Dakota woman admitted that sometimes she got so lonesome that "she would go outside and yell just to hear noise in this desolate place."

Baum's visit to the Carpenters must have been extremely welcome. Julia's sanity was beginning to suffer; Frank Carpenter was drinking heavily. The Baums visited Edgeley often, taking their boys, who enjoyed running through the grasses and playing amid the prairie dogs towns. Baum seems to have been disturbed by the sight of children (possibly his own) chasing gophers and prairie dogs and killing them for their tails, for which the government paid a bounty. In particular, the sight of Baum's niece Magdalena playing on the vast open prairie stuck in Baum's mind, splintered into his memory, and it would resurface many years later in a story about another little girl who lives out on a poor homestead on the prairies.

The summer of 1889 was red hot. Advertisements for Baum's Bazaar now stressed bargains. Notices of bankruptcy sales began to appear in the local papers. Baum plowed on, selling fancy goods on credit, pouring fountains of soda, and scooping out colorful ice cream. He was also busy now with the Hub City Nine, establishing a state baseball league and arranging games. In August, he left the store in the hands of his clerk and Maud, who was now five months pregnant, and went on tour with the Hub City Nine, traveling north in the heat, which reached 106 degrees in the shade. He sent regular dispatches to the Aberdeen papers. The team won many games that first season and became local champions, but the project wasn't a financial success. Baum had trouble finding enough teams to play against, in part because many refused to travel the long distances across the plains to Aberdeen. The Hub City Nine was disbanded, and the club took a thousand-dollar loss; the uniforms provided by Baum's Bazaar were never paid for. "I don't want any more to do with baseball," Baum told a local reporter. "I expended no little time," he went on angrily, "and worked hard for the success of the organization, but am out both money and time." The grandstand was dismantled and the lumber hauled away.

The heat and hot winds were drying the land. Baum's niece Matilda Gage, Clarkson's daughter, stood at an upstairs window in the Gage house in West Hill and watched as prairie fires, sometimes started by lightning striking the scorched earth, swept across the horizon. The dark smoke and orange glow frightened her; the fires might burn their way into town. Across Aberdeen, children chased rolling tumbleweeds, collected them into large, brittle piles, and then torched them into burning pyres, just for the hell of it.

Dakota Territory joined the Union in the fall of 1889; the borderless plains were forged into North and South Dakota, with numerous reservations carved out within them. The exact borders of the reservations were still being decided; the United States was shrinking them as much as possible in an attempt to force what had been nomadic tribes to become landowning farmers, homesteaders, Americanized people.

Baum lunged forward, bought discount goods from a bankruptcy sale in Chicago, and advertised them as bargains. In one promotion, a sad-looking doll lolled in an uncomfortable rocking chair; these and other goods were sold at half price. There were now 161 unpaid credit accounts due; despite the cheerful soda fountain and the Japanese umbrellas, a financial crisis loomed. Maud gave birth to another boy at home on Kline Street, and they named him Harry Neil. The Baums had been certain the baby would be a girl; they'd planned to call her Geraldine. Ten days later, the Baums took out a mortgage on the Bazaar's stock worth $550, to be paid in ninety days at twelve percent. But it was no good. People could no longer afford silverware, gold toothpicks, and sugar tongs, no matter how much they wanted them. Baum had misjudged the market for his goods, but he was also unlucky that a drought hit the region so soon after he arrived, and local incomes fell. The luxury goods on sale in Baum's Bazaar were the first things people stopped buying when times were hard. The North Western National bank closed Baum's Bazaar on January 1, 1890. Despite all his efforts to boost the town with baseball, and to provide people with the odd luxury item, there were larger climatic and economic forces at work. These forces had crushed the hope and ambition Baum had laid out in the new town on the prairie, under the big ancient sky. He faced 1890 with three children to support, no income, and only a hundred dollars to his name.

There was more strange news from the East: In November 1889, Maggie Fox wrote and signed a public letter, cited in all the newspapers, completely retracting her 1888 confession. She blamed her bizarre confession on strong psychological pressure from people trying to deny the truth of spiritualism, including Catholics. In her confession, she had given "expression to utterances that had no foundation in fact," she said. Her spirit guides had forced her to admit the truth: Her access to the dead was real.

Chapter 11

f Baum looked back through his memory at his working life, before the years selling axle grease and luxury fancy goods, before the brief heady years in the theater even, he would have seen the pedal printing press of his boyhood. When John Drake, a fellow Aberdeen settler also originally from Syracuse, offered to sell Baum his Aberdeen newspaper, the *Dakota Pioneer*, for a small monthly payment that would be raised through the paper's advertising revenues, Baum jumped at the chance to own and edit a weekly western paper. Here was an opportunity to rekindle his old interest in writing and printing, and take up a public position as a spokesman for Aberdeen's development, its path out of the dried-up, dusty well of drought into which it was sinking. "Ye brothers of the quill," wrote Baum in the relaunched and renamed *Aberdeen Saturday Pioneer*, "be fearless, be brave and outspoken." In Baum's "wide awake Saturday journal," he would work "zealously and energetically for the welfare and advancement of our beautiful city." The newspaper would boom the town as well as entertain a local readership.

In January 1890, as the snowpacked town shivered beneath icy winds, Baum marshaled his enthusiasm and plowed it into the newspaper with vigor. The only way out of this personal and civic hole was to promote Aberdeen and forcefully heave himself and his town into the future.

Baum and many others in Aberdeen didn't regard their brand-new state and their town so recently wrestled out of the grassland as simply a chance to build another old, eastern-style city. Here was an opportunity, as Baum saw it, to create a truly modern society fit for the final decade of the nineteenth century and the move into the twentieth. In his newspaper writing, Baum experimented with various voices and began to tell stories. His unconventional, complex nature surfaced and was made public for the first time. He now revealed his radical spirituality, his humor, his satirical eye, his politics, his intolerance, his contradictory ideas, and his volatile emotions.

This new enterprise required total dedication. The local newspaper market was highly competitive; Aberdeen already had numerous other daily and weekly papers. The only way to secure readers' subscriptions and regular advertisers would be to stand out and have a distinctive voice. Baum set himself up in the Excelsior building, an impressive brick office block on Main Street. Like many papers, he took on outside printing jobs to supplement his income.

Half of the eight-page paper was taken up with national news (bought as ready-to-print boilerplate) and advertisements. Next to ads for sea-salt soap, shoes, gloves, and Hood's Sarsaparilla, a potion "to cleanse the blood in spring after a long winter of impurities," was news of crimes and convictions, stories of who had gone mad and who had murdered whom. The other half of the paper was local political and social news, written by Baum and others. Baum's articles, with titles like "Particular Paragraphs: Pleasing Personals of Prominent People" and "Minced Giblets: Spicy Items All Can Relish," gave details of card parties, church socials, and picnics on the banks of the Jim River. Other columns, such as "Vaporings of an Idle Mind" and "Matters that Strike a Wandering Reporter's Eye," included humorous comments and silly puns. In a flashback to Peekskill Military Academy, one pun read: A "teacher tells us of her pupils being so thoroughly disciplined that they are as quiet and orderly as the chairs themselves. It was probably because they were cane bottomed."

But Baum's most extensive and imaginative writing appeared in his "Editor's Musings" and "Our Landlady" columns. He launched into an attack on his former profession as a salesman in "Editor's Musings." "There is no vice so prevalent," he announced, "than that of mercantile fabrications, or, more plainly, trade lies." He railed against what he saw as "the age of deception." But he held both salesmen and the consuming public responsible for the fabrications of promotion and advertising. The "public have to have the goods they buy pronounced superior quality, no matter how low the purchase price," he wrote. Merchants, he went on, were often unable to acknowledge "to themselves . . . the deceptions practiced" on the credulous public. "Barnum was right," he concluded, "when he declared that the American people liked to be deceived."

In these columns, he also now made explicit his attitude toward money. Baum was hardworking, an ambitious perfectionist, but he didn't believe in saving. "Live and Spend" was his motto. Those who had acquired enormous wealth, he asserted, "go to their graves misers" and in the money-free afterlife are forced "to acknowledge that their earthly course was a mistake." He tells a story about a local man recently criticized by a neighbor for eating juicy oranges for breakfast, dressing his children in the best clothes, keeping a housekeeper to free his wife for social gatherings, wearing smart clothes himself, and eating heartily well. He spends his meager salary and "never saves a cent." This was clearly a self-portrait, since Baum himself splurged on quality cigars and the best clothes for his wife and sons. After death, which is the wiser, Baum asks, "the man who can say 'I have lived' or the man who can say 'I have saved'?" "Avoid the wicked vice of saving," cried Baum, "get all the meat from the nut of life."

The whiskered businessmen of the Aberdeen Club, whom Baum criticized in his paper for failing to "hustle" sufficiently to bring new investments into Aberdeen, must have scowled at Baum's attitude toward money and found his flagrant flouting of the Protestant work ethic unpalatable.

In the column "Our Landlady," Baum expressed other opinions in an equally outspoken manner, ventriloquized through the dialect and simple horse sense of Mrs. Bilkins, the fictional landlady of an Aberdeen boarding-house. "Our Landlady" appeared in the first issue of the paper and found Mrs. Bilkins discussing with her boarders serious issues of growing poverty owing to the drought. Mrs. Bilkins bosses her boarders, pronounces on local topics, and gives her opinions of real Aberdeen people. Hidden behind the landlady's brash, slapstick persona, Baum was able to tease his fellow towns-folk, particularly local businessman Alonzo Ward, as well as put forward ideas in ways he couldn't in "Editor's Musings." In Mrs. Bilkins, Baum explored the benefits of presenting ideas in fiction.

The paper proved popular, and Mrs. Bilkins began to seem like a real local personality. Each Saturday, readers couldn't wait to find out who Mrs. Bilkins would make fun of. Baum was thrilled with the success and compiled a scrapbook of all the good things people wrote about the *Pioneer*; he would scan them when his "noble profession" forced him "into a fit of the dumps."

Like all western papers, the *Aberdeen Saturday Pioneer* followed the unpredictable shape-shifting chaos of the plains weather. If the unique land and skyscape of the western prairies was shocking to the new settlers, the extraordinary weather was more so. The prairie might look empty, but the action all took place in the dominating sky with its rolling drama as warm winds from the south collided with polar winds from the north. The climate here was all-consuming to inhabitants eking out their lives under its sway; the agricultural economy depended on rainfall. The open landscape and the strange, extreme weather patterns created an intimacy between the people and their environment that was emotionally and spiritually charged; the plains became an inner geography for those who lived there. The winters brought blizzards and colds of minus forty; the flat plains were buried in snow for months and took on a ghostly monochrome quality in the moonlight, like a black-and-white photograph. Spring and summer brought the fiercest electrical storms found anywhere on the planet. The sky would erupt. These storms had real significance in Native American belief systems. Weather events were messages; lightning was the thunderbird winking, thunder was the flapping of its wings. Severe storms, when giant, black anvil-shaped cumulonimbus clouds towered over the land, were often followed by tornadoes, which in the late nineteenth century were generally called cyclones.

These spinning twisters (which rotate counterclockwise in the northern hemisphere, as if playing havoc with time itself) can reach an estimated three hundred miles per hour and vary from two feet to two miles across. The plains are notorious for their tornadoes, and Kansas is known to experience particularly high numbers every year, accompanied by inevitable fatalities. Sixteen people had died in Kansas from tornado strikes in 1888, the year Baum moved out west. A tornado was first photographed in Dakota Territory by F. N. Robinson in 1884. In this photograph, a dark, snaking tunnel of wind, a giant, malicious elephant's trunk, reaches down from a thick black cloud to suck and gnaw at the earth. The awesome image captured the terrifying power and mysterious beauty of tornadoes. Rarely does a killer have such majesty.

Baum's paper reported western storms in detail, knowing that this was an important topic for his readers, who lived at the whim of the weather. In

May 1890, a cyclone passed through Aberdeen. Many barns and outbuildings were blown down by the swirling, destructive wind. Mr. Seelen's buggy and his pig, which was inside it, were "blown over three hundred yards." The pig, "fortunately," was "quite uninjured." When another cyclone hit the region, "thirty houses were blown away," reported Baum's paper, and Cheyenne Creek burst its banks. Three people drowned, and an Episcopal church was lifted from its foundation. When a truly ferocious storm hit a region across the country in Illinois, Baum's paper printed extensive reports on the destruction. They told how a "whirling tempest," a "death-dealing tempest," which made an "awful roar . . . distinctly heard above the rumbling of thunder," struck a schoolhouse, killing a teacher, Miss Maggie McBride, and seven pupils. Their bodies floated down a nearby flooded creek. One man reported that he witnessed the school building "raised in perfect shape some three hundred feet in the air." Others ran to their storm cellars in time to escape the tornado. The whirling wind cut a destructive path through villages, uprooting trees, tearing up fences, smashing barns and houses. The people of Aberdeen would have read these reports in horror, their fear of Dakota storms redoubled, their vulnerability to the elements reawakened.

Drought made attitudes to storms painfully ambivalent. They were both a curse and a blessing. One story of a destructive storm in the *Aberdeen Saturday Pioneer* openly acknowledged this. "The rainfall in Huron," it read, "was a little over 1.5 inches" and "at Aberdeen over three inches of water fell." The article concluded, after reporting the destruction of a church, "All in all, the rain was of inestimable benefit to South Dakota and its beneficial effects are already felt." In spring and summer, storms brought much-needed water as hail and torrential rain. The main street of Aberdeen was often flooded after heavy rains. Storms could destroy, but they also brought what was most needed to transform the dry, dusty earth into a lush, crop-yielding breadbasket.

Aberdeen's reliance on the agricultural economy, and therefore on the climate, brought the weather intimately into Baum's imagination. He also heard about storms from Julia Carpenter out in Edgeley, who kept detailed notes about exactly what to do if a storm or a tornado struck. After the stormy spring rains of 1890, Baum wrote a rather bad poem to celebrate the water. "O the mud, the luscious mud!" it went, "Mud, mud / As we scud / Through thy slime / We chew the cud / Of gratitude, for thou art a bud / Of future promise to us, O mud!"

The frequent droughts fueled Baum's anger and frustration too. He resented how reliant the town was on the climate and called for the development of irrigation and, more boldly, for the town to diversify its economic base by drawing in other industries from the East. There was a cigar factory close by, but there were, Baum asserted, mining opportunities out here too. He railed unfairly against those in agriculture: "Had our farmers the first rudiments of business instilled into their noodles," he wrote, "they could easily have withstood one season's short crop"; he also criticized farmers for buying expensive machinery on credit. But if Aberdeen was truly to be transformed "into a metropolis of unassailable magnitude," as Baum put it, what was needed was rain.

The ambitious settlers couldn't bear to see themselves as victims of this alien, unpredictable nature. There were many theories about how humans could wrest control and shape the climate. "Rain follows the plow" was one theory, the idea being that once the prairie was settled by homesteaders, the moisture trapped in the earth would be released through plowing the ground and would rise up and condense into clouds. Others suggested that the steam from trains that crisscrossed the prairie would form precipitate clouds. In their desperation to do something about drought, people turned to new experts, the rainmakers. These inventors said they could create rain clouds by bombarding the skies with gases. Mr. L. Morris from Kansas had some success and gained a contract to make rain in Aberdeen. Captain Hauser, a local lawyer, also set himself up as a rainmaker. Morris fared well and appeared to generate a half inch of rainfall over Aberdeen. Captain Hauser, from atop a roof of a business building, had less luck; the skies remained empty.

The treeless ground of the prairies seemed bald; one U.S. government advisor announced that if each homesteader planted a patch of ten to fifteen acres of trees, the climate would begin to change; trees would be magnets for gathering clouds, he said. Across the plains, settlers were called upon to plant and nurture saplings. "Plant a Tree" screamed a headline in the *Aberdeen Saturday Pioneer*. Beyond theories about how trees might alter the weather, trees and hedges would also act as windbreaks, slowing the hot blasts that bullied the settlers, their livestock and crops, lashing human faces and scoring lines into them, so they became weathered landscapes in miniature. Hedgerows would also provide livestock with shelter during snowstorms and an environment for birds, "the destroyers of insects," another dreaded curse of crops. Plagues of grasshoppers often decimated yields in years when drought hadn't prevented them from growing at all.

Trees, more importantly, would ensure that a "farm would be more homelike," as an article in the *Aberdeen Saturday Pioneer* put it. Settlers, bewildered by the treeless plains, would find the presence of trees reassuring, punctuating the vastness and marking out boundaries where there didn't seem to be any. Planting trees would also literally establish roots in the ground, and metaphorically this meant they were staking a claim to the land. Downward-pushing tree roots would be anchors in the waving grasslands that were so often compared to an ocean. "O fly to the prairie, sweet maiden, with me," read a Dakota poem, "'Tis as green, and as wild, and as wide as the sea."

The underlying goal beneath the settlement of the northern Great Plains was to transform a region that had been described on maps since the 1820s as the "Great American Desert" into a verdant Garden of Eden, alive with crops and roaming livestock. This was the vision that kept homesteaders and the townsfolk on the prairie going; it was the utopian image of the future that fueled their ambitions. The hot dusty winds and stunning blue, empty skies were frustrating this vision, creating debt and drought where there should have been progress and deep fields of corn reaching to the horizon. People didn't understand why this was happening. Wasn't it their God-given destiny to thrive in the West? Mrs. Bilkins bemoaned the ongoing drought. She described how a farmer "trying to farm Dakota dust" was out of feed for his six horses and reduced to putting "green goggles on my horses an' feed 'em shavin's an' they think it's grass."

In 1890, Aberdeen celebrated the Fourth of July in grand style, defying the drought and all that it meant. Baum helped organize the events and judged the baby show in the opera house. First prize for the prettiest baby was five dollars. There were pony races along First and Second avenues and a Slow Mule Race; the last mule won the prize of three dollars. Wheelbarrow and sack races were followed by the Animal Race, in which each contestant had "an animal in front of him through the entire race, with simply a rope attached to leg, tail or head." Suggested animals were goats, calves, monkeys, chickens, or bullfrogs. During the Greased Pig Race men chased through the dust a squealing slippery pig coated in some sort of oil or fat. The "first one catching him takes the pig," read the July Fourth events pamphlet. Two brass bands boomed and trumpeted as men hurled themselves at the pig.

Thousands of people from outlying settlements came to the celebrations. One of the most popular events was the "Band of Sisseton Indians in Native Costume." Helen Gage, Maud's sister, wrote an extensive account of this event for the *Aberdeen Saturday Pioneer*. Her detailed descriptions of what the natives wore, the "beads, necklaces of shells, head-dresses of dyed eagle feathers," and a warrior who wore "a circle of hawk's feathers hung on the back of his head, from which dangled alternate strips of fur and long quills," revealed her curiosity and fascination. Her mother, Matilda Gage, had brought her up to respect the Iroquois tribes of upstate New York. The dance, she wrote, "was one of the features of the day . . . quite a novelty to the whites and well illustrated the red man's power of endurance." The demonstration of the "war-dance" was, she said, "weird" and "impressive." She described how they rushed "rapidly around the circle," amid drumming and singing, "bending the body" and, as she put it, working "themselves into a frenzy, jumping about like an Iowa twister. . . . No one but an Indian could have endured the fatigue." But she concluded that it "was a barbaric scene and worth witnessing as a relic of customs fast passing away." Here Helen's words echo the racism and assumed cultural superiority that underpinned the settlers' cruel attitude to native peoples at this time. The native dance had been reduced to a show without real social or spiritual significance, transformed into a sort of archaeological entertainment.

The settlers of Aberdeen had a vested interest in believing that the nomadic tribes they had usurped were inferior barbarians whose culture was passing away. The event was a propaganda coup aimed at reassuring the settlers that the local Sioux, now forced onto reservations in North and South Dakota, were no longer a threat. The 1876 Battle of the Little Bighorn (called the Battle of the Greasy Grass by the Lakota) in which General Custer was killed and his troops in the 7th Cavalry were defeated by Lakota and Cheyenne warriors, including Sitting Bull and Crazy Horse, still stood out in settlers' minds as a frightening instance of native power and white vulnerability.

The day ended with an eruption of glittering fireworks that cracked and boomed, spat and sparkled in the empty darkness, lighting up the big black sky before falling back down to the dry earth as gray ash and plumes of sulfur smoke, acrid-tasting in the mouths of the windblown spectators.

Chapter 12

he brand-new state of South Dakota was drought dry but it was politically liquid. The settlers were in the process of shaping the way life would be led on the Great Plains; many important issues were undecided. Baum, not naturally political, became outspoken on many high-profile topics, his views often fueled by strong emotions and personal experience rather than sober reflection. Through his editorials and Mrs. Bilkins's humorous "chin music," Baum became super-opinionated.

He campaigned for Huron as state capital over Pierre because it was closer to Aberdeen. But the issue he most fervently supported in 1890 was women's right to vote, to be decided in the November election. Wyoming Territory had granted women the vote in 1869, and in 1890, Wyoming entered the Union as a state, with women's right to vote intact. But it was still the only state in the Union in which women had the vote. This inspired many in the women's suffrage campaign to achieve political rights for women state by state; Wyoming's success fueled hope in South Dakota. Baum offered his uncompromising and forthright views. "We must do away with sex prejudice," he wrote, "and render equal distinction and reward to brains and ability, no matter whether found in man or woman." Baum favored women of a "vigorous womanliness," who saw their right to vote as a "privilege and duty." Men who opposed women's enfranchisement were, he said, "selfish, opinionated, conceited or unjust—and perhaps all four combined. The tender husband, the considerate father, the loving brother," he added, "will be found invariably championing the cause of women."

Baum theorized from his own experience, writing that men were responsible for the atmosphere at home, women being ground down by child care and domestic chores. Maud was loving and fiercely dedicated to her husband and sons, but she had a temper that could erupt suddenly like a spring storm; at home Baum had to steady the marital waters. Maud may have been emotionally unpredictable, but she had a better head than Baum for money. "The mind of woman is more logical than that of man," wrote Baum, speaking of his own marriage for certain. Men should discuss their business matters with their wives, he went on, for "ten chances to one she will give you more wholesome advice than any of your business friends." Speaking of his own life no doubt, he asserted that women's "active brains and good judgment are responsible for the success of many a man's business which without their counsel to direct it would be irretrievably involved in ruin." Maud was intelligent and outspoken. Baum's commitment to the cause of women's suffrage must have been inspired by the absurd and painful reality that the proud woman he loved and shared his life with was denied a public voice.

When the state of South Dakota was brought into being in 1889, its constitution stipulated that the state's first legislature must bring an amendment to decide if women should be given the vote. A campaign was launched at the national and state levels. Susan B. Anthony, from the national women's suffrage campaign, set to work in earnest. Now in her seventies, Anthony traveled the state in a wagon, crossing the miles of dry, dusty plains between isolated settlements, giving speeches in schoolhouses, churches, and out in the street under the beating sun.

The South Dakota wing of the campaign was headed up by Marietta Bones, but she and Anthony disagreed on the approach of the campaign. For Bones, women's suffrage was inextricably tied to the temperance movement. Prohibition had been established in South Dakota in 1890, much to the dismay of many; Baum and others were sure it would eventually be repealed, that soon Mrs. Bilkins and her boarders would be able to legally drink the "firewater" again. Anthony wanted to separate suffrage from temperance because she saw that many men were reluctant to support women's voting rights because they thought this would strengthen the temperance movement. The two women disagreed publicly and this factionalism did nothing for the movement.

Passing through Aberdeen, Anthony would often visit the Baums and the Gages. Such was Baum's commitment to the campaign that he became secretary of the small Aberdeen Equal Suffrage Club, which included thirty-four women and thirty-six men. Baum had no doubt discussed the issue at length with Maud and Matilda; he knew the arguments inside out and was unflinching in his views.

Baum wrote in the *Aberdeen Saturday Pioneer* that "women were capable, not only of becoming politicians, but upright, moral and conscientious politicians as well, and from the moment a woman's hand is felt at the reins of government will date an era of unexampled prosperity for our country . . . An able intelligent woman will make a better politician than most men." In Baum's view, women didn't simply have the right to vote; he believed that women's entrance into politics would improve it. The movement was partly driven by disillusionment with politics at the end of the nineteenth century, and a utopian belief that women's entrance into politics would renew the public sphere.

The news of Baum's work reached Syracuse, and a local newspaper there wrote that "Louis F. Baum" was "engaged in a death-struggle for woman suffrage," a "burning theme" on fire in South Dakota in the summer of 1890, burning into a hot rage along with the prairie fires.

Baum was horrified when during the Democratic National Convention in Aberdeen in June, Mr. E. W. Miller gave an antisuffrage speech, declaring that "no decent, respectable woman is asking for the ballot." Baum responded angrily in the *Saturday Pioneer*, describing Miller's speech as a "coarse and brutal tirade," a "flow of pot-house vulgarity and abuse." He concluded, "To the eternal shame be it said . . . that the members of the convention vociferously applauded his remarks."

Mrs. Bilkins approached the issue in a different way by simply assuming a public role without having to be granted permission to do so. She tells her boarders that she didn't "see why I shouldn't run fer office as well as any other citizen o' this here Yernited States." She runs for mayor. When, after a frustrating time attempting to hold public office, the colonel tells his landlady that she shouldn't "meddle in affairs that should be left to the sterner sex," she replies, "It's the conceit o' man as is the biggest stumblin' block ter universal sufferin' o' women!"

Baum's paper was selling well. His outspoken opinions, the lively satire of Mrs. Bilkins, the unusually good layout of the paper, and its balance of news and entertainment were making an impression. Baum now had a public persona, a platform from which to speak and tell stories. Selling a product filled with real ideas invigorated him in ways that selling axle grease, gold toothpicks, and sugar tongs hadn't. Mrs. Bilkins's adventures were often vaudevillian and slapstick. In the *Aberdeen Saturday Pioneer* Baum combined his writing, printing, and theatrical talents.

There wasn't much money in the Baum household, but bathing in the tin bath in front of the stove, enjoying Sunday dinners of prairie chicken on toast for twenty-five cents at Ward's or strolling up Main Street in the heat, eating a ham sandwich, nodding to all the people he knew, Baum could feel that life here was working. He was hopeful that the suffrage amendment would be passed despite the fact that the campaigners were mired in conflict. The campaigners had hoped for support from the newly formed Independent Party (soon to be renamed the Populists), created out of the Farmers' Alliance and the Knights of Labor, but this support now looked like it was wavering. A scorching summer wind blew through Aberdeen during August 1890, and politics blew with it. The Democratic, Republican, and Independent Party conventions, the women's suffrage campaign, the vote for state capital, debates about prohibition, and arguments about how to stave off economic disaster if drought continued, created a kind of heat haze in people's minds, like the blurred and rippling horizon that blistered in the sun.

Never content to focus on one thing at a time, Baum invested energy in yet more projects, and in August he launched a new journal, *The Western Investor*, which aimed to hustle for more eastern investment in the Dakotas.

Baum hoped that politics would reorganize and reshape the modern public sphere of South Dakota; but he was equally focused inward, on re-shaping the spiritual life of his community to fit the coming twentieth century. In his belief that being "brave and outspoken" would "win both honor and prosperity" for his newspaper, he explicitly outlined his unconventional, freethinking, radical ideas about religion. His reading and extensive discussions with Maud, Matilda, and others on Theosophy, visits from mediums, and participation in séances had begun to profoundly shape his spirituality. These new ideas gave Baum a platform from which to more fully kick against his Methodist upbringing. The time had come to launch into a wider debate with the people of Aberdeen, most of them members of one of the town's several churches.

His "Editor's Musings" column opened with the bold statement that "the age of Faith is sinking slowly into the past," to be replaced by an "Unfaith" that is not "atheism" but "rather an eager longing to penetrate the secrets of Nature, an aspiration for knowledge we have been taught is forbidden." He went on to discuss many earthly religions and their prophets, Buddha, Muhammed, Confucius, and Christ. Each religion, he said, "sends praises to a common Creator—a Universal God." He took the opportunity of his new public voice to introduce his readers to Theosophists, people, he explained, of "no faith," rather a sect whose members were not part of a religion as such but were "simply 'searchers after Truth'." "The Theosophists," he went on, "are the dissatisfied of the world, the dissenters from all creeds. . . . They admit the existence of a God—not necessarily a personal god. To them God is Nature and Nature God." Here, for the first time, Baum made explicit his dissent from Christianity and his belief in an occult vision of Nature inspired by Theosophical thinking. This was a bold departure from the majority of the settlers on the plains, who had been driven there in part by economic necessity or ambition but also by a biblically inspired sense of Christian destiny. God had willed that they would make the desert bloom.

Baum's statements caused a furor. The following week, he called for religious tolerance in "Editor's Musings." But a few weeks later, he launched back into the topic. The growing interest in the occult among many intellectuals and writers of the day, wrote Baum, showed "the innate longing in our natures to unravel the mysterious." He went on, "The severe restrictions of religion against penetrating into the unknown restrained many intelligent people from exercising this natural and reasonable desire." The intelligent modern mind, he believed, was interested in the occult as a means of exploring "the inner workings of nature." Baum made it clear that he believed in reincarnation and even suggested that the popular author H. Rider Haggard was a reincarnated mystic in whose "brain lingered some latent and inexplicable knowledge" from his past life.

Mrs. Marks-Smith, a clairvoyant from Chicago, had come to Aberdeen in the spring of 1890 and visited "a private residence," likely the Baums. In his "Musings" column, Baum made clear his belief in spiritualist mediums, and he elaborated on his understanding of the spirit world, including his belief in the Theosophical concept of Elementals. He wrote that science had shown that "no portion of the universe, however infinitesimal, is uninhabited. Every bit of wood, every drop of liquid, every grain of sand or portion of rock has its myriads of inhabitants—creatures" derived from "a common Creator." All of nature was alive, including the very air. "The creatures of the atmosphere," he wrote, "are microscopically and otherwise invisible to ordinary humanity. . . . These invisible vapory beings are known as Elementals, and play an important part in the lives of humanity." Through his "numerous conversations with mediums," Baum had discovered that a clairvoyant is someone "so constituted" that she can lapse into a trance, free her soul from its body and travel about (known as astral traveling), and her "body, in its comatose and unprotected state, is taken possession of by an Elemental." These immortal creatures long for the opportunity to inhabit a human body and speak through it.

Eventually, the soul of the clairvoyant returns from its wanderings, drives the Elemental out of the body, and "resumes possession" of it. The gift of mediumship was potentially "a decided misfortune." To temporarily separate the soul from the body was "an operation of considerable danger" because there was a "liability of the soul not returning, in which case the Elemental will continue to inhabit the body until death."

The more conventional Christian readers of the *Aberdeen Saturday Pioneer* must have thought that Baum's Theosophical, dissenting reading had led him off the path of righteousness. Perhaps the unrelenting hot winds that were driving many homesteaders crazy had gone to his head; the wide-open spaces and big empty skies had opened his mind to strange influences. Readers began to write to competing papers publicly questioning the editor's judgment, and Baum was forced into silence on matters of the spirit. He stepped back for a while, but during this pause, his freethinking views of the natural world as alive with occult powers simply grew more fervent.

Aberdeen won the right to host the first South Dakota State Fair in 1890. During Fair Week in September, ten thousand visitors came to town daily by specially designated trains. They came to watch the horse racing, the tightrope act, the balloon ascensions, and to admire the varied livestock herded from across the state into town to bleat, bray, cluck, and low at one another across their pens. Baum joined amateur dramatic productions of *The Little Tycoon* and *The Sorcerer.* Politics was here too; suffragists and campaigners for state capital gave speeches. The Aberdeen Guards were a small army of daughters of Civil War veterans who drilled with long lances in uniforms of red skirts, red hats, and blue jackets with gold braiding. Mrs. Bilkins told her boarders of how she had attended the fair and found "the most soul-inspirin' thing the tight-rope act." When she got home from the crowds, the animals, the speeches, music, and furor, she "was so mixed up that I didn't know when I got home whether I was a woman-suffrage-anti-Pierre-prohibition-jack-pot woman, or a anti-Rights-anti-Huron-anti-up-anti-prohibition-anti-boodle-all-wool-an'-a-yard-wide politician." There was so much going on, the people of Aberdeen were in a spin. "Aberdeen folks is gettin' pretty near rattled," said Mrs. Bilkins, "an' nothin' but a rise in wheat will bring 'em to their sober senses."

Baum remained hopeful that women's suffrage would come into law. It was, he wrote, "a popular movement that is bound to carry all before it as a whirlwind does the particles of dust in its path." The actual climate, the rainless months and hot blasts, seemed to be outside the natural order, but women's enfranchisement was as natural and unavoidable as a spinning whirlwind. In the days before the vote in November, Baum sounded a final rallying cry. "Let no man who respects justice, no man who respects his family stay away from the polls" he wrote. "Vote as you would be glad to have your wife or mother vote in case you were a political slave." Mrs. Bilkins too was "a good deal bothered to know how to boom Ekal Suffrage at the polls."

Baum's hope for change and progress was high on polling day, November 4. He was horrified when the bad news reached him; both causes he had vigorously campaigned for lost. Pierre won state capital over Huron; women's suffrage suffered a massive defeat. "The defeat of Equal Suffrage," he wrote in the *Saturday Pioneer,* "will stand as a lasting reproach to the state of South Dakota." Mrs. Bilkins was thoroughly disheartened. "I've had enough of politics," she told her boarders, "to last me a life-time, an' if you boarders don't give the sujec' a rest," she yelled, "you can find some other boardin' house." To the triumphantly elected Independent Party (the Populists of the future), Mrs. Bilkins said, articulating Baum's disillusionment, "When you've been in politics a year or so you'll be as corrupt as a pail o' sauerkraut. It takes politics to knock the honesty out of a person."

Two days after the defeat, Baum's and Maud's spirits were raised by a Phantom Party, hosted by Harvey Jewett, a successful grocer who supplied oranges and lemons to Aberdeen. Guests wore a sheet over their clothes, and all forty were so well disguised as ghosts that husbands and wives couldn't recognize one another. Instead of conjuring spirits in a séance, the guests dressed up as them.

It would have been easy to imagine that one of the moving, lumpy bodies beneath an old sheet at the Phantom Party, and the muffled voice coming out from under it, was in fact Mrs. Bilkins. She was bound to have attended the party even though she said she didn't approve of it. Mrs. Bilkins was Baum's first believable fictional creation and she seemed very real to the people of Aberdeen. Like the famous characters he would later bring into being in his writing, she seemed to take on a life of her own and became distinct from her creator. Mrs. Bilkins was believable because Baum placed her among the real people of Aberdeen, earthing her in its dusty streets, blurring the line between the world of story and the physical world, a boundary Baum hardly recognized at all.

Chapter 13

he past, Baum liked to believe, was buried in the ground and could only be unearthed by archaeologists with an interest in "relics of a former race." The *Aberdeen Saturday Pioneer* reported recent finds out on the prairie such as Native American burial sites. The settlers might have wanted to view the native history of the region as archaeological, but they couldn't avoid the evidence that surrounded them, which suggested otherwise. The topic was painfully alive.

The "Indian Question" was fraught with tension. With the formation of North and South Dakota in 1889, the Great Sioux Reservation was carved up into six separate small reservations (Pine Ridge, Rosebud, Cheyenne River, Standing Rock, Crow Creek, and Lower Brule). The policy of the U.S. government was to force native tribes onto reservations, with the aim of assimilating them into Euro-American culture. Native Americans must be forced to become landowning citizens living in nuclear families. The 1887 General Allotment Act was aimed at breaking reservation land into privately owned plots to enforce assimilation. But on the ground, it wasn't as simple as that and many settlers knew it.

Baum made space in his paper for the ambivalence and guilt felt by many settlers toward the native peoples of the plains. He published a story by Hamlin Garland, for instance, who had lived a few miles north of Aberdeen for some years. The story's title, "Drifting Crane," is a reference to Drifting Goose, the local chief familiar to many in Aberdeen. "How the Indian Was Swept Aside by the Onward March of Civilization" was the story's subtitle, but its actual content was far more sympathetic. A settler meets a warrior out on the prairie. The settler, writes Garland, had a "fearless heart" but he was also "narrow-minded, partly brutalized by hard labor and a lonely life." He watches Drifting Crane stare out across the western sky and then, "a lump came into the settler's throat; for the first time in his life he got a glimpse of the infinite despair of the Indian." It was "as if two armies had met and soaked the beautiful prairie sod with blood." The settler, his voice cracking and trembling, tells Drifting Crane, "this is all wrong . . . there's land enough for us all, or ought to be. I don't understand—."

The *Aberdeen Saturday Pioneer* printed an interview with Senator Sanders of Montana, on "the Indian Situation," and the report superficially proposed that "breaking up tribal relations" was the "true solution," but the interview gave full reign to settler anxiety and guilt. "The Indian was found," it read, "in possession of the entire country . . . and so far as we know did not voluntarily consent to . . . intrusion." The "Caucasian" had "obtained a foothold," the article went on, because "he was adroit enough to exhort, under various forms of duress, the consent of alleged chiefs." The United States' claims to ownership of land were "the invention, however, of the Caucasian out of his own covetousness rather than after consulting with his aboriginal neighbor." The senator was unremitting. "Whenever the covetousness of the Anglo-Saxon has come in contact with the desire of the Indian to retain the home of his ancestors," he said, "processes have been found, more or less questionable, but certainly effectual, to make the Indian succumb. Without consultation with the Indian and certainly in hostility to his views we ourselves have determined that the continent belongs to civilization . . . and we have further determined that we are civilization." He added, "As to the morality of this process . . . opinions differ." There was no reversing the process, Sanders claimed, but there was also no denying that this was a tragedy. "Why call it a tragedy? Because it is nothing less," he said. In publishing the article, Baum asked the people of Aberdeen to think more about the current situation in the Dakotas as a tragic one, not a triumphant victory for "modern civilization."

The Sioux were in crisis, forced onto reservations, no longer able to hunt, their cultural and spiritual practices suppressed. They were dependent on government rations, which weren't as plentiful as had been promised. This, combined with the terrible drought that made growing food difficult, meant that they were threatened with starvation.

Hope surfaced for the desperate and despairing Sioux in 1890, in the form of a messianic religion that was moving through the plains tribes like a prairie fire, igniting weakened spirits. Wovoka, a Pawnee from Nevada, had experienced a vision on New Year's Day 1889. He told how he had traveled to heaven, where he had seen the dead and been told by the Great Spirit, or God, to return to earth and explain to people that they must be good in their earthly lives and then they would be reunited with ancestors and friends in the other world. Wovoka, sometimes known as Jack Wilson, had grown up amid United Presbyterians, with Bible and prayer. His vision for his native peoples was a melding of Piaute and Christian beliefs.

News of Wovoka's vision and prophecy spread, and representatives from various reservations went to visit him. Black Elk, an Oglala Sioux from Pine Ridge, explained decades later to John Neihardt in what became *Black Elk Speaks*, that Good Thunder, Brave Bear, and Yellow Breast went to see Wovoka from North and South Dakota. Black Elk was suspicious of the news at first. "I thought" he told Neihardt, "maybe it was only the despair that made people believe, just as a man who is starving may dream of plenty of everything good to eat." According to Black Elk, Wovoka had told these visitors from the plains that "there was another world coming, just like a cloud. It would come in a whirlwind out of the west and would crush everything on this world, which was old and dying." In this new world, there would be "plenty of meat," and "in that world all the dead Indians were alive, and all the bison that had ever been killed were roaming around again." Native Americans could get on this world, when it came, "if they danced the ghost dance" taught to them by Wovoka. Tales of Wovoka's prophecy varied. For the Sioux, it took on a more violent tone. When the new world came in the form of some kind of natural disaster, the white settlers would be buried under a new layer of soil, would "sink into the earth" along with their horses and die, to become buried remains of a former world, like the archaeological relics being unearthed in the prairie sod; the world, in other words, would be reversed. All the dead Sioux would return, along with the buffalo herds. The new world would come in the spring of 1891, as long as people danced the ghost dance all winter.

In the fall of 1890, Kicking Bear, a Miniconjou Lakota from Cheyenne River who had visited Wovoka, went to visit Sitting Bull, who was living as a herdsman and medicine man on the Standing Rock Reservation. Sitting

Bull wasn't convinced by Wovoka's prophecy, but Kicking Bear's message was powerful, a welcome utopian vision for a desperate people. "The earth had grown old and tired" was the message, "the messiah would cover it with a deep new layer of soil. Sweet grass, running water and trees would adorn the surface." James McLaughlin, who was the white U.S. government agent in charge of carrying out U.S. policy on the Standing Rock reservation (all reservations were assigned a U.S. "Indian Agent"), was suspicious of Sitting Bull and feared his local power and national reputation. McLaughlin ordered Kicking Bear to leave the reservation. Dancing began near Sitting Bull's cabin. In the early mornings, people gathered to make "ready to join the ghosts," purifying themselves in a sweat lodge put up nearby, before beginning exhausting daylong dances in a loose circle around the prayer tree, a dead sapling painted red. Bull Ghost was the dance director. Sitting Bull didn't dance, but he encouraged others to do so. Some would collapse or fall into a trance, and awaken later with tales of visits to their dead relatives.

Some of the ghost dancers wore ghost shirts, which many Lakota believed were bulletproof. These were muslin shirts decorated with sacred patterns, images of eagles and insects, and fringed with feathers. Stitching symbols into the cloth triggered powers that would protect the wearer.

Settlers were frightened by the new, violent tone of the ghost dancing on reservations in the Dakotas. The government, urged on by agent McLaughlin, told Sitting Bull to stop the dancing. The "Medicine Men" were "seeking to divert the Indians from the ways of civilization." By November 1890, just after the elections in South Dakota, the government marshaled troops to Pine Ridge and Rosebud reservations. News of the ghost dance and what settlers feared was a mounting transtribal resistance movement erupted in all the newspapers.

Reeling from the recent political defeats, Baum was anxious. "South Dakota is unfortunate," he wrote in the *Aberdeen Saturday Pioneer* in late November. "After two years of successive crop failure comes the Indian scare." This "was the last straw" for many people, he admitted. People were abandoning the state, driven away by fear of a Native American uprising or because of drought-created debt. The "Indian scare" was, he claimed, "all the work of sensational newspaper articles," whose "flashy headlines" were selling papers but damaging the state.

But then more news of the dancing came in and the people of Aberdeen became truly frightened. The *Aberdeen Saturday Pioneer* published news of "an alarming report" that claimed there were more than two thousand Lakota at Wounded Knee Creek on the Pine Ridge Reservation who "had resumed the ghost dance, with many warlike accompaniments." There were rumors that settlers' houses were being burned and livestock stolen. In early December, as the cold began to bite, the *Pioneer* announced that Company F of the National Guard, whose headquarters were in Aberdeen, had "received orders to be in readiness to march at a moment's notice." A speech by Short Bull, a Lakota leader in the ghost dance movement, was published on the front page of the *Aberdeen Daily News*, in which he described the coming of a new Native American messiah who would drive all the whites from the earth. It became extremely difficult to work out how vulnerable the settlers truly were; there was no way to assess the situation accurately.

In "Our Landlady," Mrs. Bilkins visited a reservation and talked with a chief, and Baum pointed out an injustice. The chief remarks that he "can vote an' you women can't, an' don't you ferget it." The recent elections had confirmed that Native American men could vote while women of all races couldn't, and this galled Baum. Mrs. Bilkins asks the chief about the ghost dance and he tells her that "religion is free as water an' much more plenty." Baum tried to make light of the situation, but in truth he was scared. He even counted the guns in Aberdeen, concluding that the settlers were vulnerable; they were, he wrote, "poorly equipped . . . for protection of any kind in case the Indians *should* rise." He tried to remain calm, not wanting to alarm people further, but he pointed out that the town had only fifty rifles, "and some of those are not fit for use." He feared that if the Sioux "chose to revolt," armed as they were said to be with Winchester rifles, the city would be "completely at their mercy." He added, "The troops that are left are so scattered that the Indians could easily avoid them, and then the whole state is virtually at the mercy of the redskins." Baum felt extremely vulnerable; Maud was five months' pregnant. As they huddled over the stove in December, they likely feared for their lives, as did many settlers, disconcerted by the conflicting, confused tales about the intentions of the Sioux, who were gathering together in increasing numbers to call up ancestral spirits.

The ghost dancing continued near Sitting Bull's cabin. Agent McLaughlin was alarmed by what he saw as the growing militancy and fervor of the dancing. He was also keen to get rid of Sitting Bull and was looking for an excuse to arrest him.

During a walk out on the prairie that fall, Sitting Bull had been told by a meadowlark (according to the Sioux, birds speak Lakota) that a fellow Lakota would kill him. And so it happened. The government tried to enforce law and order on reservations by creating reservation police forces out of native men; this had mixed results, and often only increased tensions on reservations, as men from different tribes began to hold sway over each other in ways that they never had done before. Agent McLaughlin sent a group of Native American police to arrest Sitting Bull on December 15. A fight broke out between the police and the medicine man's supporters, and in the confusion, Sitting Bull was shot by two officers, Bull Head and Red Tomahawk. Crow Foot, Sitting Bull's fourteen-year-old son, was also killed. News spread fast; sensational headlines reignited fear of a Sioux uprising. One paper reported that armed Sioux were gathering south of Aberdeen in the Badlands, a unique, ridged prehistoric ocean bed worn into an awkward terrain of gullies and peaks, ruts and outcrops, ideal for hiding in. The journalist feared "another Custer massacre unless the greatest caution is exercised."

The governor had sent Aberdeen one hundred Springfield rifles plus ammunition, but the people of the town were terrified. Baum's *Saturday Pioneer* report on the killing of Sitting Bull was shot through with mixed emotions of anger, guilt, regret, racism, and sorrow. He described Sitting Bull as "the most renowned Sioux of modern history," a medicine man who had risen to a position of leadership "by virtue of his shrewdness and daring." Half of Baum's article accused the settlers of gross wrongdoing. Sitting Bull had seen, wrote Baum, "his son and his tribe gradually driven from their possessions; forced to give up their old hunting grounds." The settlers, "his conquerors, were marked in their dealings with his people by selfishness, falsehood and treachery." "What wonder," Baum continued, "that a fiery rage still burned within his breast, and that he should seek . . . vengeance upon his natural enemies."

Baum's ongoing editorial principle that outspoken, extreme, and partisan opinions would attract readers was also in danger of alienating them; there was a fine balance to be struck between gaining readers' attention and offending them. Baum had come close to the latter in his campaign for women's suffrage, his radical ideas about religion, and his satirical landlady column. The second half of his report on Sitting Bull takes the opposite view of the first, possibly to counteract his earlier, more sympathetic comments. Driven by the reverse side of guilt and sorrow, namely anger and fear, Baum gave full rein to the vicious racism at work in popular attitudes toward Native Americans on the plains. In sorrow he wrote that the "proud spirit of the original owners of these vast prairies inherited through centuries of fierce and bloody wars for their possession lingered last in the bosom of Sitting Bull." The Native American spirit on the Great Plains was now "extinguished," a flame gone out. America had won the West and, he went on, "the best safety of the frontier settlers will be secured by the total annihilation of the few remaining Indians. Why not annihilation? Their glory has fled, their spirit broken, their manhood effaced; better they should die than live the miserable wretches that they are."

As this terrible outburst showed, Baum's spirit had become dry, cracked, and cold through his experiences in Aberdeen, like the dried-out ground of the plains, now iced over for winter. Sadly, his views weren't unusual or unique. The brutally racist policy of eradicating Native American culture and assimilating native people into Euro-American ways of life was widely accepted and remained largely unchallenged until the 1930s. "The stress of misfortune," wrote Hamlin Garland of the drought-ridden plains, "had not only destroyed hope, it had brought out the evil side of many men." The dried-up plains and the struggles there had indeed brought a kind of evil to the surface, up through the ground and into the settlers. Perhaps it had infected Baum when he wrote this report. He was cracking up, like a muddy hole covered in ice run over and shattered by a wagon wheel.

In the early hours of the morning after Baum's report on Sitting Bull appeared, a loud fire alarm was sounded in Aberdeen; people leapt from their beds, fearing something awful, that the Sioux had finally attacked. But the fire was put out and the rattled nerves of the townsfolk steadied.

The word "war" was now being spoken. "The Sioux War" was the headline of a news report in the *Saturday Pioneer*, and the subtitles read, "Sitting Bull's Death to Be Avenged by a Massacre of Whites" and "Reinforcements Ordered to the Front to Repulse an Onslaught of the Indians."

While the Lakota continued their ghost dancing, Baum launched into another attack on the church. His response to the defeat of his hopes for political change was to turn away from politics, but the anger created by the failure of his causes and the threat of a Sioux uprising migrated into other topics. Baum's frustration surfaced when in December he returned to spiritual issues in both "Editor's Musings" and "Our Landlady." Eyebrows had risen after Baum's previous articles on the rise of "Unfaith," and so he now prefaced his "Editor's Musings" with a warning. The column was, he wrote, his "inner sanctum. . . . This is not the newspaper, it's the man, and if you don't like him you are not obliged to read what he says." This shielded the rest of the paper from Baum's unconventional views, but it also gave him license to let himself go. "As our country progresses," he asserted, "the percentage of churchgoers is gradually growing less." He didn't hold back now, pouring into his writing his anger at the cloudless skies, at the poverty the weather was breeding, at his political frustration and fears of war with native peoples. "While everything else has progressed," he said, "the Church alone has been trying to stand still, and hang with a death-grip to medieval or ancient legends. It teaches the same old superstitions, the same blind faith in the traditional bible." Then he changed tack, calling Christianity an "ancient and beautiful religion," but he blamed its human representatives, the clergy, for the "superstition, intolerance and bigotry" that he saw as characterizing the church. "Independent Thinkers" like himself were speaking out against the authority and power of priests. Baum then turned his anger on congregations, most of whom were his readers, describing them as a "mockery"; "it is not devotion or faith that attracts them to the church," he wrote, "but policy and fashion." He concluded, "Through the Church, you can obtain more prestige on earth than you can in heaven." On Sundays, the churches of Aberdeen were filled, cried Baum, with "insincere and indifferent men," and with "fashionable and unthinking women."

Baum followed this outburst with columns promoting spiritualism. He engaged in an elongated debate with the popular Reverend Doctor Keeling of St. Mary's Episcopal Church. Keeling had given a lecture on the topic of spiritualism and declared that spirit manifestations were real but all the work of the devil. Good Christians should keep away from mediums, he said, and he called spiritualism "a delusion of the Evil One," a "deceit and imposture." Baum retorted in the paper that he didn't believe in the devil, who was an old superstition to him that had no place in the coming modern world. "I do not see," wrote Baum, "what we need fear from communication with our friends on the other side."

Mrs. Bilkins was a spokeswoman for keeping to the Sabbath, while her boarders rebelled, asking why the devil they should be forced to go to church on Sundays. Baum twisted the argument around. "A pusson as never goes to church," says Mrs. Bilkins, "can't realize the fun there is in stayin' away." And if the churches were emptied, ministers "be obleeged to work fer a livin'." This was further biting criticism of the church, sugarcoated with the land-lady's humorous blather.

In his attack on orthodox religion, Baum even questioned Christmas. The "Yule Feast," as he called it, "ante-dates Christ, and was celebrated in commemoration of pagan gods." "But the Church," he said, had tried to drive out "deep-rooted heathen customs and feasts," with a "grandly devised Liturgy." "Kris-Kringle or, Santa Claus, is a relic of the ancient Yule Feast, so that the Festival of Christmas is a curious mingling of ancient heathen and Christian customs." Relics of heathen pagan European cultures were persisting into the modern age, for Baum, even as he rejected and feared "relics" of native cultures. Christmas was always important to Baum, as was the figure of Santa Claus, precisely because this was a joyous winter festival (involving lots of rich food) connecting people to an ancient, pre-Christian story.

Baum's public promotion of spiritualism had begun at exactly the same moment as the Native American ghost religion was spreading across the plains. Although neither the Sioux nor the settlers saw this at the time, spiritualism and the ghost dance had things in common. During both a séance and a ghost dance, contact was made (often through a circle of believers) with dead ancestors and friends "on the other side." The trances and visions of Black Elk and others initiated through the ghost dance were similar to the astral traveling of clairvoyants. Spiritualism and Theosophy may have been influenced by Native American belief systems and ideas of the vision quest.

The people of Aberdeen were frightened by the ghost dancing because sensational newspapers whipped up fear, because Indian agents were scared, and because it seemed that a long-standing settler nightmare, that native tribes would unite against them, might come true. The U.S. government had been able to forward its own ends by exploiting divisions, ancient animosities, and mutual distrust among tribes. The new ghost religion offered a transtribal prophecy that could possibly unite them into a powerful resistance force.

But perhaps the settlers, Baum in particular, feared the ghost dancing for a deeper reason; perhaps in part they secretly feared that Wovoka's prophecy might possibly be true. If white mediums and clairvoyants could call up the spirits of the dead, make contact, and communicate with them, why couldn't Sioux medicine men? The ghost religion fit easily into Baum's belief system, his conversion to the "science" of spiritualism. Inside settlers' mixed feelings of racist superiority, guilt, sorrow, and anger lurked a fear about what would happen if thousands of Sioux began to dance the ghost dance, and make contact with and channel the fury of their dead ancestors. Perhaps such a collective force would indeed have the power to create a natural disaster that would devastate the settlers. They had already witnessed killer blizzards, plagues of grasshoppers, destructive whirlwind cyclones, and drought, so it wasn't hard to imagine. Perhaps the reason the ghost dance set off such panic in Baum and others, and resulted in such an outburst of unjust, fear-fueled anger from Baum, was because the ghost dancing chimed with Baum's belief in ghosts and spiritualist possession. The ghost dancing set off inner alarm bells that drowned out more just responses.

Baum and others may have imagined themselves to be potential victims of the Sioux, but terrible news reached them at the end of December 1890, which confronted them with the truth that the Sioux were the real victims. After the killing of Sitting Bull, Big Foot and his band of Miniconjou Lakotas had fled the Cheyenne River Reservation, hoping to join Red Cloud on Pine Ridge and find sanctuary there. In the early morning of December 29, the U.S. 7th Cavalry intercepted them at Wounded Knee Creek. The Lakota were told to hand over their weapons, and in a misunderstanding, shooting began; gunfire echoed across the rolling grasslands in the crisp, cold morning air. Almost three hundred Lakota were killed, including many women and children. Twenty-five U.S. soldiers were also killed, many from friendly fire. The bloodied bodies lay scattered in the white snow; three days later, they were buried in a mass grave by civilians hired to do it; they were paid two dollars for each body they buried. The tragedy of what had happened there was scored into the earth by the mass grave, to become a painful landscape memory.

News of the terrible massacre spread across the country. Baum wrote an article in the *Aberdeen Saturday Pioneer* about it in which he was utterly uncompromising and driven by anger and fear. He lambasted the military, describing General Miles, the man in charge, as weak, vacillating, and incompetent; the "battle" was "a disgrace," a "disaster." This was followed by a bizarre, terrible, unthinking outburst in which Baum simultaneously acknowledged the wrongs of the U.S. policy toward the Lakota and yet called for the Lakota's "total extermination." His rationale: "Having wronged them for centuries, "we had better . . . follow it up by one more wrong and wipe these untamed and untamable creatures from the face of the earth." Baum's vicious response was a kind of madness.

There was a certain emotional and psychological honesty in Baum's two outrageous editorials on the Sioux that bleak and troubled winter of 1890. In his unjust and venomous words, Baum expressed the settlers' ambivalence and viciousness in regard to the "Indian Question." His thoughtless comments were incoherent, full of the pain and frustration of his own life out on the prairie, which surfaced in his writing as irrational emotions fueled by fear and guilt, twisted into terrible anger.

Baum's rage against the established church, his badly expressed fury at the terrible history of U.S.-Native American relations, his frustration with the drought, and the failures of his political projects, forced him to look outside his immediate reality, to escape it by plunging into the unseen world of the spirits and imaginary futures. Concrete hope was being rubbed away and transformed into out-of-reach utopias. Others were doing the same. Edward Bellamy's *Looking Backward* had inspired a host of futurists; the *Aberdeen Daily News* imagined a South Dakota farm called The Updike Farm, which was run by electricity powered by an artesian well. All tasks were automated. There was even an electric winter garden that grew strawberries under artificial light. In January 1891, Baum satirized this vision in "Our Landlady." Mrs. Bilkins, like everybody else, was fed up. She threw her hat on the sideboard and declared, "This kind o' life ain't worth the livin', an' if ever I were sick o' this air boardin' house I am this minute!" Mrs. Bilkins explained that she had visited Downditch Farm, "a much more wonderful place," the utopian futuristic home of Aesop Downditch, a scientist-inventor. On entering the house through electric doors, steel arms removed Mrs. Bilkins's bonnet; every action was carried out by electric automatons; the scientist's nose was even blown by an electric handkerchief. Mrs. Bilkins stayed to watch an evening show performed by dummies with phonographs inside them (a phonograph had recently arrived in Aberdeen). Downditch's cigar was shoved into his mouth by a machine and lit for him, and Mrs. Bilkins discovered that even Aesop Downditch's smile was created by electricity. She was both amazed and alarmed. "I kept my thoughts to myself," she tells her boarders, "fer fear the 'lectricity should get hold o' them." But on her return, she is outraged at the prospect of doing domestic work, having seen machines perform it all. "Do you think," she announces, "that I'll be content to settle down an' wash dishes again? Never!"

Here Baum expressed his enthusiasm and excitement about new technologies but also his anxiety about their impact. At Downditch Farm, the human body had become redundant, overpowered and overtaken by technologies that perform all physical tasks, including smiling. But machines have also liberated Aesop Downditch from domestic drudgery.

Beneath these anxieties was a larger question about what it meant for something to be alive. Electricity for Baum was a natural, scientific force, but also an occult one, a vital energy at work throughout the cosmos. Humans had learned to harness it to make machines perform tasks previously carried out by humans (or by animals). Baum began to explore a distinction between the living force of electricity and the inorganic, artificial objects it powered. This tricky, slippery distinction began to trouble him. He, like Mrs. Bilkins, looked at the new force of electricity and the machines it was generating with wonder and fear; the force that powered them was a vital natural element, but the machines it powered weren't truly alive.

Later that month, Baum bemoaned "the bleak and uninviting prospects which stare us in the face during the day's scarcely requited labor" and launched Mrs. Bilkins into a happy, utopian vision of Aberdeen of the future. She falls asleep and experiences a dream-vision of Aberdeen five years ahead, when it's become a "great metropolis" in a "Garden of Eden" state. Aberdeen is at the center of the flourishing "wonderful irrigated valley o' the Jim. The most fertile an' productive land in the world," whose produce is "air shipped to all parts of the world." People drive around in electric cars, visit the Bank of Eden, which has millions of dollars in its coffers, and shop at "Beard an' Gage's" enormous department store.

The Lakota ghost dancers experienced a vision of South Dakota returned to a pre-settler past, a renewed, borderless prairie populated by plains tribes and herds of buffalo. Mrs. Bilkins, in contrast, envisioned the same landscape transformed into a technological metropolis of the future. The settler and Sioux visions of utopia were diametrically opposed. Baum's landlady's vision, though, was a satire of hope. It was absurd to think that such transformation could occur in only five years, other than by some messianic miracle maker.

Notices of mortgage sales filled Baum's newspaper. Thompson's grocery and the Hagerty Bank went bankrupt. Coal, food, and other necessities were being supplied to the desperate. Baum too was feeling the pinch. Subscriptions to the paper dwindled, as did advertising revenues. He explored the pros and cons of leaving Aberdeen in conversations between Mrs. Bilkins and her boarders. "Why should I stay?" asks Tom; "with the same amount of energy it requires to earn a crust here, I could get a full loaf anywhere else. . . . Do I owe anything to Aberdeen?" Settlers had begun to leave. The first prairie boom was over. The exodus from the Great Plains that would quickly depopulate Kansas by a quarter and Nebraska by a half had begun.

Baum launched into another controversial attack on a local leader, righteously though mistakenly criticizing the Aberdeen school superintendent for being overpaid. This infuriated many people; some wrote to the competing *Aberdeen Daily News* to complain, asking that the people of Aberdeen "refuse patronage to a public nuisance that is constantly engaged in making scurrilous attacks upon its superiors." Baum had offended churchgoers and now the school board. He responded, saying he had "the skin of a rhinoceros," but in truth he was ill. He had developed a tumor under his tongue and it needed to be removed. He was confined to bed for two weeks, unable to manage the newspaper, which limped on without him.

The *Saturday Pioneer* was now no longer covering its costs, let alone providing an income. Maud was heavily pregnant; there would soon be four children to support. Baum had invested so much in Aberdeen, in this western grassland where they were going to build a modern world. He felt "thoroughly identified with the city's institutions and enterprises." He had grown a public voice in his paper, offered his uncommon views openly, looked up into the big empty sky that surrounded him and seen an Edenic future. Now he was discouraged and disappointed, angry and bitter. Baum watched children playing marbles in the midwinter evenings under the town's electric streetlights. What future was there out here for them?

In late March 1891, having recovered from the removed tumor, his tongue healed so he could talk and smoke cigars again, Baum took the train southeast to Minneapolis, St. Paul, and Chicago to look for work. The avenues of Aberdeen houses spread out on the flat land would have gradually shrunk in the carriage window as the train chugged forward, until the town became no bigger than the palm of Baum's hand. Julia and Frank Carpenter were going mad out on the homestead in Edgeley; Helen had taken over the Bazaar and was making a modest go of it. Who knew what Clarkson would do? Baum knew he had to leave this place he felt so attached to. It was making him bitter, cracked, and hateful. He would uproot his family again, tearing the boys from the grasslands in which all children loved to play. Maud was now nine months' pregnant, days from giving birth.

Baum made the decision to leave Aberdeen, South Dakota, in early spring 1891. He would take with him a rage at the plains for what they had taken out of him; this rage was a mix of love of the vast open landscape and the big dome of the sky, and a fury at the impossibility of living there.

The Lakota ghost religion predicted that after the long winter of dancing, the new world would come in the spring of 1891. The settlers would be buried under a new layer of fertile soil, and the spirits of all the dead Lakota and all the buffalo would return. Baum left the plains at just the moment when the prophecy would either come to pass or be proven wrong, a collective delusion inspired by oppression and desperation. "Sometimes dreams," said Black Elk, "are wiser than waking."

Part III

CROSSING LAKE MICHIGAN

1891 TO 1903

Chapter 14

rom Aberdeen, South Dakota, Baum headed toward the vast blue expanse of Lake Michigan, which had gained a reputation as an aeronaut's death trap, a sort of Bermuda Triangle for balloonists. Numerous aeronauts had floated above the lake in bloated silk balloons that created an hourglass reflection on the water, risen up into the clouds, and vanished. William H. Donaldson was a dashing, daredevil aeronaut who would hang a trapeze beneath the basket of his balloon and perform dazzling, sky-dancing acrobatics. He traveled with Barnum's Hippodrome in the 1870s, promoting the extravaganza by taking local journalists from each city they visited up in his mammoth balloon, called the *P. T. Barnum*, to show them their town from above. During these flights, Donaldson would explain how the balloon worked, demonstrating, for instance, how the dragline was a three-hundred-foot rope attached to the basket to help manage ballast. The rope dragged on the ground during night flights when it was impossible to see what you were passing over, and the sounds that traveled up the line helped assess what was beneath. Traveling over leafy woods, the rope made a rustling sound; a cornfield sounded like rushing waters; an orchard would make the rope thud and jerk from tree to tree; a fence created the regular sound of a buzz saw; and in long grass the rope whistled.

"Professor" Donaldson had visited Syracuse with Barnum's annual show in 1875 (when Baum was nineteen and still living in the area) and ascended above the city to look down on Lake Onondaga. One month later, the aeronaut went missing. In July 1875, he had lifted off from Chicago to attempt a 120-mile flight across Lake Michigan. At dusk he was spotted twelve miles off the coast, flying low over the lake; the basket was so low it dipped occasionally into the water. A rescue boat was launched, but as it approached, the balloon rose into the air rapidly and blew up and out of sight. Violent storms erupted across the lake that night. Donaldson's balloon never landed and he was never seen again. The showman balloonist was swallowed up by the lake or the sky above it.

John Wise, another famous aeronaut, set off from Lake Michigan in the fall of 1879. Wise was seventy-one years old at the time and had forty years of ballooning experience under his belt. His obsession with flight had begun as a child when he had experimented on his cat, tying it to a homemade parachute and watching it float down from the roof of his local church. Wise was more a scientist-aeronaut than a showman. He had been a Union Army aeronaut during the Civil War; after that, he carried out many scientific experiments and observations during flights. While floating through the sky, he had discovered what he called a "great river" in the air, which we now know as the jet stream.

Wise rushed into that flight in 1879. It was a blustery day with strong winds blowing from the north. By eleven thirty P.M. his balloon was spotted edging over the south of Lake Michigan. Wise was never seen again. The "professor" and his airship simply disappeared. Donaldson and Wise were the most high profile aeronauts to vanish over Lake Michigan in the late nineteenth century, but in the years that followed, other lesser-known balloonists also went missing, confirming the lake's reputation as an unpredictable expanse of freshwater and weather. These disappearances created gnawing questions; the empty spaces left by the missing aeronauts of Lake Michigan could be filled only with acts of the imagination.

At ground level, Baum arrived in central Chicago, the big city on the edge of the lake, in the spring of 1891, in search of yet another new start. The impending Chicago World's Fair, under construction in 1891, was the gravitational pull that brought him to the city. Drawing on his skills as a journalist, he approached numerous newspapers for work and finally secured a job with the *Post*, on North Wells Street.

He had left the drought-ridden plains and entered a city outlined by water. A network of parks ran alongside the lake on Michigan Avenue, constructed from the rubble of the 1871 fire that had nearly destroyed Chicago. The charred remains of the city had been pushed into the lake, to claim land

and beaches from the water. Walking along these beaches created a loud squeaking sound from the high quartz content of the sand. The Chicago River wound through the center of the city. Algae gave its depths a particularly vibrant hue that moved through various shades of green as light hit the water. It was amazing that anything organic could live in such a dirty, stinking river running with the city's filth, including the dumped body parts and spilled blood of animals from the stockyards, Chicago's main industry. The city, some said, was an abattoir on the edge of a lake. Cattle and pigs were herded across the Midwest to Chicago to be slaughtered, butchered, and sent east.

Multistory stone buildings housing the headquarters of numerous growing businesses of the late Gilded Age lined the river, such as Sears, Wrigley, and Montgomery Ward. Wealthy businesses occupied Wolf Point, the central curve of the river where, one hundred years earlier, wolf pelts had been hung to show that the wild was being wiped out. Waterborne diseases flowed through the river too, infecting many of Chicago's one million inhabitants with cholera. Nobody pretended that all was well. Ambitious programs of development were under way. Chicago was determined to heave itself into the twentieth century renewed. In 1891, when Baum arrived, the elevated railway was under construction, which would soon whiz people around the city's center, called the Loop. Workmen clambered over the network of iron girders and wires that jutted up from the street, looking like spiders on a giant web.

Baum stepped off the train from Aberdeen that spring into a giant smoggy stone and brick urban center crowded with horses pulling carts loaded with barrels, and tram cars crammed with people. The streets were filled with poverty-stricken barefoot children, sidestepped by wealthy well-dressed gentlemen in silk hats and shiny leather shoes. Advertisements for Friedrickson's Ice Company, Leonard's Seed Store, and Goodfriend's Shirts were painted on the sides of buildings in letters the size of cart wheels. The Reliance Building, the first skyscraper in America, had been completed the year before, in 1890, enabled by the invention of the elevator and new ways of engineering steel.

Daniel Burnham, with John Root and Charles B. Atwood, was the architect of this miraculously tall building, and in 1891, he was embroiled in the Herculean task of building the Chicago World's Fair. Chicago had won the competition to host the fair (against New York and St. Louis), which would celebrate four hundred years since Columbus discovered (or stumbled upon) America. It would be a world's fair to showcase the nation's history as well as its utopian future. The fair had been scheduled for 1892, but delays forced it back to a spring 1893 opening. Burnham was busy almost to exhaustion transforming the boggy, pitted, desolate landscape of Jackson Park, on the edge of the lake, into a site fit for the grand fair.

From the city center at the corner of State and Adams, Baum leapt onto a street car, paid five cents, and traveled out of the business district, hopping off when he reached a residential neighborhood that appealed to him. He rented a modest house on Campbell Park, a short street with large trees growing along the curbs.

He traveled back west, returning only briefly to the small town on the Great Plains to sell the *Aberdeen Saturday Pioneer* and pack up; Maud gave birth to a boy, who was named Kenneth. The Baums couldn't afford to ship their furniture to Chicago, so they sold it all in Aberdeen to raise some funds. Baum went ahead; Maud traveled a few weeks later by train with the three boys and the six-week-old baby, and they all arrived in Chicago exhausted. The family moved into 34 Campbell Park on Baum's thirty-fifth birthday, May 15, 1891. The house was small and simple, with no electricity or gas for lighting. Kerosene alone lit the darkness, which was better for stirring the imagination. Electricity, they said, banished the darkness, whereas living flame illuminated it.

Baum worked for the *Post* for only two weeks before he discovered that his pay was lower than he had expected ($18.62 a month). He got a job instead as a buyer for one of Chicago's department stores, Siegel, Cooper & Co. His experience with Baum's Bazaar was finally of use here in a city where there really were people with money to buy fancy goods.

The Baums discovered that their new house was haunted. Years later, Rob, Baum's second son, wrote that "it is certain that some peculiar psychic phenomenon occurred when we lived there." Baum rigged up a rocking system for Kenneth's cot, and it was rocked on its own as if by an invisible force; various family members experienced "strange noises" and "mysterious visions." Matilda Gage, Maud's mother, visited often. Her room was on the second floor, and as she descended the stairs, she gripped the banisters tightly because she "could feel invisible hands trying to push her down the stairs."

The boys got into a lot of trouble in this house. Baby Ken swallowed a safety pin, and the doctor had to be called to remove the metal point from the child's throat; Harry fell while carrying a glass bottle, cutting an artery in his leg and nearly bleeding to death before he was stitched up; Frank Jr. broke an arm; and while hanging from a porch railing, pretending to be a circus acrobat, Rob fell and cracked his head open.

In December 1891, bad news arrived from Aberdeen that Clarkson and Sophie Gage's baby daughter, Alice, had died only nine hours old. Matilda Gage, Alice's grandmother, was devastated and held séances in Aberdeen in an attempt to contact her. Maud and Frank's interest in the occult was furthered in 1892, when they joined the Chicago Theosophical Society, which sent them reading materials and hosted lectures. Maud abandoned the local Episcopal church, and she and Baum decided not to send the boys to Sunday school but to the West Side Ethical Culture Sunday School instead, which taught morality rather than religion. When Baum's mother, Cynthia, a committed Methodist, came to stay in Chicago, she found her son's unconventional religious ideas disturbing and this caused tension between them.

The spirit world was an important part of Baum's life, but, in the early 1890s, the more pressing issue was the question of how to survive. Money was very tight. Through his job as a buyer, Baum met a manager of Pitkin and Brooks, a Chicago glass and china company, who offered him a job as a salesman. By 1893, Baum was traveling the Midwest by train with trunks packed with breakable pottery, porcelain, glassware, and lamps. Gilt-edged plates painted with luscious roses were packed next to water jugs with swirling gilt spouts and matching washbasins. Pitkin and Brooks used the latest technology for producing tinted glass, made out of the trapped breath of skilled glassblowers, to create elaborate kerosene lamps. Baum's trunks would have been stuffed with finely decorated chandeliers and hanging lamps. Some lights were figurines featuring cherubs and turbaned genies.

He stopped in small towns, unloaded his wares, set up a stall in a hotel, and invited local store owners to peruse the array of colored glass and china. He also sold fireworks on the side. His boys loved to set off rockets at home. The Baums were known locally to have the best fireworks in the neighborhood. Children from all around would come to see the sparks and hear the booms over their street; Maud worried that the boys would blow their fingers off.

The year 1893 brought two major imaginative resources that clearly impressed themselves deeply upon Baum. One was a book written by his mother-in-law, Matilda Gage, and the other was a grand fake city. The book and the city would blend together in Baum's mind and resurface later in his writing.

Matilda Gage's magnum opus, her "chief life work" as she called it, was published in 1893. *Woman, Church and State* was a blistering five-hundred-page assessment of women's position across the ages, part history, part anthropology, and part political manifesto. Matilda's antichurch beliefs were now far too radical for the main body of the women's suffrage movement, with its emphasis on temperance and Christian morality. She was now an intellectual outsider.

In the "many ancient nations" of Egypt, Assyria, Africa, and the Americas, she discovered, "woman possessed a much greater degree of respect and power than she has at the present age." Matilda also found an example of a society in which women had power, on her own doorstep in upstate New York, in the Six Nations of the Iroquois. The "division of power between the sexes in this Indian republic was nearly equal," she wrote. The Iroquois clan mothers chose their chiefs and possessed the "veto power on questions of war." The line of descent was through mothers, and women could own property, had custody rights over their children, and could divorce. Iroquois women also managed the tribe's agriculture, which was shaped by a female-centered creation myth: A grandmother who fell from the sky buried her daughter, so the tale went, "and planted in her grave the plants and leaves" out of which grew corn, beans, and squash, the "three sisters" of the Iroquois agricultural crop.

Nonnative American women had few of these rights in the late nineteenth century. They looked enviously at the comfortable dress and the rights and status of Iroquois women. Matilda's ideas were oddly the reverse of the American mainstream; while white religious and political leaders sought to "Americanize," "Christianize," and "civilize" the peoples of native tribes, Matilda hoped to do the reverse, to introduce native traditions into Euro-America.

After the publication of *Woman, Church and State*, Matilda was offered an honorary adoption into the Wolf Clan of the Mohawk Nation in 1893, and was given the name "Ka-ron-ien-ha-wi," or Sky-Carrier, "she who holds the sky." Matilda wrote to her daughter, Helen, explaining that "this name would admit me to the Council of Matrons, where a vote would be taken as to my having a voice in the Chieftainship." Matilda didn't have the right to vote for the president of her own nation; earlier in 1893 she had been arrested for registering to vote in a local school board election.

Woman, Church and State also contained an intriguing chapter in which she looked at the history of witchcraft. Many women accused of being witches were, she said, scientists of their day, and many had a great understanding of the hidden laws of nature. She even uncovered some evidence that witches were said to be able to conjure storms. In Scotland, "a woman accused of raising a storm by taking off her stockings was put to death," she wrote, and some "very strange stories of such power at the present time have become known to the author." A well-to-do physician from a western city told her how "a most destructive cyclone, known to the Signal Service Bureau as 'the great cyclone,' was brought about by means of a magical formula made use of by a schoolgirl." Wild western storms and their spinning tornadoes had taken the lives of many children. The idea that a violent cyclone could be conjured by a little girl was terrifying.

Woman, Church and State was banned from school libraries, and Matilda was vilified by conservatives. She relished the controversy, found it to be "like a tonic," and hoped the Pope would ban the book too. Freethinkers like Victoria Woodhull championed it. Leo Tolstoy, the famous Russian author, praised it, saying it "proved a woman could think logically."

Baum took an active interest in Matilda's work and probably read *Woman, Church and State*. In Aberdeen he had described her as "undoubtedly one of the most remarkable women of her age, possessed of the highest literary ability, the brightest thoughts, the clearest and most scholarly oratory, the most varied research and intelligent and diversified pen of any public woman in the past twenty years." Matilda spent months at a time each winter living with Maud and Frank, when she and Baum would probably have discussed her research, if he didn't read her book from cover to cover. Baum may also have liked the idea of storm-conjuring witches.

If Matilda's controversial book overturned widely held ideas of "progress," the Chicago World's Fair of 1893 did the opposite, and presented America as an advanced, technological civilization at the peak of its power.

The Chicago World's Fair was officially opened by President Grover Cleveland on May 1, 1893. The six hundred acres of scrub, mud, and dust

of Jackson Park had been transformed in less than two years by a team of
exhausted architects and engineers and thousands of workers into a fabulous
spectacle beyond all expectations. The White City at its center was two
hundred gigantic themed palaces that encircled a series of manicured waterways along the shore of Lake Michigan.

Over the next six months, twenty-seven million visitors came to witness
the spectacle, one quarter of the population of America. Baum visited the
fair several times, like everybody else in Chicago, gladly paying his fifty-cent
entrance fee. Clarkson, Sophie, and little Matilda Gage came from Aberdeen
to stay with the Baums and attend the Exposition, as did Matilda Sr. During
a visit in June, Baum arranged to meet Maud and the boys outside the
Woman's Building, at the edge of the long, thin lagoon. On that day, thousands queued up outside the building in the hope of catching a glimpse of
the Spanish Infanta, Eulalia, the "The Queen of the Fair," who was visiting
as a representative of Columbus's home nation. The Infanta had been given
a dress made from spun glass created on-site by the Libby Glass Works.
Baum failed to meet Maud as arranged and when she finally caught sight of
him chatting happily amid a crush of ladies dressed in their Sunday best, she
was furious. On another occasion, Baum visited the fair with Pitkin and
Brooks, who were hosting clients from across the Midwest. Dressed in his
best striped trousers and silk top hat, Baum was mistaken for an official in a
crowd of Spanish delegates similarly dressed.

On each visit, Baum would have arrived at the Terminal Station and entered the dominating centerpiece of the fair, known as the Court of Honor.
He would have surged forward with the crush of people and confronted a
long, rectangular man-made lake, surrounded by gleaming white palaces. As
the crowd pushed forward, they faced the magnificent Columbian Fountain,
an enormous sculpture of a galleon rowed by giant Greek gods. Cherubs and
dragons edged the boat, which was encircled by horses with fish tails. At the
opposite end of the Basin was a 111-foot-high gilt statue of an androgynous
figure named Republic. Along one side of the Basin was the Agricultural
Building, a grand structure of columns, arched windows, and sculpted por-
ticos, somewhat at odds with the farming tools, seed grain, and the latest
methods for beekeeping, brewing, and dying wool showcased inside. Opposite was the Manufactures and Liberal Arts hall, the largest building in the

known world. Inside, visitors could wander along the main indoor street that ran through the middle, called the Bullion Boulevard.

Crowds wandered along the promenades in front of the buildings, and rested occasionally on benches to take in the impressive spectacle. Large potted aloe vera plants lined the promenades; their oddly prehistoric fingers pointed at the strange sites around them.

The White City was adorned with a bizarre bestiary, with animal sculptures that were a mix of imaginary creatures from myth and America's indigenous animals. Dotted around the Court of Honor were mer-horses, lions, pumas, and unidentifiable winged creatures. Stags, one hoof raised in thought as though they had just heard a twig snap, stood on plinths at either side of the canal; an outsize moose, weighed down by a forest of horns, stared down at the hordes; a pair of bison with heads bent low eyed one another across the promenade, and a muscular bear stood ready to pounce. Oxen with garlands of flowers thrown over their long horns pulled grand chariots instead of plows across the roof of the Agriculture Building.

Beyond the Court of Honor was the lagoon, which was encircled by more magnificent white palaces, including the popular Fisheries Building, which contained an enormous illuminated aquarium. Lights were shone through the water, casting eerie moving blue shadows over the walls, making visitors feel as though they too were underwater. The Woman's Building, where Baum became lost in the crowd, was opposite, and it showcased all aspects of the Victorian woman's world but didn't represent Matilda's more radical vision of women's history.

The White City shimmered in the sun and in the glare of light from reflections in the blue water. The light was so intense that many visitors wore tinted sunglasses. This marvelous architectural display had seemed, as one commentator put it, to have risen like Venus from the watery depths of Lake Michigan. The palaces were painted white, but many had tinted glass ceilings, which filtered colored light into their vast interiors. Each building was filled with magnificent exhibits, 65,000 in total, which included artworks from around the world and more peculiar items such as an enormous chocolate Venus de Milo, a map of the United States made from pickles, a sculpted knight on horseback made from prunes, a model of the Statue of Liberty made of salt, and a 22,000-pound brick of Canadian cheese. In the eight enormous greenhouses that made up the Horticultural Building, entire environments were recreated, including a Japanese garden and a Mexican desert.

The Electricity Building, the most popular palace in the whole fair, was the size of two football fields. Inside was a kaleidoscope of fantastic gadgets, alive with the newly harnessed force; the high-ceilinged open-plan building echoed with the clicking, buzzing, and whirring of new technologies. There was a wall of Egyptian hieroglyphics electrically illuminated from behind, an ancient language made visible by a newly tapped energy that was transforming communication. There was a kitchen of the future, where every domestic task was performed by a machine, much like the one Mrs. Bilkins had discovered at Downditch Farm in South Dakota. Carved animals with electrically illuminated eyes looked out from each corner of the building.

Thomas Edison, known as the Wizard of Menlo Park (where his laboratories were located), visited the fair. His inventions filled the Electricity Building, including a small box called a Kinetoscope (meaning "moving-vision"), which enabled a single viewer to peep through a hole into an illuminated interior, where black–and-white photographs flashed in sequence across the astonished eye. This was one of the earliest forms of what would soon become cinema. The machine received little notice; nobody yet realized its significance.

At the center of the Electricity Building stood the eighty-foot Tower of Light, which was covered with 30,000 glass prisms that flashed on and off. But it was outside, in the White City beyond, that electric light made a real impact. All the palaces were studded with bulbs. The fair had more electric lighting than any "real" city in America at the time, and used three times more electricity than the whole of Chicago. For many visitors, especially those thousands who came from the rural Midwest, the fair was their first experience of electric light. In the 1890s, less than ten percent of American homes had electricity. Visitors flocked to the Court of Honor at dusk to witness the coming to light and life of a magnificent electric landscape.

The Columbus Fountain was surrounded by enormous Electric Fountains. Powerful jets lit by rows of multicolored lights spurted water 150 feet into the air. Colored water leapt into the night air, weaving patterns against the darkness. Hundreds of thousands of sparkling electric lights outlined the palaces of the White City, marking the curves and domes of their rooftops. The numerous waterways acted as enhancing mirrors, and the oddly stretched reflections of the fantastic lights in the water created a rippling backdrop.

A powerful spotlight was mounted on the roof of the Manufactures Building. During the day it resembled a big blind metal eye, but at night it became a powerful all-seeing cyclops, visible from one hundred miles away, swirling this way and that across the fair, illuminating crowds of blinking visitors and statues of mythical beasts.

In newspapers, magazines, letters home, and diaries, visitors described the fair in fantastic terms. The scene was such a contrast to the unilluminated Chicago beyond, with its poverty, gruesome meatpacking industry, dark streets, coal smog, and filthy river. Chicago was dubbed the Gray City in contrast. The White City, with its perfect, orderly buildings and promenades, bright by day and illuminated like jewels at night, was "a vision of delight unrivalled on this side of Fairyland"; it was "simply a journey into Fairyland." Others called it a "classic phantom," a "vanishing city," a "Fairy city." Asked one journalist, "What shall we do when this wonderland is closed—when it disappears—when the enchantment comes to an end?"

At right angles to the White City was the Midway Plaisance, a mile-long strip filled with an eye-popping mixture of entertainment, food, fairground rides, and anthropological exhibits. Accompanying the jingle of tambourines and booming of German brass bands, visitors could find an exotic zoo with real lions and bears, a reproduction of Blarney Castle in Ireland, German and Javanese villages, a Cairo street, old Vienna, and a Moorish palace containing fun-house mirrors.

One of the greatest engineering feats of all time had been put up on the Midway, a structure that aimed to "out-Eiffel" the Eiffel Tower in Paris. George Ferris had designed an enormous metal wheel that had a series of glass carriages attached to it, each able to carry sixty people. The gigantic wheel turned slowly around, one revolution every twenty minutes. This ride into the heavens afforded a grand view of the White City. From the top of the rotating wheel, at three hundred feet, awed visitors looked down on the domes, the colonnades, the promenades, the sparkling white buildings, and the dark trails of little figures that snaked around them.

A hot air balloon was tethered a hundred feet from the Ferris wheel. Visitors not afraid of heights, already reeling perhaps from a ride on the giant wheel, could purchase a trip in the balloon. But on July 9, a powerful storm struck. A strong wind was funneled up the Midway from the lake via the lagoon and tore the balloon from its moorings, strewing shreds of silk across the fair. Yet another ballooning disaster had occurred on the edge of Lake Michigan.

Lectures were given daily in various buildings on every subject imaginable. At a history meeting, Frederick Jackson Turner, a university professor, gave a talk entitled "The Significance of the Frontier in American History" in which he drew on the evidence of the 1890 census to argue that the western frontier was now closed; the idea of the limitless western landscape as the embodiment of American freedom and opportunity was over. The American nation now stretched from the eastern ports of the Atlantic, westward to the Pacific Ocean. There was, suggested Turner, no wilderness left.

The 1890 census also revealed, for those who cared, a dramatic decline in the Native American population. In response, many had set to work to "preserve" their cultures, by collecting items from the native world and displaying them at the fair in anthropological exhibits of dress, goods, homes, villages, and religious items. Groups of native peoples were also brought to the fair as living exhibits. If these were meant to put on show an authentic pre-Columbian America, they also displayed this old world as a museum exhibit from a disappeared past.

On the outskirts of the fair, and not officially part of it, Buffalo Bill's Wild West show demonstrated western cowboy and native skills (Sitting Bull and Black Elk had been part of Bill's show in the 1880s). This was a sideshow act that further suggested that the West was now an historical curiosity, alive only in the realm of stories.

The White City was an overwhelmingly impressive spectacle, but it was also, as many awed visitors quickly found out, as ephemeral as a dreamscape. In truth, the palaces had been hurriedly erected and were, at heart, little more than giant temporary sheds. They were designed to be quickly assembled and then dismantled equally quickly. Machinery Hall, so impressive from the outside, was in reality three train sheds bolted together. After the fair closed in October 1893, the hall was dismantled and the materials were resold for use as actual train sheds. What appeared from a distance as stone and marble structures were in fact architectural screens, a film set before cinema had been invented.

The impressive sculptures that adorned the buildings of the White City, the mix of mythological and indigenous creatures that crawled all over them, weren't carved from stone or marble. They were made from a material called staff, which was essentially a lightweight mix of plaster, cement, and jute fibers, a kind of plaster of Paris. What appeared to be artfully sculpted was in fact a rough cakey liquid poured into molds and then patted and sanded into shape.

So the grand palaces were in truth storage sheds covered in a veneer of theatrical plaster most famously used to reset broken bones.

At the edge of the White City was a replica of Santa Maria de la Rabida, the Franciscan monastery where Columbus had received encouragement for his journey. Inside this imitation monastery were displayed what were claimed to be documents and memorabilia from Columbus's explorations. Numerous visitors speculated about the dubious authenticity of the documents. They were probably fakes.

And it was soon discovered that the huge ostrich egg omelets sold on the Midway at the ostrich enclosure were really made from hen's eggs.

The fair was a unique combination of awe-inspiring beauty, marvelous new technologies, fakes, and authentic relics from Native America, all jumbled together and made magical by electric light used to conjure gorgeous jeweled effects. The White City embodied the utopian hope placed in new technologies, but it also spoke to Baum of the dangers of such powerful wizardry, of the bedazzling effects of electricity, which could distract dumbstruck viewers from the hollow fakery that lay beneath.

The mind-boggling spectacle of the fair was a stark contrast to the realities of Baum's life, lived in a house where there was no running water, let alone electricity, where once a week he would bathe in a tin tub set on the kitchen floor and filled with hot water from a kettle simmering on the coal range. He couldn't afford to buy ice, so food was kept cold in boxes of clean sand dug from the shores of Lake Michigan. The electrified kitchen on show in the Electricity Building was a remote fantasy.

After the fair closed in the fall of 1893, Jackson Park became almost deserted, and the palaces were transformed into illegal makeshift homes for many of the unemployed workmen who had built them, who were now penniless and homeless. The buildings soon became targets for arsonists. The whole Court of Honor erupted into a huge uncontrollable fire on the edge of the lake. What was left was dismantled and the materials were sold. Six months after the fair closed, all but one building had completely disappeared.

But the fair lived on in people's memories. The bright, sparkling lights of the White City illuminated recollected images particularly clearly. There seems to have been a murky, gray area in Baum's mind where memories bled into stories. The big fake White City now sank into his memory and then on into this gray area, where stories were beginning to stir.

Chapter 15

ivers, woods, small towns, expanding cities, factories, farm-land, and empty grasslands passed by out of the corner of Baum's eye as he rattled through Illinois, Iowa, and Missouri on the railroad. His sales were reasonable, but money was still very tight, as he confided to his mother in a letter. Cynthia Baum offered her son and his family a home in Syracuse, but Baum refused the offer. "While I live," he replied, "I shall somehow manage to provide for those dependent on me."

Rocked rhythmically through the heart of America, Baum listened to the anecdotes of his fellow travelers and told a few of his own. Time could always be passed in telling stories, and memories could be stretched into a good yarn. Baum told one story that drew on his past out in the "Wild West." After he had printed a typo in a newspaper article and accidentally insulted a new bride, so the story went, the groom challenged him to a duel with revolvers. Both men, he admitted, set off from the dueling spot at a pace and fled the scene, loaded guns in hand.

Wielding trunkloads of china and staying in cheap hotels, Baum became profoundly lonely. He and Maud wrote to each other almost daily. Once, when Baum didn't receive a letter from his wife for a few days, he panicked and telegraphed that he was coming right home, fearing that something awful had happened.

Meanwhile, Maud, a talented seamstress, was earning a little extra money by giving embroidery lessons to local women at twenty-five cents a class. In the evenings when Baum was at home, as Maud stitched patterns in colored silk thread, he wove tales for his captivated boys. Frank Jr., Rob,

Harry, and Ken, ages eleven, eight, five, and three in 1894, were all at a most imaginative age, when fairy tales exist in the child's mind on the cusp between literal fact and pure fiction. Baum developed a ritual of telling tales to his sons in the evenings before bedtime, around the glowing kerosene lamp. Sometimes they made taffy or popcorn, so the colorful tales would be mingled in the boys' minds with the smell of melted butter and the taste of sugar and salt. Baum never read the Bible to his children or told biblical stories; his imaginative resources were the ancient folktales. Andrew Lang's numerous editions of collected folktales were always scattered about the house; these books were living, working daily imaginative resources to be read and reread. A new Lang collection came out almost annually and included "fancies brought from all quarters," stories from the Brothers Grimm and Hans Christian Anderson, as well as ancient tales from England, France, China, Russia, Scandinavia, Japan, Africa, the Middle East, Iceland, and Aboriginal Australia. The tales featured all kinds of strange things, such as a snow queen who lives in an ice palace, a forest witch who shatters into a million pieces, a coat spun from a woman's hair, pearl-studded slippers, a flying trunk, and a tree with girls' heads growing out of the end of each branch.

Baum also liked to tell the old Mother Goose tales, which had become strange over the centuries, worn into weird, dreamlike episodes. The children would interrupt him with questions. How did the blackbirds baked in the pie escape? Why did the little pig make his house out of straw? How did the cow jump over the moon? Baum made up his own tales in response to these insistent questions.

On the road, alone in hotel rooms, staring out of train carriage windows at the passing landscape, Baum began to jot down ideas for stories on the backs of envelopes and hotel notepaper to tell the boys when he got home. Long-buried literary ambition from his youth, only partially unearthed and put to use in the *Aberdeen Saturday Pioneer*, began to resurface, taking shape in the space and time opened up by extensive, lonely travel, the silence of hotel rooms late at night, and the dull ache of homesickness.

The oral tales he told the boys were private, family stories developed as a way to spend intimate time with his children. A nickel each for a jaw-breaker candy when he got home just didn't seem enough. Stories were something unique he could give them, and they were free. He hated to return after a long trip away to find himself saddled with the role of disciplining father. He once came home and Maud told him that Ken had been naughty and needed to be punished; she insisted that he spank the boy for his disobedience. After reluctantly giving Ken a few smacks and sending him howling to bed without supper, Baum felt sick to his stomach and couldn't eat his own dinner. He took food up to Ken, who was sobbing and probably clinging to Eddie Riley, his rag doll comforter. Baum sincerely apologized to his son and swore he would never hit any of the boys ever again, and he never did.

Matilda Gage often stayed with Maud while Baum was away, to help with four boisterous boys who seemed to be at an age when they were always getting into trouble. Frank Jr. and Rob roamed the neighborhood in a gang of boys; Rob got into a fight and was stabbed with an ice pick, though he wasn't badly injured. Matilda heard Baum's intricate stories one day when he was home, and she told him he should try to publish them. Many years previously, Matilda had written a children's story called "Tom's Tale," based on the orphaned crow her children had reared. It had never been published, but she understood the ambition to write stories and was of course a published author herself. Matilda was a complex woman, sometimes impulsive and unpredictable, like Maud, but she was also extremely determined, filled with a life force that must have been infectious. In a letter to her son, Clarkson, written in 1892, as she worked frantically to finish *Woman, Church and State*, she had written, "I have simply determined that no power on Earth, or beyond, should crush me, and here I am, at 69."

In addition to penning tales for his children, Baum started to try his hand at short stories and poems for adults. He sent them in to newspapers and magazines, and kept his rejections in what he called a "Record of Failures." But he continued to write. In 1895, he started to have some success, and a couple of light poems were published in Chicago newspapers. The *Chicago Sunday Times-Herald* issued a writing contest that called for people to send in "the biggest lie" they could think of; "lying is a fine art," read the request, "and only those who have become devoted students can distort facts until they seem more attractive than the truth." Baum rose to the challenge. In May 1895, the *Herald* published his "lie." A small, seemingly insignificant anecdote more than an entire story, "A Cold Day on the Railroad" nevertheless showed Baum's imagination finally sparking into life. A "stranger" described a bitterly cold winter's day when even smoke froze. The "conductor entered the car, knocked his head against the side of the door to break off his breath, and yelled ticket! before it froze again." The word froze, "penetrated a few feet and stuck fast in the atmosphere," so the passengers could read it spelled out in frozen breath hanging in midair. The conductor then "broke his little finger off as clean as if it had been an icicle. It rattled onto the floor, but he picked it up and calmly put it in his vest pocket." This little fragment showed that Baum was good at conjuring simple but vividly real descriptions of the fantastic.

When he was home in Chicago, Baum was firmly locked inside a smoggy, bustling metropolis, a stone and steel city heaving with people hustling and striving amid the trams and trains. In a collection of what he called his "Phunniland" tales, Baum escaped internally to a rural, idealized alternative landscape where everything anyone could "possibly need grows upon trees, so they have no use for money at all." There's no poverty; the river flows with milk, the sand is sugar, candies grow on bushes, it rains lemonade, the beams of sunlight are perfumed, lightning is fireworks, and thunder is the roaring of opera music.

But everything isn't perfect, which is fortunate for the purposes of a good story. The land is full of odd creatures, silly monarchs, talking composite beasts, a good sorceress, and a wicked purple dragon. A giant cast-iron man built by miners stomps through the land, crushing fifty trees with every step. The machine eventually walks into the sea, where it remains. A "powerful magician" who lives in a cavern studded with rubies and electric lights is a trickster who changes into a crow to steal a princess's toe. Surreal events occur in Phunniland, as when an elephant swallows itself, and a kiss hardens into a small, strange solid object. The story was a light travelogue through Baum's recently ignited imagination, a warm-up for what was to come.

In his stories for adults, Baum explored the morality of the brutal economic competition of the late Gilded Age. In "The Return of Dick Weemins," a troubled gambling addict makes a fortune and returns home to become the local big shot, mill owner, and mayor. When Dick is challenged about the morality of his first fortune, he replies: "All occupations, to my notions, is gamblin'—or speculatin'," which "mounts to the same thing. Did anybody ever question Gould's or Vanderbilt's money?" In "The Suicide of Kiaros," a respectable businessman builds up considerable gambling debts, kills a local Greek moneylender, and stages the murder as suicide. He then marries the daughter of the wealthiest man in town and builds a reputation as "an honorable and highly respected man of business." The message was that the immoral acts that often put men of power in place go unpunished.

These tales were morally challenging but not particularly well written. Baum's writing came to life in tales about new technologies, magic, the occult, and the natural world. In "Yesterday at the Exposition," published in the *Chicago Sunday Times-Herald* in February 1896, he imagined a world's fair of the year 2090, with high-speed pneumatic cars, and airships projected into the sky, transporting people through the clouds between Boston and Chicago. Magical fertilizer makes wheat grow from seed in fifteen minutes, and people communicate through telepathy. A display on the midway features women wearing strange garments called "corsets, a mode of dress that was fashionable. . . . Many spectators can scarcely believe that so cramped and unlovely a costume was ever universally adopted by women." The "discomfort to the wearer," he went on, "must have been great." X-ray has penetrated the ground to discover "monster gems" that have been dug up and displayed.

Wilhelm Roentgen's discovery of X-rays in 1895 had stirred everybody's imagination; some people were seriously worried that X-ray spectacles would soon be able to look through women's clothes to see their wire and bone corsets beneath. In a short poem, also published in the *Chicago Times-Herald*, called "The Latest in Magic," Baum exaggerated the potential of X-rays to "turn tin into purest gold" and to peer into people's true hearts and illuminate their minds. These were indeed "wonder-struck days."

"My Ruby Wedding Ring" was an important short story in the development of Baum's writing because here he began to explore the realm of hypnagogia, the transitional mental state between waking and sleep. In the story, a lonely midnight traveler meets a beautiful, despairing woman on a moonlit road, and she tells him she will soon be forced to marry a brute. The traveler offers her an escape by suggesting that he marry her right away instead. After the brief ceremony, the woman melts into the night, and the traveler discovers that he has "wedded a ghost," a "phantom bride," the troubled spirit of a tortured woman who had killed herself decades earlier to escape a forced marriage. But the ruby ring she gave the traveler remains on his finger.

This story takes place on the open road, by moonlight, and begins as the traveler, weary on his way by horse and buggy, enters "a somnolent state midway between sleep and waking." This intermediate, trancelike state where memory, dreams, nightmares, and stories blend together is very productive to the storyteller. In "My Ruby Wedding Ring," Baum leapt into this important in-between state where fairy tales are weaved, and he figuratively wedded himself to it.

Back in Chicago in the summer of 1896, the Democratic National Convention selected a senator from Nebraska, William Jennings Bryan, as their nominee for president in the coming fall election. Bryan was an extremely charismatic speaker, and he won the nomination after his "Cross of Gold" speech, in which he addressed the terrible economic depression of the 1890s (which had forced Baum to leave South Dakota) and argued strongly in favor of "bimetallism," of basing the monetary system on silver as well as gold, thus breaking the gold standard, which, he said, threatened to "crucify mankind upon a Cross of Gold." The argument for bimetallism had grown since the discovery of silver mines in the West (in which Baum's father, Benjamin, had invested) after the Civil War; support for it had further developed since the economic depression of the 1890s. The new reformist Populist Party, formed in the West in the 1890s, also selected Bryan as their candidate for president, so Bryan's ticket represented both Democrats and Populists. The Populists, many Democrats, and even some Republicans supported the move to bimetallism as a way of curtailing the economic power of the railroads and banks, and helping debt-ridden farmers. Baum's interest in politics was temporarily reignited by the charismatic figure of Bryan, and he took part in torchlight parades in support of Bryan's presidential campaign. But Baum never made it clear that he supported either the Populist Party or bimetallism particularly strongly. Bryan lost that November, and the Republican William McKinley was elected president.

The year 1897 was a major turning point for Baum, now age forty-one. He was mingling with Chicago's extensive network of artists, writers, publishers, and architects, including Chauncey Williams, wealthy publisher of Way and Williams (who lived in the first house designed by Frank Lloyd Wright). Williams wanted to publish Baum's collection of Mother Goose tales, the stories Baum created in response to his children's questions about the queer tales from the Old World. He commissioned a talented artist named Maxfield Parrish to illustrate the book, which came out toward the end of 1897 as *Mother Goose in Prose*. Baum was finally in print as the author of a children's book.

The new author showed off his considerable knowledge of the history of folktales in his introduction to the book, in which he took "some pains to record the various claims to the origin of Mother Goose" from 1600s Europe to nineteenth-century America. There were competing theories about where the tales had come from, Baum explained, citing their possible creator as Elizabeth Goose, Eliza Vergoose, Martha Gooch, and Queen Goosefoot. But he admitted that nobody really knew where they had come from. He also reflected on the place of nursery rhymes in memory. "Those things which are earliest impressed upon our minds cling to them the most tenaciously," wrote Baum. "The snatches sung in the nursery are never forgotten," he added, "nor are they ever recalled without bringing back with them myriads of slumbering feelings and half-forgotten images." Baum made up realistic tales to explain the old rhymes and offered new interpretations of ancient stories. The old woman who lived in a shoe, for example, has so many children to look after because her four daughters died and she's left to care for their sixteen children.

Baum sent editions to his family back in Syracuse. In the copy to his sister Mary-Louise, he wrote: "When I was young I longed to write a great novel that should win me fame. Now that I am getting old my first book is written to amuse children. . . . I know you will not despise these simple tales, but will understand me and accord me your full sympathy." In his sister Harriet's copy, he thanked her for encouraging him to write when he was a child. "I inflict these pages upon you," he scribbled; "you have but yourself to blame for this sad result of your past rashness." It was as though he was slightly ashamed of the book. What had started as a private family ritual of storytelling, of spinning unselfconscious tales for his boys to spark their imaginations, had now become public, commercial property. In his brother Harry's copy, Baum recalled their shared childhood, when they had done everything together, before "we came to the crossways of life and stepped out upon divergent paths." He wrote that "the old life, so sweet to remember, is now left far behind"; his memories of childhood had "become a dream of the past." Writing for children had stirred up memories of his own childhood, and these memories had become dreamlike, rather like the Mother Goose stories themselves.

Baum was now fully committed to writing, but he didn't imagine that he could earn a living by his pen. After four years on the road, the traveling was becoming unbearable and he knew that he simply had to think of a new way to make money. Recent developments in glass technology had produced thick plate glass that was being used to glaze large storefronts. Department stores in America's cities now showed off their wares in large window displays. With electric lighting, windows could be illuminated even at night, which transformed sidewalks into theatrical tableaux.

On his travels, Baum had noticed that many storekeepers had no idea how to present their wares attractively, how to appeal to the roving, fickle eye of the customer, and this gave him his next idea: "window trimming." Drawing on his old theatrical experience, Baum was one of the first people to put his mind to the business of department store window display, and he became an important innovator in the emerging consumer economy. He was as ambitious about this new idea as he had been about Baum's Bazaar and the *Aberdeen Saturday Pioneer*, and he threw himself in to it.

"I have wanted to quit traveling and find some employment that would enable me to stay home," he wrote to Mary-Louise in October 1897. "I conceived of the idea of a magazine devoted to window-trimming, which I know is greatly needed." He was having trouble raising capital for the journal; he had scarcely had "time to sleep and eat from my business" efforts to get it off the ground. But the first issue of *The Show Window* finally appeared in November, published by Chauncey Williams, and it was a great success. He resigned from Pitkin and Brooks. At last he could pack away the trunks of crockery and glassware and hang up his traveling coat.

In 1897, the El rising above Chicago's Loop was finally completed. People rode the rattling rails elevated one story aboveground, and looked out as the sun glinted off large plate-glass windows of department stores like Marshall Field's. Passing the windows on street level, they saw, perhaps, their own faces reflected amid the carefully arranged toys, smartly dressed wax mannequins, and rows of kid gloves. Such images excited their desires. Baum was determined to excite their imaginations as well, by transforming window displays into fairy-tale landscapes that would absorb the amazed eyes of passersby and convince them that if they made a purchase, they too could enter a fantastic world and be transformed. The purpose of elaborate displays was, according to Baum, "to arouse in the observer cupidity and a longing to possess the goods you offer for sale." He pleaded with the window trimmers of America: "For heaven's sake, be original!" *The Show Window* rapidly became a highly successful monthly magazine, in which Baum advised the merchants of America how to innovate.

"I have always found," he wrote, "that anything which was worth doing at all was worth doing well. It may take a little more time and cost a little more money, but you will obtain the desired result in the end." As ever, he approached his new project with real enthusiasm and an acute attention to detail. He called on the storekeepers and window trimmers of the world to do the same, and filled *The Show Window* with photographs of the most ambitious, elaborate, extravagant, and theatrical displays of goods ever seen. He no doubt put together many of the displays and took the photographs himself. He showed how the most ordinary household items could be transformed into extraordinary visual spectacles. The magazine featured displays of women's stockings arranged into whirling cartwheels, blankets rolled into logs and made into a log cabin, and thousands of cotton reels strung together to make a model of the Brooklyn Bridge.

Baum showed shopkeepers how to make just about anything with enough gentlemen's handkerchiefs folded, using a skilled form of cloth origami. The magazine featured all manner of displays made from folded handkerchiefs, including a steam train, a Venetian palace with gondolas floating along a model canal, a grand pillared arch, like one from the false White City, and a Thanksgiving turkey. Goods could even be transformed into figures, such as the "Manila-Man," a man made from rope, another made entirely out of sponges, and a donkey made from tin implements.

A clever window trimmer could also transform a store window into a magical miniature landscape. Baum suggested cutting down branches and putting them into windows to create forest scenes. One article featured photographs from a store in Ohio in which a "Sylvan Glade" was created with trees, rocks, and moss; elks' horns blurred into the tree branches. Men's shirts hung from the branches instead of fruit, as though the neatly tailored cotton shirts grew on trees, as do all necessities in Baum's Phunniland.

Baum expressed his fascination with illusions and trickery in *The Show Window*. A display could attract the passerby with beguiling illusions and become a kind of magic show, he explained. Extended articles were dedicated to "Illusion Windows," which "originated with dime museums and side-shows," he said. In the "Vanishing Lady" illusion, for instance, the top half of a real woman (rather than a wax mannequin) appeared to rest on a wooden pedestal. Through the clever arrangement of mirrors that disoriented the viewer's perspective, the woman's lower half was concealed. "At short intervals," the article suggested, the "woman would disappear right into the pedestal, and presently would reappear with a new hat." This odd trick suggested to startled passersby either that a real live woman had been chopped up and transformed into a mannequin or that the top half of a wax fashion model had come to life.

Another article showed how to display a decapitated man's head in a box on a table; the head talked and moved to show that it was still alive. A man crouched under a table, poked his head up through a hole in the top, and through the clever use of angled mirrors, the table would seem to have nothing beneath it. *The Show Window* included carefully drawn diagrams, like the manuals for stage tricks and illusions popular at this time. Magician Albert Hopkins's *Stage Illusions and Scientific Diversions, Including Trick Photography* (1897) was a popular manual, for instance, of what Hopkins called "side show science," and it contained all the illusions mentioned in Baum's journal. Hopkins was a famous nineteenth-century magician. In another popular manual, called *The Modern Wizard*, A. Roterberg insisted that "it's the conjurer's business to make ordinary Things appear marvelous." Baum reveled in the use of trapdoors, invisible mirrors, false walls, and altered perspectives that enabled him to "make ordinary Things" in shop-front windows "appear marvelous."

The modern window display had the wonders of electricity at its disposal; the newly harnessed energy could bring goods to life with automated flashing lights that showed off goods after dark. *The Show Window* advertised false gems, nuggets of colored glass, which, if carefully arranged, reflected glinting kaleidoscopes of colored light across mundane products such as handkerchiefs, stockings, and work shirts. Baum's enthusiasm for these illusions, electrical scenes, and miniature fantasy landscapes was without end; his extravagant claims for their effects were worthy of P. T. Barnum.

But in *The Show Window*, Baum promoted goods and selling strategies that were in tension with ideas he expressed elsewhere. The magazine included advice on how to display corsets attractively on carefully arranged mannequins. "A dozen corsets, properly placed," he wrote, "will make an excellent display." Stuffed birds appeared in cages made from ribbons; in later stories, Baum expressed his strong dislike of the use of stuffed birds in women's fashion. He had already expressed his views about the horrible cruelty of the corset in "Yesterday at the Exposition," but here he was advising others on how to sell them.

When he wasn't at the office in the Caxton Building in central Chicago, rustling up advertising, managing subscriptions, writing, and editing the magazine, Baum was working on a new collection of stories for children, as a follow-up to *Mother Goose in Prose*. Instead of explaining the old rhymes with stories, Baum invented his own. Writing these oiled his imagination, as he wrote about a boy who invents an airship and flies to the moon, a fast-running clockwork man, a frightening jack-o'-lantern, a Native American patchwork doll, and a boy who's blown away in a storm on the end of a kite. He drew on a mix of imagination and memory in these modern nursery rhymes, which included a goose from Syracuse that thinks he is a clown and an old man called Mister Micklejohn, an amputee (from the Civil War perhaps) whose wooden leg raps rhythmically as he walks.

Through his acquaintances in publishing and the arts, Baum had met William Wallace Denslow, a talented illustrator and keen ice-skater. Den had illustrated P. T. Barnum's 1890 book *Dollars and Sense.* He had lived out West for a while, where, so the story went, he had been chased by a pack of wolves and embroiled in a shoot-out. Like Baum, Denslow had been brought to Chicago by the World's Fair and he had drawn several illustrations of the White City for newspapers. Known as Hippocampus Den from his signature, which was a sea horse, this man had a radically different personality from Baum, but the men got along well. Denslow had a loud, foghorn voice and drank too much. He was vain, gregarious, restless, unpredictable, morose, and misanthropic. He kept a human skull on his desk with "What's the Use?" written beneath it. In his diary, he had written in 1893, "I shall believe no one and pretend to trust all, and endeavor to carve out my own salvation."

Baum showed Denslow some of his new rhymes, and the two men agreed they would create a colorful, vibrant, highly illustrated book for young children together. They found a publisher in the George M. Hill Company and agreed to split royalties equally. Baum and Denslow met regularly to discuss the book. Smoke from Baum's cigars and Denslow's pipe puffed out of the workroom as they transformed their nicotine rushes into quirky verse.

The tales Baum read as a child, particularly those of the Grimms and Andersen, worked their way back into his mind when he read them to his boys from Lang and other collections, and reconnected him to his first readings as a child. But he was now an adult reexperiencing the tales. He had loved the stories as a child, but they had also frightened him. As an adult and a father, he now asked whether the Grimms were really for children, and perhaps the cruelty in many of Andersen's stories, such as "The Little Mermaid" and "The Red Shoes," wasn't appropriate for the very young. Andersen's later tales, in particular, are filled with suffering and torment. These questions had been asked before. In his preface to *The Pink Fairy Book*, for instance, Lang warned his readers that "the Danish story of the princess in the chest need not be read to a very nervous child." In their earliest editions of collected oral tales, even the Brothers Grimm had recognized similar worries. "It has been noted," they wrote, "that this or that might prove . . . unsuitable for children . . . and that parents might not want to put the book into the hands of their children."

In "Who's Afraid?" and "Civilized Boy," two poems for his new book, Baum touched on this question. "Who's Afraid?" declares that "Ev'ry Giant now is dead," "Jack has cut off ev'ry head . . . Ev'ry Goblin, known of old, Perished years ago, I'm told. Ev'ry Witch on broomstick riding, Has been burned or is in hiding." This ditty wasn't very pleased about the death of folktale fear, and longed for the ancient goblins and witches to resurface into the modern world. In "Civilized Boy," Baum asked, "Pray, what can a civilized boy do now, When all the Dragons all are dead," "And the Giants stout, that we have read about, Have never one a head?"

It was as if Baum's instinctive child reader was buried beneath the rational adult who reread the tales and competed with the grown-up perspective. The adult Baum was anxious about the frightening aspects of folktales and their possible effect on children, who often read the stories before they fell asleep, so the tales entered the child's mind in its hypnagogic state, the vulnerable no-man's-land between waking and sleep. Baum's inner child reader, however, was far more emotionally responsive to stories, and more anarchic and intrepid, like the many brave child heroes of the classic fairy tales themselves. In "Who's Afraid?" and "Civilized Boy," Baum acknowledged the buried child reader and gave him permission to include frightening things in his stories. He recognized that we need things to fear.

Chapter 16

n May 1898, Baum discovered a brilliant new idea for a story about a child who travels to a marvelous land called Oz. It seemed like a discovery rather than an invention because it came to him so suddenly, as if from outside his mind. It was seven years since Baum had left the Great Plains, but he frequently heard news from family still living back in North and South Dakota. The landscape there was etched in his memory, painfully associated with struggle and drought and the terrible wars with the Native Americans. In the spring of 1898, Baum's mind returned to the prairies and found a lonely little girl, much like his nieces Matilda and Magdalena, playing out on the dry, cracked, open plains. The dramatic, unstoppable force of wild storms out west was imprinted on his memory too. He was remembering the Dakotas, but he set his story on the Kansas prairie to create some distance from the Carpenters, Maud's sister's family, still struggling on the homestead in Edgeley, North Dakota. He conjured a "low wail of the wind" from the north and "a sharp whistling in the air from the south" that bowed and created "ripples in the grass," and imagined a giant, violent twister that spun through his mind, ripping the child he named Dorothy from the waving grasses and taking her to a faraway land. Baum worked on this new story in between editing *The Show Window* and the book of illustrated rhymes. The tale came easily, as if it were being written through him. He began to construct an alternative country that in some ways took its shape from U.S. geography, as though this new land was being dreamt up by the American landscape itself.

The story of Dorothy's journey through Oz was sifted from the sediment of Baum's deepest memories. It came out of the farmland, woodlands, and lakes of his childhood, the nightmarish Civil War amputees he must have seen, the scarecrows that had haunted his dreams, and the folktales he had read; it came out of his experiences out west, amid drought, cyclones, and rural poverty, out of the gleaming fake White City of the Chicago World's Fair, and out of his fascination with illusions and tricks. Baum shaped his stories intuitively, drawing on a mix of old buried memories, his thoughts and fears about modern technologies, tensions from the commercial world of *The Show Window*, and profound love for his children. This was a highly potent mix to bring to storytelling.

The new story took shape over the next year and a half in the real-life context of two powerful and almost opposing influences that must have deeply affected Baum while he was writing. The first was a series of painful losses in Baum's life. The second was the expansion of space around him and his entrance into refreshing wooded landscapes.

The discovery of the new story starring Dorothy was shortly preceded by two significant deaths in Baum's world. The first occurred in the realm of modern fairy tales, into which Baum was just dipping his toe. On January 14, 1898, Lewis Carroll, "the quaint and clever old clergyman," as Baum later called him, died. The following day, newspapers across America announced his death. *Alice's Adventures in Wonderland* and *Through the Looking Glass* had been bestsellers since they were first published in the 1860s and 70s. The author of the most famous modern fairy tale was dead. This sparked a renewed interest in the Alice books in Britain and America, and in the idea of a girl child hero who accidentally travels to a strange other world.

As Baum absorbed this passing in the outer world of stories, death came to the inner world of his family. He was very close with his extended family, especially to Maud's mother and siblings; it was often Baum and not Maud who wrote to them with important news or to express concern or condolences. In the early months of 1898, Matilda Gage, Maud's mother, had been staying with the Baums. She was ill and confined to her bed. She had experienced some kind of collapse in 1896 and had come very close to death. Her attention had since turned fully to spiritual matters and to the subject of reincarnation. The latest Theosophical books and pamphlets she read and passed on to her children were filled with theories about reincarnation. In a letter written in 1897 to her seven-year-old grandson, Harry Carpenter, Julia's son, living on the homestead out in North Dakota, Matilda had explained her views. "What is called death by people is not death," she wrote; "you are more alive than ever you were after what is called death. Death is only a journey, like going to another country. . . . After people have gone a while they come back and live in another body, in another family and have another name. Sometimes they live in another country."

Baum and Maud firmly believed in reincarnation too; they felt sure that they had been together in numerous past lives, and would be together again in future incarnations.

In March 1898, Matilda had a stroke that left her semiconscious and partially paralyzed. Baum wrote to Clarkson in Aberdeen. "I think your mother is near the end," he said. Her "vitality" was "at a low ebb." Five days later, Matilda died at the Baums's house, her ghost given up above Chicago, to be, if she was right, reborn into a new body.

Matilda's other children and grandchildren came to Chicago for the cremation. Clarkson's wife, Sophie, was five months pregnant at the time. The Gages believed that the dead body was an empty vessel. The grandchildren were told to treat it as such, and were given a tour of the crematorium, including the furnaces in the basement. They were shown the red-hot fires and told that in order to consume a body, the furnace would have to become white hot. Matilda, Clarkson's daughter, age twelve, was distressed by this and even more so that evening after the cremation, when the children were taken to the theater for a bit of distraction; unfortunately, the play included a scene in Hell, featuring "a great burning of red lights and flames" that reminded her of the crematorium furnaces.

A stone monument to Matilda was later put up in a cemetery near her home in Fayetteville, with the words "There is a word sweeter than Mother, Home or Heaven. That word is Liberty" chiseled into it.

Maud was extremely distressed by her mother's death. She now had no family living close by. "It is just two months ago tonight that Mother left us," she wrote to her sister Helen. "We have had a terrible electrical storm tonight, and I am very lonely. If only I could see Mother, once, if she was only up in her room. O, Mother," she lamented, "I am so lonely without you . . . Frank is good and kind, but he is different from Mother and I want her so much."

In the spring of 1898, just before Baum had the idea for Dorothy's story, fear entered his life again, in the awful form of war. The troubles were centered on Cuba, and the Cuban movement for independence from Spanish rule. Conflict with the United States had been brewing for some time, and when, in February, the American battleship the USS *Maine* suddenly and mysteriously exploded and sank in Havana Harbor, military action seemed unavoidable. In early April, President McKinley requested the movement of troops to Cuba, before he declared war on Spain on April 20. On May 1, Harry Baum, Frank's beloved only surviving brother, enlisted. He joined the 2nd Regiment and wrote to Baum the night before he left to travel south into action. Harry rarely wrote to his older brother, and Baum later complained: "You are an unsatisfactory correspondent." "The one you wrote me . . . on the eve of your departure for war—has always been kept among my private treasures." "Your letters," he added, "being like angels' visits are held in the light of miracles and treasured accordingly." Harry's letter, though precious because rare, brought worrying news of his enlistment, preserving fear as well as warm affection in Baum's mind, like a piece of glowing amber with an ugly insect trapped inside.

The newspapers were filled with stories about Cuba and Spain in the spring of 1898, as Baum began to put together his new story. The Spanish-American War sparked the public's interest in exotic foreign lands outside America.

Inside the Baum-Gage family, the pain at the recent loss of Matilda Gage and the fear of losing Harry must have been momentarily lifted when on June 11, 1898, Sophie and Clarkson Gage's daughter was born; they named her Dorothy. Baum continued to work on his tale about a fictional Dorothy, but five months later, just as Dorothy Gale was coming into being, baby Dorothy Gage disappeared. In November 1898, the terrible news reached Chicago that she had died on the eleventh from "congestion of the brain." Maud was distraught. She simply had to attend the funeral on the sixteenth. Dorothy was buried in Bloomington, Illinois, where Clarkson and Sophie had moved temporarily to escape the hard times in Aberdeen. She was buried in a tiny coffin and laid to rest in the cold ground in the children's area of the Evergreen Memorial Cemetery. A stone marker read simply "Dorothy Louise DAU of Mr. and Mrs. T. G. Gage," followed by the frightening dates: "June 11th 1898, November 11th 1898." It was a tiny window of time to have been on earth.

Maud was so upset that, when she returned to Chicago after the funeral, she needed medical attention. She wrote to her sister Helen a week later. "Dorothy was a perfectly beautiful baby," she wrote. "I could have taken her for my very own and loved her devotedly." Maud's sister was still miserable out in Edgeley, North Dakota. Maud and Frank suggested they adopt Julia's daughter, Magdalena, believing they could offer her a better life in Chicago, but Julia wouldn't hear of it. Maud was now thirty-nine (who knows if the Baums were still trying for children); it's likely that around this time, Maud and Frank were coming to terms with the fact that they would never have a daughter of their own. But it might also have been that Maud's distress was an echo of her recent powerful and painful grief at losing her mother only eight months earlier. With the death of Matilda Gage, the eldest in the family, and then Dorothy Gage, the youngest, the family was severed at its top and tail.

Chicago was locked in snow by December. On the tenth, the Treaty of Paris of 1898 was signed, officially ending the Spanish-American War, with America triumphant. The world had changed forever: Cuba was no longer under Spanish rule, and Spain ceded rule of Puerto Rico and Guam to the United States. The Spanish also sold the Philippines to the United States for twenty million dollars. America had become, for the first time, an imperial power.

Harry was safe. He left the army on December 13 and returned to Syracuse. He had been stationed in Tampa, Florida, during the conflict, and the most damaging attack on the 2nd Regiment had come not from the Spanish but from a storm that hit the camp during the night. Thunder had boomed about the soldiers' heads and a bolt of lightning struck the camp, traveling down tent poles and through the bodies of fourteen soldiers. Dr. Harry Baum and others rescued the unconscious men from their tents and brought them on canvas stretchers to the makeshift hospital. All were revived except one, Private Edward Nichols. When the regiment surveyed what looked like the aftermath of a battle, they found that the soldiers had failed to put their rubber ponchos underneath them in their tents, which would have saved them from electrocution.

The deaths of Lewis Carroll and Matilda and Dorothy Gage, and the fear of losing Harry, seemed to stimulate Baum's writing. Perhaps the colorful far-off land that Baum discovered was an imaginative act of compensation, an attempt to fill the space created by loss.

But the grief and fear Baum experienced at this time was counterbalanced by the pleasure brought on by the expansion of his living space and, more importantly, by his reacquaintence with wooded landscapes. The development of his new tale coincided with his movement out of cramped, smoggy Chicago and back into proximity with trees. He hadn't lived amid dense woodlands since he left Syracuse in 1888, and his writing benefited from moving back into the realm of what the poet Wallace Stevens called "the intelligence of trees."

In mid-1898, Baum was able to move to a bigger house now that he had a bigger income from *The Show Window*. Perhaps it was also good to escape the memories of Matilda Gage's death that lingered in their previous house. The family moved to a large wooden house, the grandest they had ever lived in, on Humboldt Park Boulevard. It was located on the corner of the street; a big bay window on the second floor curved around the corner, affording a view down streets to the left and the right. A young sapling grew to one side of the porch, casting dappled shadows across the white-painted walls. A tall lamp stood on the corner of the street, like a miniature lighthouse. Its glowing light must have crept into the house during darkness, casting shadows across the heavy oak furniture, the patterned wallpaper, the rugs, and the sea of knickknacks. Baum's home was decorated in the late-nineteenth-century style that would later be called "horror vacui," meaning the fear of empty space, used to describe the cluttered interior design popular in the Victorian age. The main living room was a riot of floral patterns. A glass-fronted cabinet filled with china ornaments stood at the bottom of the stairs, which must have rattled as the boys leapt up and down the steps.

Baum now had his own room, known commonly as his den, as though he were a wild animal that needed a retreat. He hung above his desk a quote from the Bible, reminding him who he was writing for. The line from Corinthians read: "When I was a child, I spake as a child, I understood as a child, I thought as a child." The house also had a cellar and an attic, so family members could spread throughout the house to find room for their growing interests. Rob, for instance, was fascinated by electricity and set up a "workshop" in the large attic. The boys also soon found a trunk up there filled with musty costumes and a blond wig, remnants from Baum's theater days. He had kept some relics from *The Maid of Arran*. On rainy days, the boys would dig through the trunk of old costumes and dress up, inhabiting their father's youthful past but staging their own stories.

Baum had never fully adapted to big-city life, but now he lived near a large park. Humboldt Park was one in a string of large Chicago parks and boulevards known together as the Emerald Necklace. It was filled with mature trees, remnants of the ancient forest from which it had been carved in 1869. It was crisscrossed with a network of paths that framed large areas of flower beds, rosebushes, and formal gardens of exotic flowers. Baum was fascinated by the recent innovation of the bicycle and bought one for each of his sons and for Maud and himself. Wheeling through Humboldt Park, he would have whizzed past scented flower gardens, glass conservatories filled with exotic plants and ferns, manicured lawns, topiaried shrubs, the wading pool, and the lagoon, where in winter, people would skate across the ice.

By mid-1899, the new story about a child called Dorothy was coming along well. Baum discussed his notes with Denslow, who agreed to illustrate it. They signed a document in which they agreed to produce a book "to be called *The City of Oz*, or some other appropriate name." Baum agreed to complete the text before November 1, 1899. This was the first time a place called Oz appeared in a public document.

In the summer of 1899, midway through writing his new story, Baum visited the fashionable new lake retreat of Macatawa Park in Michigan. He named the cottage he rented there that summer Hyperoodon Rostratus, which expressed the unnamable strangeness of finding himself in this new landscape, writing a new tale. The name had lodged itself in Baum's mind during a visit to the Columbian Museum of Chicago, the collection of exhibits gathered together for the Chicago World's Fair and afterward developed into a permanent museum (renamed the Field Museum in 1905). *Hyperoodon rostratus* was the Latin name of a bottlenose whale, whose giant jaw, vast arched rib cage, and knobbly spine spreading backward in a series of vertebrae each the size of a man's clenched fist, was on show in the museum where Baum took the boys. This type of whale was central to the nineteenth-century whaling industry. Its oils and fats were rendered and made into high-quality candles (very bright and odorless), soap, and perfumes. It's strange to think that such a huge beast could be transformed into such small domestic things.

Baum had heard about the summer resort at his Chicago athletic club; he was keen to be a part of the city's fashionable society and wasn't averse to the approval of his male peers. He joined several clubs, including the Chicago Press Club, where he made useful contacts. Macatawa was on the opposite side of Lake Michigan from Chicago, south of the town of Holland, south of the Sleeping Bear Dunes, where, as the Chippewa legend has it, a bear fleeing from a forest fire with her two cubs swam across the lake; the mother bear made it to the eastern shore, but her cubs drowned, forming two small islands, while the grieving bear was buried under the dunes on the shore. The dunes had buried other things along the shores of Lake Michigan too, including whole forests of trees whose top branches poked up above the sand. These were known as "ghost forests."

Baum traveled to Macatawa Park by steamboat from Chicago, on a five-hour journey across the lake. Opened in July 1898, the resort was a half-mile row of wooden cottages nestled amongst thick wooded areas of maple, oak, and cottonwoods, next to the lake and above a boardwalk. Paths led up from the boardwalk through the trees to the houses. Facilities were basic; we don't know if Baum lit whale oil candles at night inside the cottage, to illuminate the house with the rendered remnants of the poor creature it was named after. "Hyperoodon Rostratus" became a Baum family term for anything incomprehensible, nameless, or mysterious.

The whole family swam in the lake in the summer heat. Like all the women in the resort, Maud wore a dark serge swimming outfit that consisted of a blouse, bloomers, and a skirt, thick black stockings, canvas shoes, and a broad-brimmed hat. In the August 1899 issue of *The Show Window*, Baum published an enthusiastic article on the retreat. "Macatawa Park" was "the most original and wonderful place in all the world," read the report, probably written by Baum. Behind the lakeside beach "rise the great bluffs covered with dense forest." Four photographs accompanied the short piece, which Baum probably took himself. He introduced himself to this new landscape, as he had done on the Great Plains, through the camera.

This was the first time since Baum had begun to create stories that he had been able to write in woodlands and next to the mentally irrigating influence of a large body of water. Baum continued working on his new story about a lost balloonist, as he sat next to the very lake that had seen many aeronauts disappear. He liked to write outdoors on the back porch, jotting down ideas and writing some passages out in full in longhand, weaving the characters, the narrative, and the landscape together into a whole, a feat that Baum hadn't managed to achieve before in his stories, which had so far been episodic and fragmented. Writing there, Baum would have been surrounded by the intense call of tree-dwelling cicadas and the sight of flickering Ebony Jewelwing damselflies and Green Darner dragonflies, which were abundant in the area.

Back in Chicago in September 1899, the new story almost drafted, Baum and Denslow's collection of illustrated verse was published as *Father Goose, His Book* in a cautious print run of 5,700 copies. The book opened with a poem called "Father Goose," which explained that "Old Mother Goose became quite new, And joined a Woman's Club," leaving Father Goose with the children, who "called for stories by the score. . . . When Mother Goose at last returned, For her there was no use; The goslings much preferred to hear, The Tales of Father Goose." The book was a call to the modern father, whose role was changing in middle-class households where women had more independence outside the home and there were no nannies to care for children. Maud did have the help of a Swedish housemaid named Sigrid Swanson, but Maud, Frank, and Matilda, before her death, did most of the child care.

These rhymes were in truth a collection of unfinished fragments from Baum's imagination, a work in progress or series of sketches, warm-ups for the story about Dorothy from Kansas that was already on its way, roughed out in jottings and passages on notepaper.

Baum knew that it was Denslow's animated drawings, full of the brightest colors that ever splashed across a children's book, that made *Father Goose* a success. He joked in his inscription in Maud's copy that he hoped "she will find this book instructive and elevating and will remember me as the goose who wrote it." But many reviews were genuinely enthusiastic. The *Chicago Times-Herald* praised the book as "charmingly original," containing "a bunch of funny, sensible, freak-facts," a book full of "fancy masquerade, with clever yarns, bright ditties."

Beyond press applause, the book shocked Baum when it became a runaway bestseller. Hill was also amazed and printed thousands more. Mark Twain was sent a copy and was said to have liked it.

Incredibly, Baum was now the author, the "versifier" as he was called, of a bestselling children's book. It was strange that this book, which he knew wasn't his best work, was selling well and bringing in money. Baum didn't yet fully comprehend that this comic verse, written as a playful recreation outside what seemed to be his more serious commercial business, would prove to be his most profitable enterprise to date. It would become a painful truth that when Baum stopped trying so hard, success came to him. This flew in the face of his Protestant work ethic, which held that only pressing one's nose painfully to the grindstone was rewarded. Baum wrote the first drafts of his stories in longhand, which showed him that his left-handedness, his awkward, reverse way of doing things, was in fact the source of his power.

The surprising success of *Father Goose* must have given Baum a boost. He wrote quickly that fall, in his den lined with bookshelves, crammed with prints, drawings, and photographs, and finished a draft of his new tale a month earlier than predicted, on October 9. He took a new piece of note-paper and scribbled that triumphant sentence: "With This Pencil I wrote the MS of The Emerald City," and then signed his name in his distinctive curly signature. This was a bold act expressing Baum's absolute belief in his new story. The journey was over and had come full circle. In the end, he had brought Dorothy back to the dusty Kansas prairie she had left so suddenly in the tumult of the tornado.

Baum knew instantly that this tale had taken him to a marvelous new place in his mind, somewhere that had enabled him to a write a brilliant story of simplicity and depth.

Denslow sent out an invitation to ten friends to join him at Rector's Tavern on December 31, 1899, to celebrate the New Year. On the envelope containing the invite was a drawing of a bemused goose dressed in top hat and tails, staring at a grandfather clock showing midnight. The perplexed expression on the goose's face embodied the problem being called the "century question." Nobody could agree where the year 1900 would be located in the calendar. Some said that January 1, 1900, was the first day of the last year of the nineteenth century, whereas others insisted that it was the first day of the twentieth century. The party would last, read Denslow's invite, "until A.D. 1900," but no mention was made of the century.

Baum and Maud joined the celebrations. *Father Goose* had now sold over 75,000 copies; it was the bestselling children's book of the Christmas season. To his utter joy and amazement, Baum passed over midnight, December 31, 1899, which was widely recognized as a mystical divide, as the author of a bestseller, but also, as he knew, with a new and powerful story in the wings. This new tale would come to light in 1900, a transitional year lodged between the past and the future. Scholarly studies of the ancient, mischievous figure of the fairy suggest that these creatures often appear on cusps and during transitions. It was wholly appropriate, then, that Baum's new fairy tale would emerge in this cusp between times, in this troubling, unidentifiable conduit between centuries.

When the clock chimed twelve on that cold midnight in Chicago, nobody could put a name to what came next.

Chapter 17

The early months of 1900 were filled with blizzards. The snowfall in Chicago was the heaviest on record, as though the sky were whitewashing the earth, creating a blank canvas for the new century. The cold wind off the lake blew the snow into icy drifts. The streetcars came to a standstill, and railroad carriages filled with livestock were stranded on the edge of the city. But by the time Baum wrote to his brother, Harry, in April, Chicago had thawed. "The young'uns are all great readers," he said, and Rob, his second son, was still fascinated by electricity. "Rob fills the house with electric batteries," wrote Baum, "and we are prepared to hear a bell ring whenever we open a door or step on a stair." Rob's workshop was up in the large attic. But Matilda Gage's ashes were kept up there too, and Rob feared that the ghost of his grandmother might appear suddenly amid the sparks of electricity. The "family ghost," wrote C. W. Leadbeater, a Theosophical author Matilda had much admired and whose work Baum also read, "may really be an earth bound ancestor still haunting the scenes in which his thoughts and hopes were centered during life."

Baum now identified himself as a writer and bragged to Harry about the success of *Father Goose* and about the fact that "my work is now sought by publishers who once scorned my contributions." But he also admitted that "my work in *Father Goose* was not good work, and I know I can do better." Numerous stories and verse were to be published in the coming year, including a series of musical scores created from *Father Goose*, two highly illustrated alphabets, and, at last, the first story he had written for children, set in the exuberant valley of Phunniland. "Then there is the other book," he added, "the best thing I ever have written, they tell me, *The Wonderful Wizard of Oz.*"

Baum's publishers were particularly excited about this new book, he explained, and predicted "a sale of at least a quarter of a million copies." He added, "But the queer, unreliable Public, have not yet spoken."

The author and illustrator had struggled to find the right title for their new book. It had begun as *The City of Oz* and then mutated into *The Emerald City*, but the publishers rejected this title because of an old publishing superstition that any book with a jewel in its title would flop. It had changed to *From Kansas to Fairyland*, then to *The City of the Great Oz*, to *The Fairyland of Oz*, and to *The Land of Oz* before finally settling at the last minute on *The Wonderful Wizard of Oz*.

On a personal note, Baum admitted to Harry that "I miss friends at times. . . . Here I have many acquaintances," but "outside my home no intimacies. I do not make friends easily, nor does Maud." If he became more successful, he would "be able to go home often." Baum had left Syracuse over a decade earlier, but he still called it home.

The Wonderful Wizard of Oz was finally published in September 1900. Its cloth cover was a deep green color, like the Chicago River, and the title leapt out in bright red ink. It was one of the most elaborately illustrated children's books ever published, far more vibrant than any other on the market at the time. It was illustrated in an unusual way, with color images blended into the text. The walls of Dorothy's wooden house, for instance, merge into the text that describes it. Words reach up into the blue sky of Munchkinland, weave in and out of the corn in the Scarecrow's cornfield, are laid over the bark of the trees in the Tin Woodman's forest, and run along the yellow brick road up to the gates of the Emerald City. The layout of the first two illustrated pages made it look as if the Good Witch of the North conjures the tornado with her wand, like one of the witches discussed in Matilda Gage's controversial book.

On the endpaper the initials "B" and "D" were wrapped around one another in an entangled embrace, representing the fact that this was a joint project. Baum and Denslow shared royalties equally and had already received an advance of five hundred dollars each before the book was published.

Baum collected reviews of his work in scrapbooks. He eventually compiled a total of 202 reviews of *The Wonderful Wizard of Oz*, only two of

A popular image from the 1870s of
the unearthing of the Cardiff Giant

Artist unknown

Baum on his
wedding day, 1882

Courtesy of
Gita Dorothy Morena,
The Wisdom of Oz

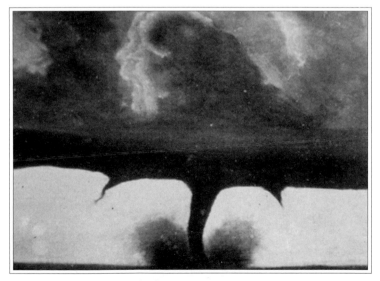

The first known photograph of
a tornado. It was taken in 1884 in
Dakota Territory.

Photographer unknown

Above left:
Maud Gage Baum

Courtesy of Gita Dorothy Morena,
The Wisdom of Oz

Above right:
Matilda Joslyn Gage

Courtesy of the Matilda Joslyn
Gage Foundation

Above: The building in
which Baum's Bazaar
was located on Main
Street in Aberdeen

Courtesy of the
Alexander Mitchell Library,
Aberdeen, South Dakota

Left: A photograph
of Aberdeen, Dakota
Territory, taken by
Baum in 1888

Courtesy of the
Alexander Mitchell Library,
Aberdeen, South Dakota

The White City, the Chicago World's Fair, 1893

Photographer unknown

Below: William Wallace Denslow at work, 1900

Photographer unknown

Above: Baum's scribbled note: "With this Pencil I wrote the MS of The Emerald City," signed and dated October 9, 1899

Special Collections, Syracuse University

Above: Envelope that contained the invitation from William Wallace Denslow to Maud and Frank Baum, for a party to celebrate New Year's Eve, 1899, and the entrance into the cusp year of 1900

The Baum Bugle

Left: The cover of *The Wonderful Wizard of Oz*, 1900

The Wonderful Wizard of Oz, 1900, by L. Frank Baum, illustrated by William Wallace Denslow

Above: Illustration of Chapter 1 of *The Wonderful Wizard of Oz:* "The Cyclone," 1900

"'This is a great comfort,' said the Tin Woodman."

"You ought to be ashamed of yourself!"

Other images on this page:
Illustrations from *The Wonderful Wizard of Oz*, 1900, William Wallace Denslow

Frank, Maud, and their four sons
Courtesy of Gita Dorothy Morena, The Wisdom of Oz

Baum and his four children at home on Humboldt Park Boulevard, Chicago

Courtesy of the Alexander Mitchell Library, Aberdeen, South Dakota

Left: A poster from the 1902
musical extravaganza
The Wizard of Oz

Courtesy of The Library of Congress

Below: Publicity photograph of
Baum in a white suit, 1908

Courtesy of The Library of Congress

Below: Baum typing outdoors
probably in the woods of Macatawa Park

Courtesy of Gita Dorothy Morena
The Wisdom of Oz

Above: 1904 cartoon of
Baum and Walt McDougall
peering out into space
awaiting the arrival of the
"Queer Visitors from the
Marvelous Land of Oz"

The Philadelphia North American

Right:
Ozcot, Baum's
Hollywood Home

Photographer unknown

Below: Baum dancing
on a table as a cowboy
with The Uplifters

Courtesy of
Gita Dorothy Morena,
The Wisdom of Oz

Above: The founders of the
Oz Film Manufacturing
Company: L. Frank Baum,
Louis F. Gottschalk,
Clarence Rundel, and
Harry Haldeman, 1914

Courtesy of Gita Dorothy Morena,
The Wisdom of Oz

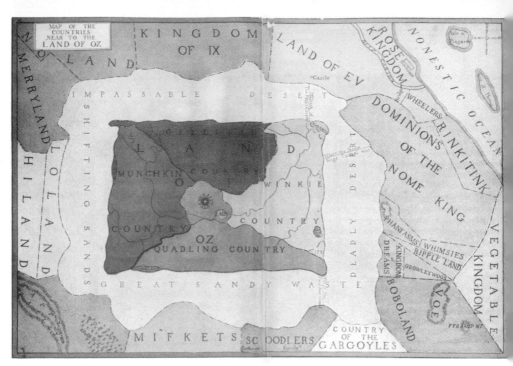

Above: Map of the countries near to the Land of Oz, from *Tik Tok of Oz*, 1914

Tik Tok of Oz *by L. Frank Baum,*
illustrated by John R. Neill

Right: 1939 MGM
publicity photograph
of Maud Baum and
Judy Garland reading
a 1900 copy of *The
Wonderful Wizard of Oz*

Courtesy of Warner Bros.

which were negative. The *Grand Rapids Herald* praised the book for its "comingled visions of multifold opium dreams." It was "the most fantastically delightful child's book of the year." Baum was praised for a story that "never insults childhood intelligence by writing down to it," and *The New York Times* lauded the book as "ingeniously woven out of commonplace material," humorous and filled with "bits of philosophy." The odd characters had a "living and breathing quality"; it was "bright and joyous." It "will indeed be strange," concluded one review, "if there be a normal child who will not enjoy the story."

Kindergarten Magazine suggested that "impossible as are the little girl's companions, the magic pen of the writer, ably assisted by the artist's brush, has made them seem very real." This review noticed Baum's ability to write realistic yet fantastic characters, which was one of his greatest strengths. His ability to create magical characters who seem entirely lifelike stemmed in part from the fact that Baum's "reality" accommodated the invisible presence of both immortal Elementals (as outlined in his Theosophical reading) and the spirits of the dead.

The New York Times suggested that Baum had produced "something new in the place of the old, familiar, and winged fairies of Grimm and Andersen," but also recognized that the story seemed "in some respects like a leaf out of one of the old English fairy tales that Andrew Lang or Joseph Jacobs has rescued for us." Baum must have been thrilled to be put alongside the collections of folktales that had inspired him. The new story seemed both ancient and original.

Baum was now in middle age. He couldn't have written such a wise story so full of complex ideas as well as simple ones if he hadn't suffered and strived for so many years, trying to succeed in the late Gilded Age. His experiences as a child and as a man, his extensive reading through which he'd absorbed the oldest archetypes from folktales, had all jumbled together in his mind to make a brilliant cocktail, which surfaced intuitively as this brilliant, hyperreal story.

The best thing about *The Wonderful Wizard of Oz* is its interpretive openness, its clarity of vision and psychological depth. Readers could see so many things in the story. It was (and still is) impossible to exhaust its hypnotic simplicity and the many-layered interpretations it offers. Ultimately, this breadth and depth of the story was Baum's greatest achievement.

But there might have been particular things about it to strike readers in 1900, recognizable features of their world folded up inside it.

For those used to the tales of the Grimms and Andersen and Carroll's Alice stories, all set in ancient or reimagined Europe, the distinctly American landscape of Dorothy's home "in the midst of the great Kansas prairies" felt familiar and real. Dorothy's life contained wagons, a storm cellar, and a wooden farmhouse; the roaring tornado that captures Dorothy in her house, rips her from the ground, and whistles her into the sky was a known phenomenon, although the event itself was as otherworldly and frightening as anything from a fairy tale. Many of the characters in Oz, such as the Scarecrow, had their equivalents in the immediate world of Baum's readers; Dorothy is a real child, though an unusually fearless one, and Aunt Em and Uncle Henry were all too recognizable as poor homesteaders out on the unforgiving prairie. In Oz, Baum's eye for small details made extraordinary things feel real. He explains, for instance, that while staying in the Wizard's palace in the Emerald City, the Scarecrow stands by the door of his room all night because he never sleeps, and that the Scarecrow also finds it difficult to pick up small things because his hands are old gloves clumsily stuffed with straw.

The recognizably American elements of the story won Baum's readers over in 1900. When Baum took them off in the tornado, spinning them through the sky with Dorothy to a land where things aren't quite so ordinary, his readers already trusted him and let their imaginations follow.

At first, the world in which Dorothy lands doesn't seem so peculiar. It's a country of "marvelous beauty," full of meadows, "stately trees bearing rich and luscious fruit," blossoming flowers, and birds with brilliantly colored feathers, an idealized, natural place, the flowering land the prairie homesteaders had hoped to create out of the Great American Desert. The story is rooted in 1900 America, where homesteaders continued to struggle out on the prairies, but it took readers off into the realms of the collective American imagination, sometimes called the American Dream, the idea of what America was supposed to be or would soon become, a fertile, lush landscape with a gorgeous, glowing city as its capital. Dorothy lands in Uncle Henry's utopian dream.

In the Land of Oz, Baum takes his readers into a world familiar from ancient folktales. There's a good old-fashioned everyday Scarecrow here but this one's alive, talks, walks, and has ideas, even though he thinks he has no brain. Dorothy then discovers a living man made entirely out of tin, an animated metal man filled with empathy and kindness even though he has no heart beating drumlike inside his chest. The long-established role of charmed shoes in the oldest folktales is at work here in the form of magic silver slippers (not ruby red as in the 1939 MGM movie, whose makers wanted to take full advantage of the power of Technicolor). And at the center of Baum's new story is an old-fashioned wicked witch.

But Baum also blurred together the America of 1900 with the old world of fairy stories, writing into Dorothy's adventure things that were true of both worlds, muddying any clear distinction between the two. When the Wicked Witch of the West spies Dorothy and her companions traveling through the yellow plains of the Winkie country, for instance, she sends a pack of wolves, a flock of crows, and a hive of black bees to kill them. The travelers fight creatures familiar in both the realm of fairy tales and the western frontier.

In the four witches of Oz, the Good Witches of the North and South and the Wicked Witches of the East and West, Baum clashed the old world of folktales with a modern perspective. The witches of the East and West are old-fashioned evil witches of witch-hunting folklore, while the witches of the North and South are good and wise witches from Matilda Gage's *Woman, Church and State*, powerful figures like the Iroquois Clan Mothers of upstate New York. Baum also provides a glimpse into the prehistory of Oz, before the witches reigned and the Wizard arrived, blown off course from Omaha in his free-floating balloon. Before this, Oz was like the ancient matriarchies Matilda wrote about, ruled by a benevolent matriarch called Gayelette, a powerful sorceress who lived in a palace built from blocks of rubies.

When Dorothy first meets the Good Witch of the North, after her house lands with a bump on the Wicked Witch of the East and kills her, she admits that she "thought all witches were wicked." "Oh, no," replies the witch, "that is a great mistake." Dorothy persists: "Aunt Em has told me that the witches were all dead—years and years ago." The witch asks Dorothy if Kansas is "a civilized country." "Oh, yes," Dorothy says proudly. "Then that accounts for it," replies the witch. "In the civilized countries I believe there are no witches left; nor wizards, nor sorceresses, nor magicians. But, you see, the Land of Oz has never been civilized. . . . Therefore we still have witches and wizards among us." Uncivilized wilderness is alive and kicking in Oz even if Frederick Jackson Turner was right when he said that the American frontier had closed, the wilderness civilized, populated, and plowed. The inner geography of Baum's mind had to conjure a spacious place of wilderness because there was no wilderness left outside the imagination.

Dorothy and the Scarecrow stumble upon the Tin Woodman standing like a statue in the forest. He explains that he "was born the son of a woodman," but the Wicked Witch of the East cursed his ax, which then chopped him to pieces. A local tinsmith built him a prosthetic tin body and he "could move around as well as ever," he says, but "alas! I had now no heart." The figure of the Tin Woodman raised all kinds of relevant questions. His tin body recalls underlying questions about what happens to the amputee Civil War veteran's sense of self once his body has been merged with prosthetic limbs; Baum perceptively suggests that his traumatized heart might be frozen. The Tin Woodman also echoes Baum's ideas about reincarnation: He remains himself even though his entire body has been removed and replaced. Perhaps this was a stark image of Theosophical reincarnation; The individual's spirit remains intact as it moves through and inhabits many different bodies. In the Tin Woodman, Baum also explores the difference between organisms and machines, and questions which is superior. Machines of all kinds were entering life in 1900 and doing jobs previously performed by humans and animals. Baum's story suggested that this might have consequences; riding to work on an electric streetcar was very different from being pulled along by a horse-drawn cart, with the horse's heart pumping blood through its veins. Talking to someone over the telephone was very different from speaking to them face-to-face.

Baum combined realism with old archetypes brilliantly. Nothing is out of place or extraneous to the story, and each character is both a unique individual and an elemental or archetypal force. Toto, for instance, is a realistic little dog who never speaks, but he's also Dorothy's familiar, the animal spirit attached to its human counterpart, the speechless beast who makes Dorothy complete ("in toto," meaning whole or entirely) by embodying instinct and animal intuition, a kind of intelligence that works beyond language. It's Toto, after all, who discovers the humbug Wizard behind the curtain, as though Dorothy already suspected him but didn't have the nerve to nose about for herself. It's worth remembering also that for thousands of years, dogs have been imagined as creatures who stand at the threshold between life and death, and as guides through the spirit world. In Oz, everything feels at once fully real, earthly, and believable and yet purely symbolic at the same time.

All the Theosophical "elements," the building blocks of the universe, are contained in the story: The Lion is the animal, the Scarecrow the vegetable, and the Tin Woodman the mineral. And the life-giving, purifying, baptizing element of water destroys the wicked witch. The story is filled with a life force, and in Oz everything is alive. Baum's Theosophical literature haunts the tale. There's "no such thing as dead 'matter'," wrote the prominent Theosophical leader Annie Besant in her 1897 book, *The Ancient Wisdom*. "All matter is living," she said, "the tiniest particles are alive. . . . Matter is form, and there is no form which does not express life." Theosophy claimed to have revealed the "ensouling force in every particle." Besant discussed rocks and minerals, whose living particles made them alive. "Metals . . . are living things," she wrote. The "occult doctrine" regarded all matter as existing on a continuum. Rocks were at one end of the living spectrum, which moved on through metals and vegetable matter to animals and finally to human beings. The Theosophical answer to the question of whether the Tin Woodman is alive was simply yes, as a man made of metal he was alive, like everything else.

Each of the characters set out on the journey to see the Wizard because they believe they lack something. The Scarecrow seeks a brain, the Tin Woodman a heart, and the Cowardly Lion courage. But throughout their quest, first along the yellow brick road to the Emerald City and then to kill the Wicked Witch of the West, each demonstrates that he has in abundance the qualities he thinks he lacks. The Scarecrow is always coming up with clever plans, the Tin Woodman is filled with empathy and love for his fellow creatures, and the Lion courageously faces his enemies. The only thing the characters lack is belief in themselves. This leads us to the troubled heart of Baum's tale, to the humbug Wizard.

Having trekked through the frightening forest and the deadly poppy field, the weary travelers finally gain an audience with the mysterious Wizard in his Throne Room in the heart of the Emerald City. The Wizard booms and roars at them and insists that he will help them only if they first kill the Wicked Witch of the West, for in "this country everyone must pay for everything he gets." The Wizard tells Dorothy, "If you wish me to use my magic power to send you home, . . . you must do something for me first." Disheartened and afraid, the group sets off for the yellow plains of the West, where the witch rules from atop her castle. The witch sees them coming, captures them with the help of the flying monkeys, and enslaves Dorothy as her Cinderella servant. The Wicked Witch steals one of Dorothy's silver shoes, and in anger, the girl throws a bucket of water over the witch, who immediately melts into the floor, to become a sticky pile, like melted sugar.

The travelers fly back to the Emerald City with the help of the flying monkeys. During their audience with the Great and Terrible Wizard of Oz, the Cowardly Lion roars in frustration as the Wizard continues to vacillate. He frightens Toto, who runs off and tips over a screen in the corner of the room, to reveal "a little, old man, with a bald head and wrinkled face." His voice trembles as he admits that he is indeed "Oz, the Great and Terrible." "Are you not a great wizard?" asks Dorothy. "I'm just a common man," he replies; "I am a humbug." The Wizard admits that he is just a skilled circus trickster, ventriloquist, and common illusionist, who appeared to the bedazzled travelers as first a giant head, then a beautiful woman, and finally a huge monster by the use of humdrum, earthly methods known to any half-decent magician. The humbug explains that he was born in Omaha and became a circus-promoting balloonist until one day his balloon was carried by the wind and taken up into the clouds. He floated for many days through the sky until he finally landed in Oz, where he was received by the people as a great Wizard and settled as the humbug ruler. He built the Emerald City, which could have been designed by Daniel Burnham, and made all the people wear green-tinted spectacles to make the city, plain white in reality, appear to glow in emerald green.

The Wizard explains that he feared the witches, "for while I had no magical powers at all I soon found out that the witches were really able to do wonderful things." The witches of the North and South he knew were good and wouldn't harm him, but he was able to stave off the Wicked Witches of the East and West only by pretending to be powerful. The Wizard exploited Dorothy's longing for home in order to have the Wicked Witch of the West destroyed. But now, "I am ashamed to say," says the humbug, "I cannot keep my promises." This humbug Wizard embodied many contemporary figures in 1900. He was the politician who offered more than he could possibly deliver; he was the pushy salesman who claimed that his flashy new product could change lives; he was the trickster showman who displayed all kinds of exotic wonders that were really costumed fakes.

But Baum's story uncovered something else even more disturbing about humbugs. Once the Wizard has been unmasked, the disappointed travelers don't know what to do or who to turn to for help. "Can't you give me a brain?" pleads the Scarecrow; "how about my courage?" demands the Lion; "how about my heart?" asks the Tin Woodman. The humbug tries to convince all three that they aren't lacking these qualities. "You don't need them," he tells the Scarecrow. "Experience is the only thing that brings knowledge," he says. "You have plenty of courage," he tells the Lion; "all you need is confidence in yourself." Less satisfactorily, he tells the Tin Woodman that "you are in luck not to have a heart," because a heart "makes most people unhappy." The humbug Wizard clearly has a broken heart himself.

But Dorothy's companions simply won't listen to the "false wizard" and continue to make demands of him even though they know he can't fulfill them. "Well," he sighs, "I'm not much of a magician, as I said; but if you come to me tomorrow morning," he tells the Scarecrow, "I will stuff your head with brains." He's forced to keep up the pretense that they all know is false. The Wizard gives his visitors tokens of the things they think they lack: bran and pins stuffed into the Scarecrow's head, a silk and sawdust heart for the Tin Woodman, and a quack's potion for courage for the Lion. But as he performs these rather meager acts of transformation, the fake Wizard complains: "How can I help being a humbug . . . when all these people make me do things that everybody knows can't be done?" And here's the painful truth Baum points to: Humbugs successfully deceive others because people are willing to be deceived. Baum's story is a particularly devastating critique of power not only because it attacks false and undeserved authority, but because it shows how easily people who lack belief in themselves can become willing participants in the deceptions practiced by manipulative figures who rule over them.

Between the spring of 1898 and the fall of 1899, when Baum was writing *The Wonderful Wizard of Oz*, he had also been putting together a collection of articles, photographs, and diagrams from *The Show Window* to gather together as a book with the catchy title *The Art of Decorating Dry Goods Windows and Interiors*. This was also published in 1900. The book was a guide to creating alluring illusions, dazzling electrical displays with false gems, magic tricks, and transformation scenes to catch customers' eyes. The humbug Wizard used tricks and illusions to convince the people of Oz of his powers, and perhaps the Wizard expressed some of Baum's anxieties about the deceptive arts of selling. He wasn't entirely comfortable with putting his energy and theatrical imagination into selling corsets.

But the humbug Wizard also embodies a much deeper anxiety about Baum's role as author. Before *The Wonderful Wizard of Oz,* Baum wasn't particularly pleased with the books he had published, and he knew the poems he had collected in a handmade book called *By the Candelabra's Glare* were largely light doggerel. As he admitted to his sister, Mary-Louise, he had secretly dreamed of writing a great novel. Baum often felt like a literary impostor, a trumped-up salesman with ideas above his station. He read Shakespeare, Dickens, John Bunyan, and the dark tales of Edgar Allan Poe, but he was acutely aware that, unlike Maud, he hadn't gone to college, had barely been to school in fact. He thought of himself as "a rather stubborn illiterate." Baum lacked intellectual and creative confidence. Perhaps deep down he felt like an illusionist posing as a writer.

When Toto uncovers the false Wizard behind the curtain, the little dog reveals a man trapped at the center of his own hoax, living alone in his Throne Room, his only company the levers, wires, and pulleys to maintain the illusion of his power. "I am tired of being a humbug," he admits, "I'd much rather go back to Kansas with you and be in a circus again." With Dorothy's help, he builds a giant balloon to take her and Toto up into the skies over Oz and return to America. But the balloon takes off prematurely and Dorothy is left behind, forced to seek an alternative route home via a visit to Glinda, the Good Witch of the South.

On their journey south, Dorothy and her friends confront the Fighting Trees, clamber through the Dainty China Country, where the Lion acciden-tally smashes the church with his tail, battle a giant spider, and fight the armless Quadlings, which, like jack-in-the-boxes, attack the travelers by head butting them from their extending necks. Glinda finally tells Dorothy that she can return to Kansas easily by clicking the heels of her magic shoes together three times. Dorothy's desire to return home to Kansas has been the motivating force of the story, and it's in this knotty region that part of the story's power resides. In order to write this tale, Baum's best and most truthful, he had returned imaginatively to a place he identified with struggle and failure: the Great Plains. It was as though the dry, treeless prairie had opened a portal in Baum's mind into imaginary landscapes: The vast openness and suffering there forced a person to imagine better elsewheres of forests, water, and abundant growth. *The Wonderful Wizard of Oz* is filled with Baum's memories of the western skies, and with the immense distances over which the eye could roam and imagine strange things rising out of the heat haze that shimmered on the horizon. At the center of *The Wonderful Wizard of Oz* is a profound ambivalence about the western prairies in particular and about home in general.

The brainless Scarecrow intelligently opens up this problem at the beginning of the story when he asks Dorothy about Kansas. "She told him all about Kansas, and how gray everything was there . . . The Scarecrow listened carefully. . . . 'I can't understand,'" he tells Dorothy, "'why you should wish to leave this beautiful country and go back to the dry, gray place you call Kansas.'" "That is because you have no brains," she replies. The rest of the tale is, of course, designed to show off the Scarecrow's intelligence. "No matter how dreary or gray our homes are," Dorothy claims, "we people of flesh and blood would rather live there than in any other country, be it ever so beautiful." "There is no place like home," she says, delivering the line that appeared only once in the book but would become the central mantra of the 1939 MGM movie. The Scarecrow's response to Dorothy's feeble explanation of why she wants so badly to return to Kansas reveals Baum's complex feelings about the idea of home. "If your heads were stuffed with straw, like mine," says the Scarecrow, "you would probably all live in beautiful places, and then Kansas would have no people at all. It is fortunate for Kansas that you have brains," he concludes. This opens up the idea that perhaps the Scarecrow is right, perhaps it's strange to want to return to gray, dusty Kansas. Dorothy's desire to return flies in the face of the very idea that had brought many out west to homestead on the plains. If the dissatisfied Americans of the East, and the Norwegians, Bavarians, Germans, and Russians, had held Dorothy's view, they would never have left the East or Europe, driven by a desire to leave old homes to start new ones somewhere better. For a whole nation largely made up of immigrants, the message of gripping on to someplace you identify as home no matter how awful it is made no sense.

Baum knew this. He had left Syracuse in search of a better life in the

West; he had been forced to leave the plains when his plans there had failed. Perhaps his troubled sense of home (or homelessness) out there was shaped by the terrible wars between the settlers and the native tribes. Julia Carpenter had abandoned the homestead in Edgeley and moved to town. Harry Carpenter, Julia's husband, drank and would eventually take his own life; Julia was losing her mind and would visit an asylum.

Baum's new story was shaped by anxieties about infant mortality, thankfully in decline by 1900 but still a constant fear and common reality. Like many nineteenth-century and early-twentieth-century fairy tales (such as Charles Kingsley's *The Water Babies* and J. M. Barrie's *Peter Pan*), *The Wonderful Wizard of Oz* was haunted by the specter of dead children. Oz was in some ways a children's heaven, a place where the souls of dead children might go to play and have adventures. Spiritualists named the higher plane where the souls of the dead reside the Summerland, which called up ideas of a sunny, magical place. Baum's deep knowledge and experience of living with the souls of dead children, his siblings, cousins, and nieces, enabled him to write so convincingly about children disappearing and traveling to other worlds. If a baby died, there was virtually no memory to hold on to, especially if she died only a few hours old, like Alice Gage. If a child couldn't be kept alive in its family's memories, it was possible to create an imaginary life for them in fiction. The orphaned Dorothy was difficult to age in the book, but she was probably meant to be between five or six years old (unlike in the MGM movie, where she's much older), the age of Baum's sister Cynthia-Jane when she died back in 1848, before Baum was born. He only ever knew her in the collective Baum family memory. In many cultures, stories are said to come from dead ancestors. It wasn't so hard to imagine that this tale was whispered into Baum's ear by the spirits of ghostly shadow-children, his dead siblings, cousins, and nieces.

The Lion's clumsiness in knocking down the church in the Dainty China Country suggested Baum's attitude toward earthly institutionalized religion. Matilda Gage had refused to have any of her children baptized, and her children, Maud included, likely followed by not having their children baptized. Baum and the Gages were distancing themselves from orthodox Christianity, attempting to carve out a separate space for their own distinctive spirituality. But Baum had grown up with the ghostly shadow presence of his dead siblings, Cynthia-Jane, Oliver, Edwin, George, and Benjamin, who would all certainly have been baptized by their strict Methodist parents. Baum now had shadow-nieces, Alice and Dorothy, who probably weren't baptized before they died in infancy. This was perhaps, deep down, quite alarming for Baum, and raised the awful question that haunted so many people in the era of high infant mortality: Where did the souls of unbaptized babies go after death? Some old local superstitions held that white moths and mischievous fairies were the spirits of unbaptized children.

Matilda had been convinced that a family could remain in touch with its dead children, and she attempted to contact baby Alice Gage in séances in Aberdeen. When Dorothy returns to Kansas by clicking her heels (an odd echo of the Fox sisters' supposed toe-clicking during séances), they took her instantly "whirling through the air, so swiftly that all she could see or feel was the wind whistling past her ears," and she reappears on the plains all of a sudden, like a conjured spirit brought back from the dead.

Baum dedicated *The Wonderful Wizard of Oz* "to my good friend and comrade, My Wife." This was fitting in so many ways, not least of all because Baum had written the story while Maud grieved for her dead mother and niece, and possibly for the daughter she would never have.

Baum wrote a short introduction to the book in April 1900, just before it went to press. He wrote it in a mood of reflection, with the adult, self-conscious and rational side of his mind, with an eye on his role as a father responsible for the vulnerable, shape-shifting imaginations of a group of boisterous boys. "The winged fairies of Grimm and Andersen," he wrote, "have brought more happiness to childish hearts than all other human creations . . . Yet the old-time fairytale," he went on, "having served for generations, may now be classed as 'historical' . . . for the time has come for a series of new 'wonder tales.'" In this new story, "the stereotyped genie, dwarf and fairy are eliminated, together with all the horrible and blood-curdling incident." "*The Wonderful Wizard of Oz*," Baum declared, "aspires to being a modernized fairy tale, in which the wonderment and joy are retained and the heart-aches and nightmares are left out." Anyone who read Baum's introduction might have noticed that it conflicted with the story that followed, which includes plenty of bloodcurdling events and characters. The story is full of friendship, hope, and trust, but it also includes evil, mean-spirited characters that spread fear and suffering. The actual story was written by a different part of Baum's mind, by a much murkier, irrational region featuring gray areas and ambiguities, a place where memory and intuition blended together.

In 1900, Sigmund Freud first published his book *The Interpretation of Dreams*. It would take some years for the book's influence to spread across Europe and America, but it was written in a wider culture fascinated by dreams. Freud's contemporary, Karl Jung, saw dreams as the key not only to an individual's mind but to the collective unconscious. Lewis Carroll's *Alice's Adventures in Wonderland* strongly suggested at the end of the story that Alice's journey was one long dream. Baum wrote *The Wonderful Wizard of Oz* against this idea, and tried to make it clear that Dorothy's trip to Oz was *not* a dream but a real experience, strange though it was. He underlined this, for instance, when he explained during a sleepless night in Oz that "Dorothy fell asleep only once, and then she dreamed she was in Kansas, where Aunt Em was telling her how glad she was to have her little girl at home again." Baum wanted to save fairy tales from being collapsed into dreams, where they'd be cordoned off, removing any sense that there were other worlds outside our minds, beyond this one.

The Wonderful Wizard of Oz sold reasonably well but not as well as *Father Goose* at first. But sales picked up by December 1900, and the book became a Christmas bestseller; Hill kept running out of copies and printing more. Baum requested a royalty check just before Christmas and received well over three thousand dollars; Maud was so shocked and thrilled when she saw the check, she burned a hole in the shirt she was ironing.

One of the greatest engineering feats of all time was completed in 1900. The Chicago River, which flowed out into Lake Michigan, the source of Chicago's fresh water, was so polluted and disease-ridden that a plan had been hatched a decade earlier to solve the problem. The city would build a canal, drain the river and then reverse its flow, sending the green waters south, away from the lake, toward the Mississippi basin. Many people predicted that this wouldn't work, that it was impossible to reverse the flow of a river and alter its natural course. But by 1900, the extensive canal that would make it possible was completed, and the river was turned around. It began to flow through the city, under bridges and past Wolf Point in the opposite direction. The reversal in Baum's fortunes so late in his life might have seemed to him almost as extraordinary. He entered 1901, the definitive start of the twentieth century, as the famous author of a new kind of best-selling American story. He didn't yet know that he had created an American myth, one that would take over his life, take him spinning, like Dorothy in the twister, away into a realm he barely understood and over which he had little control.

Chapter 18

he triumphant success of *The Wonderful Wizard of Oz* expanded Baum's desire to experiment further, and so began a prolific era of storytelling. He set about writing a series of tales that did the reverse of his Oz novel; rather than taking an ordinary American child to a magical wilderness, he brought magical characters to America. These tales were serialized in various newspapers between March and May 1901. In "The Enchanted Types," a mischievous fairy called a "knook" visits "a great city" and explores it at night when it's quietest, clambering through dark rooms while people are asleep. He enters a hat shop and is horrified to see various women's hats decorated with real stuffed birds posed in stagnant postures amid ribbons and lace. The knooks, explained Baum, are guardians of birds; this knook brought the stuffed birds back to life and released them. But he soon discovers that the only way to truly safeguard birds is to change the style of the day, so he enchants newspaper type, which then magically runs stories denouncing the fashion for stuffed birds. Baum understood the power of the press.

In "The Dummy That Lived," a "ryl," another mischievous fairy, flies to a city and brings a wax shop mannequin to life. The confused dummy leaves her shop window and travels about the metropolis. On seeing the animated wax woman, people run away as if they've "seen a ghost."

Baum showed his children how to use a camera and set up a darkroom in the basement at home on Humboldt Park Boulevard, where they watched grainy images of the world around them develop in dishes of chemicals. In "The Capture of Father Time," a boy imprisons time and the world stops short, arrested in an instant, like a photograph. But strangely, the boy remains animated and explores the frozen world. He examines a horse captured "in the act of trotting," its head and hooves in the air, like one of Eadweard Muybridge's photographs of galloping horses. A penny is caught in midair as it falls from a man's hand into a beggar's hat. In "The Runaway Shadows," a pranking Jack Frost tricks two children by separating them from their shadows, which then flee "and never stopped till they had reached the forest," where they hide among the trees. Baum imagined shadows as extensions of bodies, like the black-and-white images of people captured in photographs. The shadows run to the forest of Burzee, a place that would resurface in Baum's later stories as an archetypal forest and the source of fairy tales. People stare in horror when they discover that the children have no shadows. This tale touched on anxieties of the time about what photographing a person did to them, stealing something from them, their spirit or essence perhaps.

Baum wrote convincingly about the cold, having lived through so many freezing winters; he knew what it felt like to wake up to mornings of minus twenty degrees and to have to break the ice in the washbasin. "The King of the Polar Bears" was set in "the far north," a place imagined for centuries as somewhere between a real place and a fairyland. The king of the white bears is shot by men and skinned for his precious coat, but he lives on by some magic. A flock of gulls give him their feathers, which coat him in a white layer of warm down and grow on him "as they had grown upon the bodies of the birds." The odd bird-bear fights to retain his position as king. The small details make the story believable, as when the bear "sharpened his claws in the small crevices of ice."

From his new position of success, Baum was able to rediscover some of his old interests. He now returned to the first site of his storytelling, the theater. He met a young composer called Paul Tietjens, who saw an opportunity to combine their skills to create comic operas. After several dead ends, someone suggested turning *The Wonderful Wizard of Oz* into a stage musical extravaganza, a popular type of show at the time, and Baum embarked on an adaptation of the story. Tietjens and Denslow joined Baum in Macatawa in the summer of 1901, to eat lake perch and work on the project. Tietjens bashed out upbeat numbers at the piano while Baum sang the lyrics and danced around, playing the scatterbrained Scarecrow, the stiff-limbed Tin

Woodman, or the chorus of Fighting Trees. The Baum boys watched their father jig around the wooden cottage like a veteran of the vaudeville stage. The walrus-moustached Denslow, brought in to design the set and costumes, looked on severely.

The story was altered. The Wicked Witch of the West was taken out and replaced by the minor character of a "forest witch." The production was aimed more squarely at adults, with puns, jokes, and a gruesome romance added. The humbug Wizard gives the Tin Woodman the fleshy, bloody heart of a man who killed himself over a lost love. Baum envisaged using the latest in stage illusions to bring his scenes to life with electric lights, trapdoors, hidden wires, mirrors, revolving platforms, sound effects, and moving canvases called cycloramas.

Tensions over royalties surfaced. Denslow suggested they should take one-third royalties each, but Tietjens and Baum said they had done more to develop the script than Den. The men finally grudgingly agreed to a royalty split of 1.88 percent to Baum and Tietjens each, and 1.25 percent to Denslow. They sent the script off to Frederick Hamlin, a renowned Chicago theater producer. Hamlin passed it over to Julian Mitchell, a successful director of musical theater who would later work with the Ziegfeld Follies. Mitchell didn't see its potential and wrote "NO GOOD" across the script. But Hamlin sent Mitchell *The Wonderful Wizard of Oz* book, and the director saw how the Scarecrow and the Tin Woodman could be shaped into the comic vaudeville duo of the clown and the straight man. But the script would have to be radically redrafted, so Mitchell brought in a team of script doctors.

This was Baum's first experience of having his story, the characters he had created, and the land he had discovered taken out of his hands and meddled with. He found this unpleasant and disorienting.

While Baum's script was being broken into pieces, his reputation as a writer was growing. He had three more books published in 1901. His recent short tales were collected and published as *American Fairy Tales*. *Dot and Tot of Merryland* was another project illustrated by Denslow, the last book they produced together. In this story, Baum turned back to early memories and stories. The tale opened in "Rose Lawn," a "cool but sun-kissed mansion" with a vast velvety lawn. Baum recalled a slightly idealized version of his childhood home and conjured a weird world at the end of its garden. Two children set off in a boat on the river at the end of the garden and are swept into a tunnel made by the tangled branches of trees. They float beneath low branches into Merryland, an odd place of valleys each inhabited by different creatures. The story was a travelogue or a tour of a circus sideshow. The world was vividly imagined and some aspects were frightening in their dreamlike weirdness. In the Valley of Candies, where everything is edible, the people even eat each other. Their hard stick-candy bones and soft marshmallow flesh are tasty. Another valley is a forest filled with mechanical toys wound up daily by a wooden man whose voice is "made of birch bark."

The last valley is a melancholy place called the Valley of Lost Things, a flat plain covered in objects lost from the outside world. There's a giant haystack of needles, a pyramid of thimbles, and piles of buttons, rings, pencils, caps and coats, odd shoes, toys, pennies, gloves, and handkerchiefs. This place resembles the prairie and had "no trees at all." It's revealing that Baum imagined the sad place where lost things gather as a western plain.

This story is a surreal dream without obvious plot or meaning (or one so buried, as Freud would have it, as to be hard to decipher). Perhaps Baum's lifelong and abiding passion for cheese was giving him odd dreams, if there's any truth behind the idea that, eaten before bed, cheese stimulates vivid dreams. Baum ordered one hundred pounds of cheese one summer in Macatawa, and his signature dish was Welsh rarebit, toast dripping in a coating of melted cheese.

The other book Baum published at the end of 1901 was a modern technological fairy tale in which magical characters from folklore are brought to modern America. *The Master Key: An Electrical Fairy Tale, Founded Upon the Mysteries of Electricity and the Optimism of Its Devotees* was inspired by Baum's son Rob, whose fascination with electricity intrigued and perhaps worried his father. While experimenting in his workshop, wires and circuits tangled across the room, the fictional Rob accidentally strikes the combination of the "master key," conjuring a spirit, not that of his grandmother as the real Rob feared, but the "Demon of Electricity." This "wondrous apparition," a "wavering mass of white light, edged with a braid of red flames," gives Rob several ingenious devices, each powered by electricity and unimaginable even to inventors Thomas Edison and Nikola Tesla. These included a traveling machine that looks like a wristwatch, which taps into the earth's electromagnetic field and enables Rob to rise into the air and fly. The story revels in the possibilities opened up by extraordinary devices, but it's also a cautionary tale, warning of the dangers of harnessing a power that even scientists barely understood.

The Master Key was also clearly influenced by Theosophy. The title echoed Madame Blavatsky's magnum opus, *Isis Unveiled: A Master-Key to the Mysteries of Ancient and Modern Science and Theology*. Other Theosophical writers drew on the electromagnetic field to describe the "ethereal" planes in which Spirits dwelled. There "are great etheric currents constantly sweeping over the surface of the earth from pole to pole," wrote Charles Leadbeater in *The Astral Plane*, a Theosophical manual given to the Baums by Matilda Gage. For Baum, electricity wasn't simply a scientific force; it had magical, spiritual, and moral dimensions.

While flying through the air, Rob discovers two castaways on a desert island. The men are shipwrecked sailors from a sunken boat called the *Cynthia Jane*. Baum continually used the names of family members in his stories, and particularly in this book. A wrecked ship sunk to the bottom of the ocean to become barnacled and covered in coral was a moving and strange image to attach to the name of one of Baum's siblings who had died in infancy. It was perhaps an image of what these shadow-siblings had become in his mind: broken, half-rotten vessels lost at the bottom of the mind, through which living thoughts, like fish, occasionally swim.

The Master Key also reflected Baum's view of his creative process. Rob strikes the key and conjures the demon by accident; this is how the story-writing process worked for Baum. Characters, he said, could "strike at any time." The book received excellent reviews but didn't sell particularly well. Neither did the collection of American fairy tales. Readers weren't responding to stories in which magical things come to modern America. They wanted to be taken elsewhere, it seemed, out of this world.

Baum's fame was growing and he was now frequently interviewed by newspapers and magazines. In a 1901 article, he was photographed at home. His sons, described as his "best critics," were also pictured, each playing a musical instrument. Maud was described as his "business manager." Baum felt no deep obligation to telling journalists the truth and he began to create a somewhat fabricated version of himself for the media. The press was simply a branch of marketing and he seems to have decided early on to protect himself from the intrusive, distorting potential of the media, which could so easily become a warped hall of mirrors.

In the Valley of Lost Things, there's a mountain of wallets packed with money, but a pile of sharp needles make it impossible to reach. This suggested Baum's continuing anxieties about money. *Father Goose* had been a bestseller and *The Wonderful Wizard of Oz* was catching up, but there was no guarantee of how long these books would sell. These financial uncertainties were magnified when, in March 1902, Baum's publisher went bust. Way and Williams had gone bankrupt too. This latest bankruptcy led to extended legal wrangling over money owed Denslow for royalties, money advanced Baum in unearned royalties, and other complexities about who owned what. The problems were finally settled out of court.

In the spring of 1902, Baum found himself a bestselling author with no publisher and no illustrator, his long strained relationship with Denslow having now completely deteriorated. His experience with Denslow disturbed Baum so much that he never worked closely with an illustrator again. His work had become too closely entangled with Den, like the entwined "B" and "D" on the end page of *The Wonderful Wizard of Oz*. By 1904, the men were not on speaking terms.

The unpredictable, precarious economics of publishing and of the U.S. economy in general added to Baum's difficult relationship with money. Baum's tendency to spend money when he had it rather than to save, and his general inability to manage his finances, stemmed in part from his personality and the role model of an extravagant father, but also from the sense that money might be taken away at any moment, lost or sunk in some legal tangle that Baum hadn't realized he was in, or by wider, deeper economic forces that were as mysterious as the electromagnetic field pulsing around the planet. Financial uncertainty turns some people into misers and others into spendthrifts.

In spite of financial worries, Baum directed his energy into the script for the Oz musical in early 1902. This was a rocky, grueling process. Mitchell and others tore his script apart, pared back the plot, and added new characters. Only later in 1904 did he publicly acknowledge the difficulties. His "original story was practically ignored," he said, "the dialogue rehashed . . . and several other characters forced to conform to the requirements of the new schedule." Some of the "laughs" added to his story, he admitted, "I laugh at myself; some do not appeal to me."

In June, Baum, Maud, and the boys attended opening night at Chicago's Grand Opera House of what was billed as *The Wizard of Oz*, the "wonderful" now dropped for the first time. The author watched from a theater box in amazement. The show was a truly extravagant spectacle, with a large cast dressed in elaborate costumes; the army of chorus girls was clothed in outrageously short outfits that showed off strong dancers' legs in racy, patterned lace tights. The range of hats on show included sequined Napoleonic caps and jeweled turbans. A teenage Dorothy is blown to Oz from Kansas by a cyclone, along with her cow called Imogene and a waitress from Topeka. The plot made as much room as possible for set pieces by the clowning Scarecrow and the straight Tin Woodman, and the cast was filled out with several other characters, such as Sir Dashemoff Daily, a poet; Trixie Tryfle, the waitress; and Lady Lunatic, a mad woman, unsurprisingly. The Land of Oz was transformed into a patriarchy. In this version, the humbug Wizard has usurped the King who, in the end, regains his kingdom. Power was back in the hands of men.

Audiences were dazzled by the show's elaborate transformation scenes. With the use of gauze, electric light, and a spinning disc, a tornado seemed to twist across the stage as cymbals and a kettle drum sent crashing sounds around the audience's ears. One man vividly recalled the startling sight of "many flying objects" whirling about, including "barns, houses, cattle, poultry, and people." In the poisoned poppy field a chorus of women in huge red hats and leafy green dresses swayed in unison and dissolved in a snowstorm of frosty blues and greens. Fast, high-pitched tinkling piano music chimed as the scene transformed. Outside the Wizard's palace a "phantom patrol" of charming marching women soldiers appeared and disappeared with the use of silhouettes and electric light to create "ghostly geometric designs." Baum invented a contraption made from ropes, a drum, a barrel, and resin to create a huge lion's roar offstage, which was thrown forward so it appeared to come from the lion, a heavy eighty-pound costume with a man inside, wielding it like a puppet master trapped inside his puppet.

Mitchell had created a dazzling, flamboyant spectacle. After the audience had applauded the gigantic cast until their palms ached, Baum was called from his box to the stage. Dressed in an elegant dark suit, he thanked the generous audience and reminded them that he wasn't the only one who had created the exuberant spectacle. He likened the production to a plum pudding that combined "the flavor of many ingredients." Mitchell was the "stage chef," Tietjens' music the spice; the chorus girls were "the plums and peaches." The production was indeed a sugary pudding. The audience ate it up in the especially sticky, humid heat of the Chicago summer (the theater had no air-conditioning). People dressed in evening gowns could be heard singing songs from the show in the streets outside the theater. "There is nothing so divine," they sang, "there is nothing half so fine, as the gladness of your madness when you love, love, love." Chicago reviewers adored *The Wizard of Oz*, and called it superb, beautiful, humorous, the "handsomest show of its kind," full of "marvels, of shimmer and glow," featuring "gorgeous panoramas of mystic scenes and fairy incantations . . . and such indescribable achievements of light, movement and color as Chicago has never before beheld."

The show was sold out for weeks in advance, despite the unremitting heat, and it recouped its considerable costs after only seven weeks. Baum's royalty money was soon rolling in. He dispelled the rumors about his dissatisfaction with the production in an interview in the *Chicago Sunday Record-Herald* in late June, describing the "strange sensation of wonder and awe" he experienced on seeing the Scarecrow, the Tin Woodman, and the Lion, "real children of my brain," come to visible life before him on stage. He was genuinely amazed by the spectacle, and his doubts about what Mitchell had done to his story were temporarily lifted.

In the blistering heat of the Chicago summer, the Baums moved out of the city and crossed Lake Michigan, leaving the clowning scarecrow and the dancing girls of Oz to work their magic. Baum's financial success with *Father Goose* enabled him to buy a cottage in the lakeside resort of Macatawa Park. By this time he had earned about $4,500 in royalties from the book, roughly the equivalent today of $150,000. That summer he set about transforming the cottage into a kind of joyful wooden magic box filled with reminders of the stories he had written that had enabled him to buy it. He called the cottage the Sign of the Goose, and stenciled a dark green frieze of flying geese around the top of the walls of the large living room. Standing in the middle of the room, it looked as though a flock of geese were flying around it, bringing the sky inside. Baum commissioned a stained-glass window of a goose, which threw green-tinted light into the room.

The broad veranda at the back of the house looked down through trees to the lake. Here Baum often wrote, edited, and read. He had submitted *The Wonderful Wizard of Oz* to the publishers as a handwritten manuscript, but he typed up all his other stories from notes on a Smith typewriter, bashing frantically at the keys with his two index fingers. He would edit the story as he transformed his handwritten notes into neat machine-made letters. The sound of the typewriter must have clattered through the woods.

Baum received ongoing monies from *The Wizard of Oz* musical, so he sold *The Show Window*, finally releasing himself from the last remnants of his former life. The shop mannequins dressed in corsets were finally out of his hands. The Oz musical set off from Chicago on tour in the fall of 1902, traveling all over the country and into Canada in a specially designed train, playing to sellout shows. The musical would be in production with a revolving cast on and off for the next eight years, and Baum would earn during that time between $90,000 and $100,000 from it, the equivalent today of approximately $2,000,000.

Joseph Jacobs, the English folktale collector of the 1890s, encapsulated the vagueness of time in fairy stories in the opening of "Jack and his Golden Snuff-Box," which begins: "Once upon a time, and a very good time it was, though it was neither in my time nor in your time nor in any one else's time . . ." His feet now firmly in the twentieth century, Baum wrote a story set in the indeterminate past of the fairy tale. In the woods of Macatawa, he wrote a pagan backstory to the figure of Santa Claus, set in the archetypal forest of Burzee, called *The Life and Adventures of Santa Claus*. Burzee now took its place in Baum's mind as the source of the creatures that inhabit fairy tales. A bored forest immortal finds a tiny human baby on the edge of the forest and takes him in. Claus grows up as a feral child in the forest, but soon "the sweet, wild life of the forest was over." Baum found it difficult to include explicit evil and villainy in his tales for young children, but here Claus leaves the forest for the wider world and discovers human suffering. He concludes that adults "must bear the burden Nature has imposed upon them," and face "the trials of humanity," including aging and death. But children, Claus decides, ought to be protected from the burdens of adult life, and especially from "thoughtless or selfish parents." Baum offered sympathy to unhappy children and acknowledged that not all childhoods are happy.

A new publisher, Bowen-Merrill, published *The Life and Adventures of Santa Claus* in 1902. The book received favorable reviews and sold reasonably well, but the painful truth remained that the work Baum was least proud of, *Father Goose* and *The Wizard of Oz* musical, made him the most money.

The musical Oz extravaganza opened in New York City in July 1903, at the new Majestic Theater, owned by newspaper magnate William Randolph Hearst. The entire city was plastered with gaudy, colorful posters featuring the poisoned poppy field and a swooning Dorothy. New sets were built. A network of ghostly white tangled branches and roots swept across the stage; painted landscapes and turrets of the Emerald City peered from behind. A flyer advertised the show as a "gorgeous feast for eye and ear!" and promised "a hundred people—mostly girls!" Baum's name appeared nowhere on the flyer, although Julian Mitchell's was centered in capital letters. New York reviewers weren't crazy about the show and saw it as provincial and unsophisticated. But audiences loved it. It was a sellout hit in New York for months. Many New Yorkers went to see it twice. The stars of the show were the Scarecrow and the Tin Woodman, played by Fred Stone and David Montgomery; the comic double act was the beating heart of the production.

Drawing on the success of the stage musical, Bobbs-Merrill (the publisher's name had changed from Bowen-Merrill) republished Baum's original story as *The New Wizard of Oz* in 1903. Either the publishers or the author himself seem to have planted a story in the press about where the idea for Oz came from. This anecdote claimed that Baum had come up with the idea during a storytelling evening with his children and their friends, when a child had asked where the tale he was telling took place, and Baum had glanced down at his filing cabinet and seen the drawers marked "A-N" and "O-Z." Oz! This anecdote had the strong whiff of publicity about it. It was almost certainly made up. Now that Baum's stories were famous, people began to wonder where they came from. People often ask storytellers about the source of their stories; few are able to adequately answer such questions. A more truthful though oblique response from Baum might have been, "the forest of Burzee," but nobody would have been able to make sense of this.

So Baum now started to make up stories about the origins of his imagined tales.

But there could have been another reason why such anecdotes began to appear. Composer Paul Tietjens' wife, Eunice, a successful writer herself, noted in her diary after a summer visit to Macatawa that Baum's imagination was so vibrant that he was almost unable to distinguish reality from story. He "had come to the place," she wrote, "where he could honestly not tell the difference between what he had done and what he had imagined. Everything he said had to be taken with at least half a pound of salt." Perhaps Baum didn't know how he came across his tales, and made up answers to questions about their origins to please himself as much as journalists. It was all too easy to start believing anecdotes about the shape-shifting trickster that is the inner storyteller, once you told them a few times.

Baum was now free to write full-time, unencumbered by less meaningful work. Money was flowing in from book royalties and the musical, and he took every opportunity to spend his new wealth. He sent five dollars to his niece, Matilda Gage, back in Aberdeen (roughly one hundred dollars today) and told her to splurge. "Not a sensible thing must be bought with it," he wrote to her. Live and spend was the principle, of course.

In May 1903, the Baums moved to a large house on Forest Avenue in the swanky south Chicago district. The house had no electricity, but it did have gas and a telephone, so Baum could enjoy talking to disembodied voices down a wire from the comfort of his own home. Maud owned all the royalties to Baum's books, and she managed the family finances well, as this fancy new house demonstrated.

But Baum didn't sit back and enjoy his success. Quite the opposite; he now couldn't stop writing. The strain of his demanding writing schedule, of keeping up the production of new tales, editing others, anxious to keep money coming in to sustain a lifestyle of expensive cigars, tailored suits, school and college fees, and, of course, Maud's weekly box of candies, erupted in an episode of Bell's palsy, a painful partial paralysis of one side of the face that makes it hard to smile or close one eye. Bell's palsy is often accompanied by headaches, a loss of taste, and an echoing amplification of sound in the affected ear. Baum's doctor prescribed rest and a break from writing. During the summer, Baum returned to the Sign of the Goose cottage and as a break from scratching out tales in longhand, Baum built things out of wood. He made a grandfather clock, two rocking chairs, bookshelves, and other furniture, all out of hard oak. The details as ever were important. A friend's brass foundry made up brass tacks with a goose head, and Baum banged them into the furniture. There were geese on the clock face, raised figures from his books on all the pieces, some of which he burned into the wood using a technique called pyrography. Leaning back in his rocking chair, Baum might have felt the raised shapes of characters from his stories press into his back.

These homemade items reflected the folk art style of Baum's writing, which had a similarly homespun, authentic, and handcrafted appeal. Baum's voice was vernacular rather than literary, and so his stories were closer to the old oral folk tradition collected by the Grimms, Jacobs, and Lang than to the more self-consciously literary work of late-nineteenth- and early-twentieth-century European authors of new fairy tales, like John Ruskin, Oscar Wilde, George MacDonald, and Lewis Carroll.

Baum wrote another old-fashioned fairy tale that was published in the fall of 1903 as *The Enchanted Island of Yew.* The island took its name from the yew tree, the slow-growing evergreen long associated with paganism. In his introduction, Baum explained that this was a story from an old world where tales of wonder were told orally. In the modern age, he suggested, people were "keyed up to a high pitch of excitement" by "automobiles" and "flying-machines," which were filling the modern world with wonder. In the past, tales of flying carpets and fairies had amazed people instead. The story is episodic, but the creatures were vividly imagined. A dragon, for instance, has had each tooth "carved into various fantastic shapes—such as castles, horses' head . . . griffins." Baum enjoyed playing chess with his sons; here he imagined chess pieces lined up as giant teeth in an angry dragon's mouth.

The story included an Enchanted Mirror (an iconic object from the world of fairy tales) that traps reflections and makes the original bodies that cast them disappear. At this time, some people feared that photography captured a person's image, trapped it, and then duplicated it into frightening reproducible doppelgängers. An angry king is trapped in the mirror, and people assume that the odd reflection they see in the mirror is that of a ghost.

The Bell's palsy subsided and Baum set to work on new theater scripts. The enormous success of *The Wizard of Oz* show stunned him and convinced him that in addition to writing books and short stories, he should return to the theater. The boys were growing up and were getting too old for evenings of storytelling. In 1903, Frank was nineteen and about to graduate from college, Rob was sixteen, Harry was thirteen, and Ken was twelve. For Baum, the appeal of working on collaborative theater productions might have been the opportunity they provided to tell his stories orally to a breathing, reactive, live audience. And planning the staging of transformation scenes and stage illusions enabled Baum to look behind the scenes at the mechanisms of storytelling, at the levers and pulleys behind the curtain.

He worked with several collaborators, including the novelist Emerson Hough and children's author Edith Ogden Harrison, the wife of the mayor of Chicago. She had written a story that Baum adapted for the stage. Although many of Baum's scripts failed to move beyond the early stages, this project really looked set to go ahead as *Prince Silverwings*. But on December 30, 1903, fire broke out in the new Iroquois Theater, which had just opened in downtown Chicago. Its owners trumpeted its highly fireproof security system, but during a matinee performance watched by a packed house of almost two thousand people, a spark from an electric spotlight caught on a canvas; the spark became an ember, a back door was opened, and a gust of cold air rushed onto the stage and fanned the ember into a raging fireball that rolled over the heads of the audience. Panic erupted. Smoke filled the auditorium. The crowds pushed back toward the rear doors, which, it turned out, opened inward. The firefighters outside couldn't get the doors to open against the crush. The horror must have been reflected in the many large gilt mirrors that lined the interior of the theater. In total, 602 people died; 212 of them were children. More people died in the Iroquois Theater fire than in the 1871 Great Fire of Chicago. In response, the mayor closed down all the city's theaters and banned New Year's Eve celebrations, including fireworks.

By the end of 1903, the riches from *The Wizard of Oz* musical extravaganza were carrying its creators away from Chicago. Denslow had left for New York City and then bought an island in Bermuda. He named it Denslow Island and proclaimed himself King Denslow the First. His friend Archie and a Japanese cook accompanied him. Paul Tietjens was able to fund a trip to Paris, where he continued his music studies. The winter of 1903 marked a distinct shift in Baum's life. He and Maud headed southwest to the warmer climates of California, to the far western state that had ideas of the fantastic written into its history. The word "California" had been coined in the sixteenth century by a Spaniard who imagined the land to be a matriarchal island filled with gold and diamonds, populated by amazons riding griffins and ruled by a queen called Califia. Baum reached the far western shore that winter of 1903, and saw the Pacific Ocean for the first time. It rolled before him beneath the cold, clear light. This was the ideal place for digging a new story out of the imaginative ground of Baum's mind. This new outer geography began to work its way inside Baum and reshape his image of the Land of Oz, which he hadn't by any means finished with yet.

Part IV

LIVING BETWEEN LANDSCAPES

1903 TO 1910

Chapter 19

aum had been brought up to believe that hard work in the brutally competitive business world of the Gilded Age was the only route to a man's success. But, in contrast, he had become rich and famous by listening inwardly to his buried childhood stories and tapping into an intuitive area of his mind that even he didn't fully understand.

After much hardship, he had achieved astonishing success relatively late in life by writing modern fairy tales. His real life soon began to resemble them; he spent money to make it so. It was only possible, after all, to live in a fairy-tale world if you bought your way into it. On their first trip southwest in the winter of 1903, Frank and Maud toured vastly expensive luxury resorts. They stayed at the Potter in Santa Barbara, a brand-new, rambling, six-hundred-room hotel overlooking the Pacific. It reared up out of thirty-six acres of verdant gardens, which included a giant ancient fig tree. An orchestra played all day as well-dressed guests explored the grounds or took drinks on one of the many rooftop gardens. In Monterey, they stayed at the Hotel Del Monte, a giant luxury resort built by railroad tycoons. The enormous, labyrinthine hotel was built on a 126-acre park planted with rare trees from across the world. Guests liked to have their pictures taken beneath the giant feather palm, whose waving fronds reached up from the trunk and arched right back down to the velvet lawn below. A big glass conservatory full of potted plants doubled as a bathhouse, so bathers steamed amid the unfurling fingers of fern leaves.

The Baums had traveled to California by train, but when they arrived, they explored the Southwest in the extremely novel form of an automobile tour, and drove on dirt and dust roads through New Mexico and Arizona back to California. Auto touring was so new that there were still no major roads or road maps or gas stations. They visited Pasadena and San Francisco, and in San Diego they stopped at the Theosophical community at Point Loma and then stayed at the Hotel Del Coronado. This luxurious resort at the bottom western tip of America was built on an island on the edge of the city. It was surrounded by palm trees and immaculate lawns on one side, and a long white sandy beach on the other. It had opened in 1888; one of the two men who built it was called Mr. H. L. Story, as though the place had been brought into being by a form of fiction. Thomas Edison supervised the lighting himself, and the hotel was filled with sparkling electric illumination, which lit the winding corridors leading to the nine hundred rooms. It was a huge wooden castle with a mazelike red roof covered with turrets and towers, and flags flew on the highest peaks.

Kate Morgan had checked into room 302 in 1892 and died that night from a gunshot wound to her head. It looked like suicide but might have been murder. Guests since had reported cold breezes and flickering lights in room 302 and in the corridor outside it; others claimed they saw the ghost of the tragic woman, whose background in crime and gambling was at odds with the glittering surface of the Del Coronado. The ghost of Kate Morgan was a bleak, frightening counterweight to all that sparkle.

When he wasn't writing or redrafting stories, bashing away at the keys of his typewriter outdoors, Baum enjoyed archery and golf. Raising your bow to fire a straight arrow at a distant target was perhaps the opposite of writing stories, which was a far less linear, rather more meandering task.

From 1903 to 1910, Baum lived between landscapes. He traveled between California, Michigan, and Chicago each year, living in hotels and rented houses as well as in his cottage in Macatawa. He sold the big house in Chicago and lived part of each year in an apartment in the city on South Michigan Avenue. He wrote on the move, as he had done when he first started writing back in the 1890s. But this time he conjured tales in luxury hotel suites and first-class carriages, dressed in tailor-made suits, chewing on the best cigars, with Maud at his side rather than by himself in run-down motels writing on the backs of envelopes, where his storytelling had begun. As ever, Baum had come a very long way and gone full circle.

He sought out landscapes and living arrangements that could have

stepped out of a storybook. Macatawa Park, where Baum spent each summer, was, he wrote, "an imitation paradise," a "summer haven." If Macatawa
Park echoed fairy-tale woodlands and the forest of Burzee, Coronado was
the glittering palace on a magic island. Those "who do not find Coronado a
paradise," Baum told a journalist who interviewed him there, had the kind
of personality that "would render heaven unpleasant." He called Coronado
"the queen of fairy land" in a poem to the place, the "empress of the sea,"
the "grim ocean's bride, high priestess of the sun!" He wrote a short story
called "Nelebel's Fairyland," which, like an old native tale, explained the
origins of the Coronado landscape. A disobedient fairy called Nelebel was
exiled from her home in the forest of Burzee to the shores of the Pacific; she
was accompanied by some immortals from the forest who transformed the
shoreline into the glorious Coronado peninsula. "What matters our exile,"
cries Nelebel after the transformation, "when the beauties of this earthly
paradise are ours to enjoy."

If Baum's life now looked on the surface like a graceful swan gliding on
the clear waters of wealth and success, he was in reality working frantically
to make it appear so, like the swan's rough, scaly legs that pedal beneath its
gleaming body to keep it afloat.

In January 1904, spurred on by the success of *The Wizard of Oz* musical,
Baum signed a contract with a new publisher, Reilly & Britton, for a book
he had never originally planned to write, a sequel to *The Wonderful Wizard
of Oz*. By the spring, he had completed a draft of this Oz book, written another full-length tale and five short stories. "Never could I have done all this
in so short a time, if I had not gathered such a fine collection of vim out
here," he wrote to a friend. New landscapes seemed to climb inside Baum
and unleash a new batch of stories.

The Marvelous Land of Oz was published in 1904 by Reilly & Britton,
a company formed by two men Baum had met through the George M. Hill
Co. They were just starting out and Baum would be their star author. Although the publisher wasn't an established firm, Baum could be sure his
books would get their full attention. They promised to develop innovative
marketing campaigns for Baum's books.

This first sequel to *The Wonderful Wizard of Oz* opened in the imaginary
Land of Oz rather than in Kansas, and starred an Oz native, a boy called Tip.
Baum assumed his readers would already be familiar with this other world.

Tip builds a man out of sticks and a pumpkin jack-o'-lantern head into which he carves "a mouth shaped like a new moon." He brings the wonky, homemade man made of wood, old clothes, and a big orange vegetable head to life with a magic powder. Tip had stolen the powder of life from a wicked old woman called Mombi, who kept Tip as a suffering servant. She had another powder that she intended to use to transform Tip into a marble statue. Mombi's wicked designs mirrored Baum's anxieties about the modern world of electrified machines that threatened to immobilize the human body, and make it redundant and inanimate. Tip flees Mombi with the pumpkin-headed man and has a grand adventure across Oz, involving the Tin Woodman and the Scarecrow. He brings more objects to life along the way: a wooden sawhorse becomes a speedy steed, an odd collection of junk is tied together—two sofas, a clothesline, palm fronds, and the stuffed head of an elk—and comes alive as the flying "Gump."

Jack Pumpkinhead is "butchered," his left leg "amputated" to make a prosthetic leg for the Saw-Horse, thus continuing Baum's fascination with amputation and false limbs. The Tin Woodman makes the pumpkinhead a new leg from a table. "It seems strange," remarks the jack-o'-lantern man, "that my left leg should be the most elegant and substantial part of me." Baum continued to be conscious of the conventional view of the left side of the body as the least capable. He often inserted little comments in his stories promoting the left hand or leg; perhaps he was attempting to reassure left-handed children and counteract their cruel treatment in schools.

Baum wrote intuitively, without much preplanning; his stories developed organically, and this sometimes meant he forgot the details of his previous stories, and inconsistencies arose. But perhaps Oz wasn't supposed to be a fixed, determined place but one as flexible and shape-shifting as the imagination that created it. In this sequel, the Emerald City appears to be truly green, rather than simply appearing so through tinted spectacles. And the Wizard has real magical skills. Baum didn't simply return to Oz to produce a new book for children. He clearly wrote *The Marvelous Land of Oz* with the intention of transforming it into another profitable musical extravaganza. The Scarecrow and Tin Woodman, the main characters in *The Wizard of Oz* stage play, are central to this new story. Baum even dedicated the book to Montgomery and Stone, the comedians who played the characters on stage. And he created ample opportunity for chorus lines of girls in the Army of Revolt led by General Jinjur, which conquers the Emerald City with an army of girls brandishing knitting needles. They force the men of the city to do all the housework while they eat fudge and drape themselves in emeralds pried from the city's walls with their knitting needles.

At the end of the book, Glinda captures the evil Mombi, who then confesses that Tip is in fact a girl, Princess Ozma, and the rightful ruler of the Land of Oz. Girl children were always Baum's favorite rulers, allowing him to make a carnivalesque world in reverse, where little girls are in power.

The Marvelous Land of Oz was a hit and soon became a bestseller. In New York, a department store window display featured a full-size carriage pulled by the Saw-Horse and driven by the Tin Woodman. Reviews declared that the book established Baum's reputation as "a creator of fairy myths, worthy of rank with Hans Christian Andersen." Reilly & Britton had found a new illustrator, John R. Neill, from Pennsylvania, who made many vivacious drawings full of movement and energy. He drew Mombi as a crooked, haggard figure out of the old European folktales, and the Saw-Horse and the Gump flew across the page.

This new Oz tale didn't include any characters from the outside world, but in one scene the Gump, laden with Tip and his fellow adventurers, flies too far during a night flight and unknowingly crosses the desert that surrounds Oz, and he reaches America, "the terrible outside world that Dorothy told us about," as the Scarecrow puts it. They look down on wide plains, villages, and cities before turning back. For a moment, children could feel that the characters from Oz had briefly entered their world; the geography of the United States and Oz were somehow connected.

In August 1904, a month after the new Oz book had hit stores, the *Philadelphia North American* printed a strange item penned by Baum announcing that an astronomer had seen an object careening toward earth. Daily updates followed the progress of the alien object as it flew past Neptune, Saturn, and Jupiter. Finally, on August 28, the "Thing" arrived. "From the Land of Oz to the United States" was the headline. Beneath was a big, white round moon with a silhouette in front of it, showing the Gump flapping through the stars. Beneath this was a drawing of Baum seated on top of the world, smoking a cigar and peering through a telescope, searching the sky for the visitors. The image prevented Baum looking far out into space for the contents of his inward imagination.

The article began with a "Proclamation Extraordinary" from Ozma, reigning princess of Oz, to "Mr. L. Frank Baum, by Royal appointment Historian to the Land of Oz." So that was it: Baum didn't consider himself the author of Oz but its chronicler.

Ozma had given permission, the article explained, for the Gump to fly her subjects to visit America, "your most prosaic country" wrote Baum, "Well, I felt like shouting hurrah! when I got the above letter." The curious airship had arrived somewhere in the United States but exactly where it had landed was a mystery. Baum and newspaper illustrator Walt McDougall planned to find and follow the characters and report back weekly. For several months, illustrated, multicolored tales of the *Queer Visitors from the Marvelous Land of Oz* appeared in Sunday "funny pages" across the country. The disoriented, mischievous Ozites would start a riot, fight fires, visit a beauty parlor, and tell fairy tales (here were stories within stories within stories). The Tin Woodman is struck by lightning and becomes magnetic: He runs down the street as knives, coins, hairpins, and buttons fly after him. Jack Pumpkinhead meets an amputee from the 1898 Spanish-American War whose right leg was "carried away" by a cannonball. The characters visit Kansas, meet Dorothy, and give her some magic trees to plant out on the treeless prairie.

The adventures of the *Queer Visitors* were hurriedly dashed off, and McDougall's drawings were equally rough. They were ephemera designed to keep Oz in the public mind and copies of *The Marvelous Land of Oz* flying off the shelves. But if the motivation for the series was primarily marketing, the outcome for readers was a thickened sense that Oz and its strange inhabitants were in some way real, and had a life beyond their creator. The giant papier-mâché figures of characters from Oz put up in Chicago in the summer of 1905 must have added to this sense.

Baum had successfully returned to Oz and appointed himself Royal Historian of that strange land. But he didn't feel confined in this role and continued to direct his energy into other projects, into new stories and theater scripts. *Queen Zixi of Ix* was serialized in *St. Nicholas* magazine and then appeared as a book in 1905. It reflected the luxurious California environment in which it was written. As Baum's life was starting to resemble a fairy story, the luxury resorts in which he spent time (and money) crept into his writing and shaped his vision of fairyland. Zixi is a vain and flawed witch queen who rules the land of Ix, and lives in a magnificent palace at the center of her kingdom. "The splendid palace of the queen was in the center of a delightful park," full of "gleaming white statues," fountains, flowers, shrubberies, and marble walkways, explained Baum. The rich visitors of the Del Coronado would have felt quite at home in the queen's castle. Queen Zixi is over six hundred years old but appears to everybody as a beautiful young woman, except when she looks in a mirror, which throws back a truthful image of a haggard ancient face, wrinkled and toothless, her head bald. Zixi searches for a renowned magic cloak that will enable her to wish that mirrors would lie too so she may see herself as others do and not as she is. She steals the cloak, which destroys its wishing powers, and she's forced to learn to live with her true reflection.

Animals have always been central to the most ancient folktales, and are often human characters dressed in animal bodies, like pantomime horses. Old favorites such as *Aesop's Fables* and Kipling's 1902 *Just So Stories* were popular. Andrew Lang had published a collection called *The Animal Story Book* in 1896, which included stories starring buzzards, dogs, otters, horses, and sea creatures. Baum wrote a series of animal tales, many of them written in California, published in *The Delineator* in 1905. They featured various exotic creatures, including chimpanzees, tigers, and jaguars. In *The Enchanted Buffalo*, Baum drew not on the old European animal tales but on the rich body of Native American folk stories that he would have encountered out west in the Dakotas. Native tales translated into English had begun to appear, such as Zitkala-Ša's 1901 book, *Old Indian Legends*, which included the story "Dance in a Buffalo Skull." Tiny field mice have a party inside a bone-white buffalo skull they find lying out in the prairie grass. They build a fire inside it, and light from the flames streams out of the eye sockets into the black night. Two disembodied balls of fire then materialize out of the river bottom and slowly float across the prairie into the eye sockets, chasing the dancing mice away, out the back of the skull. In Baum's buffalo tale, the main characters compete for leadership with the help of hidden powers. Barag the Bull is chased across the plains by his rival. "We know the Ut[e]s saw him," writes Baum, "and the Apaches, for their legends tell of it. Far to the south . . . lived the tribe of the Comanches; and those Indians for many years told their children of Barag the Bull." Baum dressed his story up as a reworking of an old native tale. Here he explicitly tried to blend old European folktales with a Native American tradition.

Baum's stories were modern American fairy tales that, in some ways, wove together features of two warring old worlds, to create something distinctly new and uniquely American, with imagery and archetypes that originated in both native and European cultures. If a nation's folktales are shaped by its landscape and climate, then certainly the native stories of the Great Plains and *The Wonderful Wizard of Oz* have much in common.

In an interview published in the *Chicago Tribune* in 1904, Baum publicly acknowledged the difficulties he had experienced when preparing *The Wizard of Oz* musical. "I confess," he said, "after two years of success for the extravaganza, that I now regard Mr. Mitchell's views in a different light. The people will have what pleases them and not what the author happens to favor." Mitchell's success, which was continuing to line Baum's pockets, was that he knew how "to serve the great mass of playgoers." Baum acknowledged that his "chief business is, of course, the writing of fairy tales, but should I ever attempt another extravaganza . . . I mean to profit by the lesson Mr. Mitchell has taught me and sacrifice personal preference to the demands of those I shall expect to purchase admission tickets." Baum took what he thought he had learned from the success of the Oz musical and threw himself into adapting *The Marvelous Land of Oz* into a stage show. *The Wizard of Oz* was still playing across the country by two parallel touring companies, so Baum was under pressure to create something distinctive. The second musical, called *The Woggle-Bug*, opened in June 1905 in Chicago. It was a total flop. Reviews were searing. The show was "a shabby and dull repetition of a cheapened *Wizard of Oz*," featuring "torrents of silly tunes and tag-you're-it class of low comedy." The success of *The Wizard of Oz* had sparked a series of imitations, so *The Woggle-Bug* looked like a copy of something that had already been copied. Jack Pumpkinhead, said one review, "was about as inspired as the sight of a happy cow extricating its feet from the mud."

The show copied the successful parts of *The Wizard of Oz,* including a chorus of dancing girls in flower costumes and one scene that featured a rainstorm instead of a snowstorm, as in the first musical. The script was also weak, filled with Baum's unfortunate love of silly puns. The plot was thin, and most of the songs had no connection to what little story there was. Baum had drastically misjudged what his audience wanted. The success of *The Wizard of Oz* musical had shocked him and filled his pockets with cash. He thought he could easily repeat that success but failed to appreciate what had made Mitchell's production work so well—the double act of Montgomery and Stone and the novelty of the show. Baum had entered the process of creating the second Oz musical with a misplaced conviction in his theatrical ability and a lack of respect for his audience.

Baum's rare storytelling skills worked best when he wrote intuitively and when his imagination was given free rein within the intimate realms of the written fantasy story. He had more respect for his child readers, whom he never patronized, than he had for adult theatergoers, whom he wrongly assumed would laugh and cheer at any old slapstick or sideshow antics if they were dressed up with enough distracting illusions and sparkle. Baum kept coming back to the stage because it was the site of his first storytelling endeavors; he pushed on, writing doomed scripts that dissipated his energy and never came to life on the stage. But he couldn't see this. Distraught, he fled to Macatawa to escape Chicago. He was overwhelmed by this unexpected failure when things had seemed to be going so well. This was a disaster. He tried to recover some composure in the woodlands around the Sign of the Goose before returning to Chicago. "I collapsed last week from the strain and worry," he admitted in a letter to Emerson Hough in late June, as *The Woggle-Bug* limped on like a swatted wasp. He had arrived in Macatawa, he said, "in a used-up condition." The show continued for another couple of weeks until there was no money to pay the salaries of the cast, and the extensive electric lights were taken away by the unpaid lighting company. The show closed in July, having been on stage for less than a month.

This catastrophic flop convinced Baum that he had to return to books. In October 1905, he signed a contract with Reilly & Britton in which he committed to a packed schedule of relentless storytelling. The contract seems to have been written by Baum because it was humorous and self-deprecating. He contracted for a total of six more books (and another was already under contract). Baum agreed to produce stories at a rate of knots, but in order that the market wasn't flooded with L. Frank Baum books, a plan was hatched: He would try his hand at books for different audiences under pen names, or noms de plume, as the contract put it. Many of these were female. As "Laura Bancroft" or, as the contract put it, "some female of equally dignified comprehensiveness," he would write a series of shorter tales. As "Helen Lesley," or possibly even as "Maud Gage Baum," he would write a novel for "young folks." As "Ida May McFarland" or "Ethel Lynne," "or some other mythological female," he would write a "book for young girls in the style of Louisa M. Alcott stories but," it went on, "not as good." As "Captain Arthur Fitzgerald," Baum would produce an adventure story for boys. Only a slight publication of a Father Goose calendar would be published under Baum's own name. This contract spelled a new direction; Baum would cloak himself in disguises, put on different voices, drawing perhaps on his old skills as an actor. Reilly & Britton also agreed to publish a novel for adults, titled *The Girl in the Harem*, a rather racy story unlike Baum's other work, which would also have to be published under a pen name.

The contract stipulated that "Reilly & Britton Co further agree" that "in case said Baum should at any time become hard up to provide for him upon demand any sum or sums of money that he may wish to squander that will not total more than two thousand dollars." The men signed the contract in the presence of witnesses. They were, it stated above their curly signatures, "sane, . . . well fed and not under the influence of any intoxicating beverages." The jovial tone of the document couldn't conceal the fact that Baum had committed himself to a demanding, possibly grueling writing schedule. The contract made no specific mention of another Oz book.

In 1905, fourteen years after he had left South Dakota, Baum returned once more to the western plains, to the memories of poverty, the grasslands, and simple children playing out there, in a series of six short tales written under the pen name Laura Bancroft, published as six pamphlets called the *Twinkle Tales*. The first, *Prairie-Dog Town*, opens on the Dakota prairie. Baum's descriptions are vivid, his memories of this landscape still fresh. "On the Dakota prairies there are no shade-trees at all, and very little water except what they get by boring deep holes in the ground." Drawing on specific memories of visits to the Carpenter homestead in North Dakota, Baum set his story there. "On the great western prairie," he wrote, "is a little town called Edgeley, because it is on the edge of civilization. If people walked out their front doors they were upon the little street . . . if they walked out the back doors they were on the broad prairies." Baum knew that the openness and desolation of the prairie made it a rich ground on which to find stories. In these tales, children explore the plains and find magic in the natural world around them, inside prairie-dog holes, in a ditch where a talking stone lives, and in a brook. As Laura Bancroft, Baum integrated his love of the natural world with the magic of fairy tales. As well as promoting ideas of animal welfare in these stories, Baum asked children to look around their own neighborhood and imagine where hidden magical worlds might be lurking.

In one episode of the "Queer Visitors from the Marvelous Land of Oz," the Scarecrow meets a girl who longs to own an automobile. She can't afford one, but the Scarecrow conjures one for her, using the Oz magic he has brought to America. The car seemed to the Scarecrow to be "like a thing of life," a marvelous living machine as great as anything found in Oz. This "child had especially wanted an automobile," wrote Baum, "because she believed it impossible for her ever to possess one." He knew all about longing for things he couldn't afford, though he usually gave in to his desires. In 1905, he bought his first automobile. Henry Ford had created his first proto-auto in 1896, when he had engineered a one-seater machine with a long lever rather than a steering wheel. But 1905 was a turning point in motoring history, in which Ford made automobiles more widely available to well-off amateurs rather than simply to the super-wealthy enthusiast. Baum had enjoyed the driving tour of the Southwest in 1904; now he wanted his own automobile to drive around Lake Michigan in the summers at Macatawa. As with the 1888 first Kodak amateur portable camera, Baum took the first opportunity to get his hands on the latest form of technology. He bought a pre–Model T Ford that was handmade in Detroit (well before the era of the assembly line) for around one thousand dollars. Rob, Baum's second son, was at college near Detroit, and he supervised its assembly. It had brass carriage lamps at the side and a loud honking horn. Nobody needed a driver's license in those days; the manual explained how to work the machine, how to crank it up to a hair-raising thirty miles per hour. Maud learned to drive along with Baum. She sat at the wheel in long billowing skirts and gripped the big black circle of the steering wheel tightly. At the wheel, she wore a big broad hat tied over the top and under her chin with a long scarf to prevent it from blowing away. There were no side windows or windshield to protect drivers from the rushing wind (and inevitable onslaught of insects). It was best to wear goggles.

In the fall of 1905, Baum was locked into a contract for books for the next few years. He was tied to writing commitments, but he was geographically free. He headed to the Del Coronado for the winter, to a California palace fit for a witch queen. He would have to work hard to keep his place in this luxury fairyland.

Chapter 20

n early 1906, Baum launched out beyond the geographical borders of America for the first time. He and Maud crossed the Atlantic Ocean on the steamship the *Princess Irene*, for a six-month trip visiting North Africa and Europe. Baum set off for the Old World whose old folk stories he knew well but whose landscapes he had never seen. Son Rob and brother Harry waved Frank and Maud off in New York City Harbor on January 28. They stayed in one of the two best (and most expensive) first-class cabins on the ship. Stormy seas rocked the boat as they crossed the waters that separated the two worlds. Still, the robust pair managed to eat tongue sandwiches in the mornings and twelve-course evening meals. Maud wrote continually to her children, describing the "wildly exciting" trip. Baum took reels of photographs to record the strange new sights.

In February, the giant Rock of Gibraltar reared up as they crossed the strait, passing the small mountain at the tip of southern Europe that juts out toward North Africa. They traveled through Egypt, Italy, Switzerland, and France over the next five months, sampling Europe's finest hotels, including the grand Shepherd's Hotel in Cairo, a Capuchin convent on the Amalfi coast and the hotel Castillo a Mare in Sicily. The vibrant scenes, like nothing they had witnessed before, made them feel like "plain American folk," as Maud put it, but she also wrote: "Never have we enjoyed anything more or been so intensely interested."

They visited ancient crumbling tombs and temples across Egypt, and circled giant stone monuments that glinted in the sun and dust, including the tombs of Mereuka, Thi, and Serepeum, and the temples of the Sacred

Lake, Karnak and Luxor, where seated stone men guard the crumbling entrance to pillared, roofless buildings. At the temple of Rameses, they gazed in awe at huge carvings of the ancient sun god. Many of the sites were tombs of ancient rulers; Maud experienced the trip as a journey through a "vast cemetery of a dead civilization." Staring at the tombs and temples, she "had a feeling that I was linked to all the centuries of the dead and gone civilizations of this mystic land." Egypt, and perhaps old Europe, seemed to her to be a vast land of the dead, a sort of ancient heavenly cemetery. They saw the palace and temple of Rameses III and were stunned by its carved pillars showing scenes from the king's life, including, noted Maud, "a pile of tongues cut from prisoners." Maud and Frank rode donkeys around the giant pyramids outside Cairo, both in hats, Baum with a cigar hanging from the corner of his mouth. Their minds swam with images of stone giants, painted pillared palaces, hills with images of kings and queens carved into them, crumbling remnants of bygone civilizations, all slowly collapsing under bright blue skies. Baum took a photograph of Maud standing on the roof of a temple.

Maud climbed 515 feet to the top of the Great Pyramid. "Few women," she wrote proudly, "undertake the feat." Baum didn't feel up to it. He watched Maud scale the steep stone steps of the enormous tomb, hiking her long skirts up with her.

Baum's fame pursued him. As he strolled into the dining room of a fancy hotel in Cairo, a band launched into a selection of songs from *The Wizard of Oz* musical. His fame was in part fueled by songs and music he hadn't written, for a production only loosely based on his original story. But he was very pleased when he met a child during one visit to an ancient temple whose mother told him, amongst the sun-bleached ruins, that her daughter had been allowed to bring only one book on her trip across the desert in a caravan of camels, and she chose *The Wonderful Wizard of Oz*. The trip showed Baum that his story had reached beyond the shores of America. Letters from children followed him wherever he went; he received over a hundred on the steamship.

In Italy, Baum witnessed earthly sights more powerful than anything created by human hands. In Sicily, he and Maud climbed Mount Etna, a slumbering volcano, and in Naples in April, they watched amazed as Vesuvius erupted in its most powerful explosion of liquid rock for centuries. They "could see the hot lava flowing from its sides," wrote Maud. They walked "ankle deep in ashes" in a park, and saw trees drooping under the weight of ash. They visited towns destroyed by the erupting mountain. Boscotrecase "was overwhelmed by the streams of lava," remarked Maud, and "looked as if a cyclone had struck it." The still-hot earth burned her shoes. In San Giuseppe, more than one hundred people were killed in a church when the roof fell in. "They had assembled there," Maud explained, "to pray for deliverance from the rain of stones that descended upon them." The town of Pompeii, which the Baums also visited, had been preserved in volcanic ash after a giant eruption over a thousand years before. Maud found the infamous erotic wall paintings at Pompeii "coarse and sensual."

In that same month, April 1906, as the Baums watched Vesuvius bubble and boil, a terrible catastrophe hit California, where they would have been if they hadn't taken the trip to Europe. As newspapers delivered to Baum's hotel would have explained, at around five A.M. on April 18, an enormous foreshock rumbled across California. Twenty seconds later, a giant heaving quake shook the earth for less than a minute, but it brought catastrophic destruction in its wake. The San Andreas Fault (although it wasn't called this in 1906) ripped apart, sending the ground rippling back and forth from Oregon in the north to Los Angeles in the south. The epicenter wasn't far from San Francisco. Across California the ground was torn open; a whole steam train was thrown off its tracks after the ground wobbled and rippled up and down. The quake reverberated across the entire continent and was felt as far away as Europe.

The labyrinth of pipes, tubes, and wires beneath the surface of San Francisco, running underground, hidden between walls, under ceilings and floorboards, the very signatures of a modern city, became tangled, displaced, rerouted, blocked, and knotted, all torn out of shape by the quake. This caused havoc. Fires broke out across the city as stoves overturned, chimneys blocked, noxious chemical mixtures from drugstores spilled, gas escaped from pipes, and electrical wires crossed and sparked. Thousands of buildings caught fire across the city. The fire department was rendered helpless by the overwhelming fury of the fires and by the lack of access to water. Horses that still pulled many of the fire trucks became too frightened to pull hoses and gallons of water. This would hasten the transition in cities across America from horse-drawn fire trucks to steam-powered fire engines.

The fire roared for three days, and when it subsided, so many buildings were destroyed that 225,000 people were left homeless. San Francisco City Hall was reduced to a crumbled ruin, with only a few walls left standing. It looked like one of the many ancient ruins the Baums were exploring in Europe and North Africa when the earthquake struck. The ruined and preserved city of Pompeii, its people captured in frozen, ash-gray poses after the volcanic eruption, became a weird visual echo of the ruin in California. Some of the luxury hotels the Baums had stayed in on their first trip to California had partially collapsed. What had seemed to Baum to be the glistening, sunny fairyland of California was shown to be a vulnerable crust balancing precariously on the surface of a dangerous fault line in the earth. This horrifying reality seared into Baum's mind and had a profound influence on his conception of Oz and fairylands in general. The earth was dangerously alive and shifting in unpredictable ways.

Contemporary research on tectonic plates suggests that these distant events of 1906, the volcanic eruptions in Naples and the catastrophic San Francisco earthquake, weren't unrelated. Tectonic shifts seem to affect the whole planet; the volcanic eruptions in Italy and the earthquake on the other side of the world were part of far bigger and deeper shifts in the slowly moving plates that make up the earth's crust.

The Baums pushed on into Italy and visited Rome, Venice, and Florence. Maud found Florence, the town of art galleries and museums, educational, but Baum found it all rather intimidating and inaccessible. "L F grieves me," wrote Maud; "he says he can tell one old master from another as soon as he reads the name on the frame, and makes other slighting remarks when I grow enthusiastic." Baum photographed rooms crowded with paintings and sculptures in the Uffizi Gallery, where gilt-framed portraits of pious queens and louche harlots modeling for Venus stared down at seminaked male marble figures.

Moving from one room of artifacts to another and another was exhausting. The "constant succession of scenes grows bewildering," admitted Maud. In Paris they saw Notre Dame, the elaborate buttressed cathedral, and marveled at its mix of saints and gruesome Gothic gargoyles. They also visited Victor Hugo's house, which was a museum to the author's life. Maud noted how Hugo had painted characters from his life and from his fiction all jumbled up together on the walls of his writing room. They also attended

vaudeville and sideshow entertainments in Paris, as a bit of light circus relief
from the onslaught of high art.

In June, they left Europe on the steamship *Kaiserin Augusta* from Cher-
bourg, and were relieved when they saw the Statue of Liberty looming out
of the mist as they sailed into New York Harbor a few weeks later.

This grand tour had been a baffling, exciting whirligig of unimaginably
old and strange architecture, art, and landscapes. All the while Baum was
touring, he also continued to write, fulfilling the demands of the 1905 contract with Reilly & Britton. In Sicily, he wrote on the terrace of his hotel,
from which he could see Mount Etna, and he commented to Maud that
the volcano smoked nearly as much as he did. He worked on his potboiler
adventure stories to be published under pen names; these surfaced later in
1906 as *Aunt Jane's Nieces Abroad* by "Edith Van Dyne," and *Sam Steele's
Adventures on Land and Sea* by "Captain Hugh Fitzgerald." He also stored
up memories, photographs, and impressions, which he would pour into his
writing over the next couple of years, using Maud's extensive letters as
memory aids.

The trip also fully reignited Baum's old ambition to write a novel for
adults. He had tentatively returned to this ambition with *The Emperor's Spy*,
a story serialized in the *Philadelphia North American* under the pen name
Schuyler Staunton in 1905. Reilly & Britton published it as *The Fate of a
Crown* later that year. This was followed by *Daughters of Destiny* in 1906, but
neither book sold well, and Reilly & Britton encouraged Baum to concentrate on his more profitable children's books. Baum wrote to his publisher at
the Century Company in New York (which had published *Queen Zixi of Ix*
in 1905) to try and drum up some enthusiasm for his writing for adults
there. "By the way," he wrote, introducing the subject as an aside, "I'm writing a novel! . . . It's based on material I picked up in Egypt." His lack of
confidence surfaced: "It will have to be published under a penname (if it has
the luck to be published at all) because I cannot interfere with my children's
books by posing as a novelist." This was a revealing statement. Baum couldn't
imagine writing *as* a novelist; he could only envisage *posing* as one, playing
the part, like one of his acting roles in the melodramas of his youth. The
specter of the humbug Wizard continued to haunt Baum's image of himself
as a writer.

The Century Company didn't consider the novel good enough to publish. Baum finally published it with a friend he met on the trip, and *The Last Egyptian* appeared anonymously in 1908. This stab at an adult adventure story set in the exotic "Orient" was, like his serial adventures for boys and girls, workaday and lacked the imaginative, authentic reach of his Oz tales. Baum just couldn't write convincingly about the real, external world. His gifts lay in bringing to life a homespun version of the fantastic, as in another book published in 1906, *John Dough and the Cherub*. The story stars a gingerbread man who comes to life (he's named after the slang term "John Doe," meaning an unidentified corpse), and he flies to the magical isle of Phreex on the back of a July the Fourth firework, where he meets Chick the Cherub, a genderless "Incubator Baby." When his publishers asked Baum what sex the Cherub was, he said he didn't know; the baby was just a child, he said, so it didn't matter what sex it was. John Dough and Chick have numerous adventures and meet the "freaks of Phreex," including a two-legged horse, a little girl executioner, and a rubber bear.

Now the author of a raft of books published under his own and various pen names, Baum attempted to maintain clear distinctions between his different kinds of writing, and hold on to a sense that his fairy tales, published under his own name, were his true work. He kept scrapbooks of clippings and reviews of his books and articles about him (a "Record of Success" perhaps, as a rebuff to the "Record of Failures" he had kept in the 1890s). He might have noticed, turning the leaves of the scrapbooks, reading through the glued clippings, that the image of himself that appeared in interviews varied considerably. The media portraits differed, presenting him variously as leisured, eccentric, a genius, an overworked hack, a gentleman, a dreamy outsider with an artistic temperament, an astute businessman, a child-man, an aloof celebrity living in luxury, a hardy midwesterner, and a successful, ambitious easterner sojourning in California resorts.

He was often presented as eccentric, vague, and otherworldly, as in a portrait by Walt McDougall, the illustrator of the 1904 "Queer Visitors from the Marvelous Land of Oz" series. The report explained that Baum had visited McDougall, and apparently, the author of Oz forgot to bring seasonal clothes and had to borrow old clothes of McDougall's, which made him look like a scarecrow. McDougall claimed that Baum was forever losing things, put sugar in his wine, used moustache wax on his shoes, and once buttered a heat-proof mat, thinking it was edible.

"I found . . . Mr. Frank Baum, hovering over the beautiful flower bed which graces the front yard of his pretty cottage," began one interview in Macatawa Park. Another journalist pursued Baum to Macatawa and claimed to find the author with "his hands stuck in his back pockets, his hat pulled low over his eyes, a big white flower in his buttonhole and an expression of whimsical enjoyment on his face." Baum was the "goose man," whose home in Macatawa had a "fantastic air."

Other press portraits presented Baum as remote from the cares of the world. "The only work Mr. Baum does at present," read an interview in 1907, "is to answer the dozens of letters which come to him every day from children." The paper claimed that Baum never read newspapers or magazines, to ensure that his mind remained "simple, unencumbered by the concerns of the world, free to wander in the realms of the imagination." "Unlike the world at large," the report went on, "Mr. Baum is not troubled with money matters. . . . Thus he has only to work at his convenience with no hurry and no worry." Either the journalist totally fabricated this portrait or Baum purposely misrepresented himself to conform to the stereotype of the children's author as a dreamy eccentric. The portrait grossly misrepresented both Baum and his imagination, which was worldly in a far deeper way than the ephemera of the daily press. Another report quoted Baum as saying, "I think I am the laziest man in the world, . . . for I write but three hours a day and play all the rest of the time." This was far from the truth.

The image of the leisured author, "wreathed in cigar smoke," as another report had it, was a smoke-and-mirrors trick in part designed to "misdirect" attention from Baum's frantic writing schedule to produce numerous potboilers printed under pen names; it may have looked publicly as though Baum worked at a gentle pace on a few Oz novels and some musical theater adaptations, but he was actually writing under at least five pen names, running several writers' careers at once.

These media portraits may have created an inconsistent picture of Baum, in part, because Baum's ideas were inconsistent and his personality was hard to fathom. He believed in women's rights and yet also feared the rising power of the New Woman who cycled to work in bloomers and smoked cigarettes; in Oz, he showed that he respected each individual's uniqueness no matter how strange they were, but he also harbored more conventional ethnic prejudices that became visible in his potboilers for older children. His energy, drive, and ability to attend to the minutest of details conflicted with his total lack of financial know-how. His fascination with new technologies was in tension with his fear that they would take over and petrify the natural world. He was fascinated with illusions but also motivated by a desire to look behind the curtain to understand the mechanisms by which they were created. His outward appearance was shaped by dapper tailored suits, a fob watch, polished shoes, neatly parted hair, and trimmed moustache, and this image was rather at odds with his inner scarecrow, his childish, carnivalesque, vivacious, and gently subversive imagination.

Baum thought of himself as an expert in fairy tales, old and new. He wrote a number of short pieces for newspapers and magazines on the history of fairy tales, and inserted himself into this tradition. In several articles for newspapers and magazines, he explained that fairy tales had evolved from oral folklore, found in the collected tales of the Brothers Grimm, Charles Perrault, and Andrew Lang. Hans Christian Andersen, "the glorious Dane," as Baum called him, had been the first author, as far as he knew, to originate new folktales. Andersen's tales were an intimate melding of oldest Danish folk stories and new inventions of his own, and this was the model of the modern writer of fairy stories for Baum; stories were a mixture of pure invention and ideas gathered from the cultural soup that sloshed around the author. "I appear to be the only American," Baum declared, "whose fairy tales have become widely known." He was aware of the novelty of his position and saw himself as the first Euro-American to create authentic modern American folktales. Baum took himself seriously even if some parts of the press didn't.

Chapter 21

etters from child readers piled up on Baum's various doorsteps. Sometimes several hundred would arrive in a week. Reading the funny handwritten notes, letters askew, and with unconventional spelling, Baum realized that children desperately wanted to find out what happened to Dorothy. The success of the first two Oz books (as well as the musical) convinced him that he had to return to the Land of Oz once again. He at last recognized that Oz was his most successful discovery. In the summer of 1906, he launched into a new Oz story, which would be called *Ozma of Oz*, writing on the porch of the Sign of the Goose cottage, amid the trees and lake waters of Macatawa Park.

Drawing on his experience crossing the Atlantic, Baum sent Dorothy back to Oz by tipping her overboard a steamship during a ferocious storm. He exercised his energetic imagination to the fullest in this story and conjured a number of new creatures, some frightening in their strangeness, such as the Wheelers, whose toenails grow into wheels and they roll along as though on roller skates. He introduced Tik-Tok, one of the first robots to appear in literature. The machine man had to be regularly wound up to think, talk, and walk. Baum introduced the new set of feelings and questions aroused by the growing intimacy between humans and machines. Dorothy and the other characters she meets on her travels develop an emotional attachment to Tik-Tok and consider him their friend, even though Tik-Tok is emotionless because he's a machine.

While questions about emotions and machinery circle the story, Baum included living creatures that have been reduced to objects. Princess Langwidere is a vain, mannequin-woman who collects numbered heads in velvet-lined cabinets. She spends her time swapping heads and admiring her appearance in a cold room covered from floor to ceiling in mirrors, so that her image is reflected "hundreds of times" all around her, until the room resembles a warehouse full of identical mass-produced dolls. Baum had distanced himself from his days publishing *The Show Window*, thinking of new ways to sell corsets and ribbons, but the specter of this era of his life lived on. And many of the magazines in which Baum's short stories were published were women's fashion journals with subsections for children. Next to his tale "A Kidnapped Santa Claus," published in *The Delineator* in 1904, for instance, was an article entitled "The Art of Looking in the Mirror" and an advertisement for "a plaster bandage for removing chin wrinkles." Baum's experience working in the press meant he was fully aware that such advertisements promoting female vanity paid the fee for his stories.

Ozma of Oz also features a wicked Nome King who transforms his enemies into ornaments, which he collects in a vast underground cavern. Ozma is turned into an emerald grasshopper, the Scarecrow becomes a gold visiting-card holder, and the Tin Woodman becomes a tin whistle. The king's collection of statues, antiques, and artifacts echoed the numerous museums Baum had visited on his tour of Europe. Dorothy's animal companion in this adventure is a talking hen that saves the day by producing eggs that terrify the Nome King; an egg embodies female fertility, and in Oz it has the power to defeat evil.

In the opening of *Ozma of Oz*, Baum again commented on his role as author, first mentioned in the "Queer Visitors from the Marvelous Land of Oz" series. He was the Royal Historian who merely "recorded" Dorothy's adventures. Baum explained that the children who wrote to him were "responsible for this new Oz book." "Indeed," he went on, "could I do all that my little friends ask, I would be obliged to write dozens of books to satisfy their demands, and I wish I could," he added. Baum knew from his extensive reading of folktales that you must always be careful what you wish for. He might have heeded this ancient advice.

Tik-Tok describes his creator, Mr. Smith, as "an artist as well as an inventor." He painted a "river which was so natural that, as he was reaching across it to paint some flowers on the opposite bank he fell into the water and drowned." Mr. Smith was the first of several minor characters in Baum's Oz books who are subsumed by their creations, trapped and even killed by the things they have made, which are so believable and successful they swallow their creators.

The third Oz book was a roaring success. Reviews championed Baum as "the greatest inventor of modern fairy tales," a writer whose commitment to his craft was so great that "he would rather write fairy stories than eat." One overwhelmingly enthusiastic review read, "The joys of this new Baum book are almost beyond the power of imagination."

In the sunny luxury of the Hotel Del Coronado, Baum set about writing the fourth Oz book in 1907, in what was now definitely a series. *Dorothy and the Wizard in Oz*, as it was titled, was the first Oz book Baum wrote in Coronado. Despite the luxury, the California sunshine, and bracing sea air, the story was the darkest of the Oz tales. The specter of the earthquake, the erupting volcanoes, and the parade of ancient burial sites Baum had witnessed in North Africa and Europe shaped the story. Plus, Baum was beginning to feel the strain of continuing the Oz series. "It's no use; no use at all," he wrote in his introduction. The "children won't let me stop telling tales of the Land of Oz. I know lots of other stories, and I hope to tell them . . . but just now my loving tyrants won't allow me." The loving tyrants had sent him hundreds of letters asking for news of Dorothy and Oz; "they have flooded me," he said, using a word that echoed the artist in *Ozma of Oz* who drowned in a river he painted, with thousands of suggestions for story lines. This introduction was in part tongue in cheek, offering children a sense of control over what was increasingly looking like their Oz. It was a children's world ruled by a child entirely without adult intrusion, except in the remote presence of good and bad witches who had taken a backseat by now.

Dorothy travels to Oz in *Dorothy and the Wizard in Oz* once again by way of a natural disaster; on her way in a horse-drawn buggy to visit her cousin Zeb in California, the earth shudders, rocks from side to side, and rips open to create a huge crack down into the earth. Dorothy falls through in the buggy with Zeb, Eureka, a mischievous kitten, and Jim the horse, and they all float down through the earth. They encounter many odd creatures on their perilous journey back up to the surface, passing through tunnels, caves, staircases, and pyramids on their way. Baum's vision of the underworld was a mixture of Jules Verne's *Journey to the Centre of the Earth* and his own trip abroad. The Old World seemed like a buried cemetery culture beneath the sparkling surface of modern America, the New World laid, as it were, over the old.

The humbug Wizard floats in his balloon down into the fissure opened up in the ground by the earthquake. Baum had noticed that many letters from children asked after the Wizard. He was surprised that "the jolly old fellow made hosts of friends in the first Oz book, in spite of the fact that he frankly acknowledged himself a humbug."

Dorothy lands in a place that resembles the luxury resorts in which Baum now spent much of his time. The land of the Mungaboos is made of glass houses inhabited by beautiful people dressed permanently in finery. There are no children or animals there. Dorothy discovers that the people are vegetables. They are solid all the way through and have "no hearts, so they can't love anyone—not even themselves." The beautiful and perfect vegetable people, who live in grand glass palaces, are cruel. They decide to kill Dorothy and her friends because they don't fit into their perfect world. This touched on an increasingly dominant concern in Baum's writing, which seemed to grow stronger, the more successful and rich he became: Perfection can be stale and deadening.

Above the land of the cruel vegetable people, Dorothy and her companions encounter violent invisible bears and angry flying wooden gargoyles. One of the most frightening creatures beneath the surface of the earth is the Braided Man, another figure who has been consumed by his creation. When he lived on the earth's surface, the Braided Man had been an inventor of holes—for Swiss cheese, doughnuts, buttons, and holes in the ground for fence posts; he had buried his postholes in the ground because he had nowhere else to store them. The hole he'd dug had reached far down into the earth, and the man had accidentally tumbled into it. Here he was, trapped miles below the surface of the earth. This was a bleak image of a man who fell into his own creation. Now underground, the odd fellow makes strange items for department stores. "I manufacture my products in this lonely spot," he admits, boxing up "Assorted Flutters for flags and bunting, and superior grade Rustles for ladies' silk gowns." The Braided Man specializes in making rustling sounds and breezes. He is another kind of humbug; the Wizard acknowledges a fellow faker and nods in recognition.

Baum's ability to create vivid, odd characters and varied, weird kingdoms wasn't matched by an ability to build well-structured and satisfying plots. Dorothy and her friends reach a dead end close to the surface of the earth and become trapped in the rock, in the dark, unable to go forward or back. This was an extremely depressing predicament to put Dorothy in, as Baum took in the California sunshine, practiced archery, played golf, strolled the Pacific shore, and generally lived it up in the luxury of the Del Coronado. Ozma finally intercedes and saves Dorothy by magically transporting her and her companions to the Land of Oz.

Having brought his travelers up through the bowels of the earth and whisked them magically to Oz, Baum takes a moment to explore his fascination with the motorcar and his nostalgia for horses. He races Jim, the suffering Chicago cab horse, against the Saw-Horse, who's really a proto-automobile. Horses slowly disappeared from the mainstream of human life during Baum's lifetime. These organic, breathing, sweaty, muscular, hoofed creatures were gradually removed, to be replaced with grinding gears and roaring engines (measured in "horsepower"). In rural areas, horses were gradually replaced by tractors and other machinery. Baum witnessed the rapid disappearance of streetcar horses between 1888 and 1892, to be replaced with electric cars. By the late 1920s, horses were a rare sight in city centers. All over the country, horse racing tracks were adapted for racing cars.

Many were relieved to see horses disappearing from cities, in particular. Nineteenth-century urban life had become a constant battle against the piles of manure that built up in the streets, attracting flies in the heat of summer, "the queens of the dung heap," and spreading disease. The mess swilled into revolting, stinking mud slides after rainstorms. The deafening clatter of iron horseshoes on cobblestone streets made talking outside impossible. Many city dwellers complained of being tormented by the noise. Others were horrified by witnessing the constant abuse of horses, as exhausted beasts heaved loaded streetcars, carts, cabs, and coaches back and forth. The life expectancy for a Chicago streetcar horse, for instance, was only four years. The sight of rotting horse corpses was a common one in cities too. New York and Chicago found it difficult to dispose of the thousands of dead horses that piled up in the streets.

The disappearance of horses was largely welcomed, but it was also accompanied by regret and nostalgia. In Baum's story, the Saw-Horse easily wins the race against Jim the cab horse, but his victory is tinged with sadness for the end of an era in which daily human life was lived in intimate proximity with animals. Life in the twentieth century would become increasingly removed from other living creatures, to be lived instead amongst machines.

Dorothy looks into Ozma's "Magic Picture," a screen on which it's possible to see anything anywhere in Oz or the great Outside World exactly as it's happening, like a kind of proto-webcam, and she sees Aunt Em and Uncle Henry in mourning clothes, grieving for her because they assume she has died. The child reluctantly returns to Kansas from the magical land to reassure her family she is safe. The Wizard remains in Oz as an entertaining magician humbug this time and not a deceiving ruler. The Wizard makes Oz his home; perhaps this reflected Baum's recognition that Oz was now his imaginative home.

In early 1908, *Dorothy and the Wizard in Oz* was being prepared for publication, with Neill's vivacious illustrations woven into the text. The vibrant gilt cover featured the magician Wizard doing tricks in a bright blue tailcoat. Neill drew the frightened expressions on Jim the cab horse's face and the manic, grinning Wizard particularly well. Baum, meanwhile, was busy preparing a new venture beyond books that involved a brand-new technology. This next project would take him in a completely new direction and reshape his future. It would also ruin him.

Chapter 22

tories could now be told with a stream of light projected through dust onto a screen. In 1908, Baum toured the country in a traveling show called the *Fairylogue and Radio-Plays*, which was a mixture of the very oldest forms of storytelling and the most novel. Baum was at the forefront of a pioneering new technology, the moving picture, which would soon transform America. The phenomenon was still in its infancy in 1908. The Lumière brothers had unveiled the first machine that could project moving images in France in 1895, but the pioneer of the kind of film Baum was interested in was another Frenchman, called Georges Méliès.

Méliès was a highly skilled conjurer who performed illusions in his Theatre Robert-Houdin in Paris. He had attended the Lumière brothers' 1895 demonstration of moving images and was immediately captivated. He bought his own filming equipment and set about experimenting. He soon made an extraordinary discovery. Film could do more than simply record the world, as the Lumière brothers thought; it could transform the appearance of reality. While Méliès was filming in the Place de l'Opera in Paris, his camera jammed for a minute or so until he fixed it and it rolled on. When he projected the footage he had taken that day he noticed, to his surprise, that a trolley car suddenly transformed into a hearse, and even more oddly, men changed before his astonished eyes into women. Méliès had discovered stop-motion trick photography. Over the next fifteen years, he made dozens of "trick films." He gained a reputation as a "cine-magician," and a "grand prankster." Méliès made illusion films in which all kinds of impossible and extraordinary things clearly take place before the eye. He disoriented, amazed, and bedazzled audiences in his Parisian theater with short, black-and-white, silent films in which, for instance, people leap into the air and disappear in a plume of smoke. In one film, Méliès holds a woman in his arms who transforms into a handful of fake snow that he triumphantly throws up into the air like confetti. Méliès reveled in dismembering and duplicating his body. In one film, he replicates himself seven times and creates an orchestra out of the many versions of himself. In another, he pulls off his own head and throws it onto a giant musical score; he grows another head and pulls that one off too and flings it onto the score to join the other. So it goes on. The heads then metamorphose into birds and fly off. He chops off his own head again in another short film, places it on a table, and then inflates it with a pair of fire bellows, like a large balloon, until it pops and disappears in a puff of smoke. In *The Living Playing Cards*, man-size cards, the king of clubs and queen of hearts, come to life and leap off their flat backgrounds. Méliès enjoyed transforming men into women, making furniture disappear, and conjuring objects out of thin air.

By manipulating the camera and film, Méliès created moving pictures that gave "the appearance of reality to the most chimerical of dreams and to the most improbable inventions of the imagination." With Méliès, the future of cinema moved from documenting the outside world, as the Lumière brothers had envisaged it, to revealing the bizarre, complex, interior realms of the imagination, which ancient folktales had been doing for hundreds of years. It's little wonder, then, that Méliès immediately used his newfound tricks to make old fairy tales, such as "Cinderella" and "Bluebeard." He also made the first-ever horror movie, *The House of the Devil*. The horror film was an inevitable outcrop of the trick film. The devil, after all, had long been imagined in Christian thought to be a trickster and illusionist, unlike God, who can work real miracles.

Méliès showed his "cinema of attractions" as a sideshow in his magician's theater in Paris. Maud mentioned in her letters from Europe that she and Frank had enjoyed sampling the vaudeville and cheap sideshows of Paris; they may well have visited Méliès's theater. But Méliès's films were shown across America, so Baum probably saw them there if not in Paris.

The *Fairylogue and Radio-Plays* opened with Baum stepping onstage in a dashing white suit and introducing himself as a storyteller. He then retreated into the wings, and a velvet scarlet curtain was drawn by two jesters to reveal a large, square, gilt-framed screen. The lights went down and a large map of the Land of Oz appeared flickering on the screen. This map externalized the interior lands of Baum's imagination and made Oz seem like a geographical and geological reality. There then appeared flickering onscreen a large storybook. A boy opened the book to show a black-and-white image of Dorothy. Baum then appeared in the film dressed in the same white suit, as though he had stepped directly from the wings onto celluloid. He beckoned to Dorothy, who, amazingly, stepped out of the storybook, gradually grew in size, and emerged in full bright color. The book was closed and reopened to reveal the Scarecrow, who also stepped out into moving multicolor. He was followed by the Cowardly Lion, the Tin Woodman, and other characters from Oz. This was the first time Dorothy was transformed from black-and-white into full bright color onscreen, a process the 1939 MGM movie would make more than famous.

Baum then stepped out from the wings and narrated the story of *The Wonderful Wizard of Oz* while still slides were interspersed with tinted silent moving pictures of scenes from the story. Versions of *The Marvelous Land of Oz* and *Ozma of Oz* followed, and then after a short intermission, Baum narrated with more slides and moving picture scenes from his 1906 non-Oz tale *John Dough and the Cherub*. The filmed scenes from the Oz tales used the trick photography pioneered by Méliès to make moving characters leap into the air and disappear, melt away into ghostly visions in dissolving scenes, and transform a boy into a girl. The Gump flew through the air, and Dorothy was washed overboard from a ship in a storm at sea. The many children who made up the audience squealed with delight throughout, amazed to see John Dough shoot up into a cloudy sky, clinging to a sparkling firework.

A live orchestra played twenty-seven original pieces of music to accompany the stories. This was the very first musical score written for the moving pictures. Frank Jr., age twenty-five, was the projectionist. He hid in a fireproof room and worked the film and slide projector. The actors who played the characters from Oz on film also appeared live, dressed in their costumes, so that the Scarecrow, the Lion, Tin Woodman, Jack Pumpkinhead, the Wizard, and Tik-Tok leapt around the stage before projected moving images of themselves, to create a weird doubling effect, as though the screen were a magic mirror that had stolen their reflections and given them separate lives of their own.

The title of the show was as odd and novel as its content. The "fairy-logue" was a play on the "travelogue," a popular type of illustrated lecture accompanied by slides or magic lantern projections. But the idea of "radio-plays" was more peculiar. In an interview with the press, Baum claimed that "the Radio-Play takes its name from Michel Radio, the inventor of the process of Parisian transparent coloring." This was very likely a nonsense explanation Baum invented to tell curious journalists. The moving film footage was hand-tinted by Duval Frères in Paris and no such person as Michel Radio existed. This was another instance of Baum making up a tale to tell journalists rather than answering complex questions about the origins and meaning of his work, much of which he didn't fully understand himself.

Baum didn't name the lecture tour "Radio-Play." It took the title from a small organization called the Radio Play Company of America, which promoted the show. Baum may not have understood the significance of the word "radio" in 1908 and perhaps made up his reply to cover the fact. Radio or wireless hadn't yet been invented, and wouldn't be fully developed by Marconi and others for several years. But radio waves had long been known to exist. Scientists knew that information could be sent without wires, pipes, or tubes through the air to be received and decoded by machines that in 1908 were in the process of being invented. The idea and potential of radio waves was traveling fast through the scientific world and out into the general public, where it was mixing with existing ideas about ether, an invisible, soupy zone in which spirits and information were thought to be traveling about. The word "radio" was vague and ambiguous in 1908. It suggested radiant energy, an exotic higher plane on which stories as well as spirits and fairies were sloshing about, awaiting a medium through which they could be transformed and decoded into a form comprehensible to humans down here on the mundane ground.

Applied to new moving pictures, the idea of "radio-plays" also pointed to the invisible, electrically powered process of projecting light onto a screen, of passing images through the air wirelessly, as it were, and bouncing them off a flat surface.

Baum was involved in every stage of the process of filming the moving picture scenes from his tales. He "superintended everything," as the marvelously named Romola Remus, the actress who played Dorothy, put it. He "went from one set to another to give directions to everyone," explained Romola, "but always in a calm voice . . . not aggressive, very calm. But when he gave an order, they respected it." The film footage was shot at the Selig Polyscope Company in Chicago, whose brand-new filmmaking studio had opened in 1907. It was a grand glass building designed to allow in as much natural light as possible to enable filming. This glass building was likely the inspiration for the peculiar glass houses under the earth in *Dorothy and the Wizard in Oz*.

In an interview with Baum printed in the *New York Herald* magazine, it became clear that he fully understood the intricate details of the new world of trick films and was, as ever, as fascinated by the trickery behind the illusions as he was by their startling effects. The article suggested, quite rightly, that the new phenomenon of the moving picture trick film was a form of modern magic from the "fairy land of motion pictures." After seeing the marvelous visual effects, the author of the report was left wondering, "which was the more wonderful," the moving picture illusions, "or that of the old witches and fairy godmothers themselves." Baum called his techniques "fairy photography" and proudly explained how by freezing the camera, changing a scene, and then restarting it characters appear and disappear before the astonished eye, how moving characters step out of a storybook. Through clever editing and the use of double exposures, layered effects were created, as well as by slowing film footage down or speeding it up. By the "simplest of tricks," said Baum, a "camera can be made to be a fine liar." Baum's in-depth understanding of photography enabled him to grasp the workings of moving picture techniques quickly and to develop his own innovations. The Lumière brothers and other early innovators who developed moving picture technology had envisaged film as a method of simply showing recorded reality, of capturing the world as it was seen through the mechanical glass eye of the camera. But Méliès had taken film in a totally new and radical direction by showing how clever tricks that confused the human eye could present ideas and images taken directly from the interior of the human imagination, where fairies, ghouls, and witches had been conjured, animated, and snuffed out for millennia. "Today, American children by the thousands are seeing [the] miracles of Fairyland with their own eyes," announced the journalist. Baum admitted that his moving pictures were created through "an applied knowledge of many small mechanical tricks welded together. . . . But," he added with a wink, "it makes one almost doubt the fairies . . . did genii have tricks too?"

The *Fairylogue and Radio-Plays* opened in Grand Rapids, Michigan, in September 1908, and then set off on tour, traveling through the Midwest and Chicago as winter closed in, stopping in St. Louis, Milwaukee, St. Paul, Minneapolis, and Rockford and then moving east to Syracuse (where Baum met old friends and family), finally arriving in New York City in December. In Chicago, the show played to a full house in the newly opened Orchestra Hall. The interior of the new theater was painted in rich silver and gold, which must have flickered under the colors of the tinted moving pictures. Reviews of the "Ozologue" complimented Baum on his deep, sonorous voice and marveled at the ingenuity of the production. "Nothing more cleverly mystifying," read one review, "has been achieved in moving picture devices." It was "a curious and novel entertainment, and so admirably worked out in all its details that manifestly it has cost a great deal of money." The report was right. Baum had ensured that every detail in the show was perfect. He had poured his own money into it and borrowed thousands of dollars to pay for the hand-painted film footage. The show was a sellout success, but it cost so much to keep the large cast, orchestra, and elaborate fire-hazardous technology on the road that the show couldn't pay for itself, let alone make a profit. Despite its success, the *Radio-Plays* closed in New York City before Christmas 1908. Baum returned to Chicago with reels of innovative and bewitching color film, and with a yoke of debt. He hadn't yet realized that this extravagant technological spectacle had financially ruined him. He would be forced to face the truth soon enough.

Baum still had grand ambitions for theater productions and continued to work on numerous projects, none of which had come to fruition. There was nothing to do now but keep writing stories and try to stave off the creditors. He reworked some of his adventure stories for boys that Reilly & Britton had published under the name Captain Hugh Fitzgerald in 1906 and 07, and published them as a new series called *The Boy Fortune Hunters* under the name Floyd Akers. This fictional gentleman's name could be written as "F. Aker," which pointed to the inauthentic nature of these gung-ho potboilers; they were "fakes." Baum was now financially dependent on serial adventure books written under pen names and on the Oz series. Inevitably, he was forced back to Oz to retrieve yet another story, and he set about writing the fifth Oz tale, but he was now determined to close the series, to get out of Oz. This would be the penultimate in the Oz series and then he would finish them off and release himself. He made his position clear in an interview in Coronado in 1909. "I will write one more next year," he stated, "and that will close the series of the chronicles of Oz."

Baum dedicated *The Road to Oz* to his first grandchild, Joslyn Stanton Baum, born to Frank Jr. and his wife, Helen, in 1908. Baum nicknamed the baby Tik-Tok because he was fascinated by his grandfather's loudly ticking pocket watch. In his introductory address to *The Road to Oz*, written in the sunshine and luxury of the Hotel Del Coronado despite his mounting debts, Baum presented a confused picture of his writing process. His army of tyrannical child readers had demanded a new Oz book, and Baum had tried to include things they had asked for, such as for Toto to be reintroduced. But, Baum wrote, not all "the wishes of my little correspondents" were in the new story, because "a story has to be a story before it can be written down, and a writer cannot change it much without spoiling it." He made it clear that "I discovered" stories and characters from Oz, rather than made them up. Here was the profound confusion at work in Baum's relationship with Oz and the source of its brilliance: on the one hand, children could write to Baum and make suggestions for plots and characters; on the other, Oz was a place Baum had simply discovered, like a modern-day Christopher Columbus. There seemed to be a fine line between discovering something and inventing it.

The introduction concluded with a warning that the next Oz book "will be the last story that will ever be told about the Land of Oz."

In *The Road to Oz*, Dorothy and Toto are whisked away to Oz while out on a stroll in the Kansas countryside; Ozma magically conjures a whirling cartwheel of roads and secretly directs Dorothy and Toto to the Emerald City. There seems to be an invisible membrane between Kansas and Oz in this book because Dorothy simply walks to Oz, passing through a sideshow of strange miniature lands on her way. Baum introduced some new characters, such as Polychrome the rainbow's daughter, a fairy made from pure light, rather like the moving picture characters projected onto the screen during the *Radio-Plays*. And there was the Shaggy Man, a homeless tramp Dorothy meets roaming the dusty tracks of Kansas. Baum had witnessed many such destitute people in the years after the Civil War and in the wake

of the 1890s economic depression. The tramp finds a permanent home in
Oz because he cannot be accommodated in America, which was emerging
as a cruel and intolerant place rather than a much-loved home yearned for
when lost in fairyland. Oz was beginning to seem like a utopian retreat from
America, a destination rather than somewhere to escape.

Dorothy and her friends arrive in Oz in time for a banquet in the Emerald City, in which, like a theatrical finale, Baum gathered all the many
characters and creatures from all his previous fairy tales, including those
from outside Oz. The forest of Burzee is emptied and the crooked knooks
and other immortals that live there flock to Oz. Baum joined all the worlds
he had discovered through his stories together into one interlinked continent
of the imagination. Queen Zixi of Ix, Claus, and John Dough all attend;
even the scary Braided Man, the strange character who dwells under the
crust of the earth, halfway up a giant spiral staircase, making rustles for ladies' skirts and flutters for flags, shows up. Dorothy "remembered the Braided
Man well." This minor character who was trapped and doomed to reproduce
curious objects for sale in department stores obviously stuck in Baum's
mind too.

Baum now clarified the utopian nature of Oz; "did you suppose," cried
the Tin Woodman, that "we are so vulgar as to use money here?" It's no
surprise that this aspect of Oz became clear to Baum at a time when his finances were in total disarray. There are no rich people in Oz, "for what
one wishes the others all try to give him . . . and no one in all Oz cares to
have more than he can use." This socialist aspect of Oz would worry a certain type of patriotic American during the Cold War, and get Baum and Oz
into all kinds of trouble. The Shaggy Man joins the Wizard as a new
immigrant who takes up permanent residence in Oz. Dorothy decides to
return to Kansas only because Uncle Henry and Aunt Em think she is dead.
She can't bear to see them mourn for her, and ever practical, she knows they
can't afford the expense of mourning coats and a funeral.

The Road to Oz was handsomely illustrated by Neill and innovatively
printed on multicolored paper that moved through the spectrum of the rainbow. This was the least plotted of the Oz books, and reviewers, like Baum,
were becoming exhausted with the series. The *New Orleans Times Democrat*
expressed it well. Children were forcing Baum to write more Oz books and it
"really seems time that someone in authority should interfere," read the report,

"for if this goes on we shall by and by have no room in our libraries for anything but Oz books." The journalist called for "an injunction from the Supreme Court, or even a prohibitive act of Congress if nothing else will do."

But Baum couldn't stop there, no matter how exasperated he and reviewers had become. *The Road to Oz* sold very well. Baum had to finish the series and a year later, in 1910, he set about his royal duty as Historian of Oz and wrote the sixth book in the series. In a rented cottage next to the Hotel Del Coronado, on a sunny beach surrounded by waving palm trees, Baum conjured a new tale; he threw his storytelling energy into it and developed a well-plotted narrative filled with fully imagined creatures. At last, Baum allowed himself to turn one of his characters into a real villain, an evil mean spirit suffused with the desire to cause mayhem. The Nome King, who lives beneath the ground, digs a tunnel into the Emerald City and plans to conquer it. Back in Kansas, the bank is about to foreclose on Uncle Henry's mortgage and claim the farm; the Gales are threatened with bankruptcy. Dorothy's only escape is to take her uncle and aunt with her to Oz, to live there permanently. It has become impossible to live and thrive in America. Uncle Henry and Aunt Em are magically whisked to Oz with Dorothy, where the simple prairie folk amble awkwardly around the grand palaces of the Emerald City, as out of place as the Beverly Hillbillies. Aunt Em worries that her hair isn't done up right and that her and Henry's clothes are out of place amid overdressed princesses and good witches in diaphanous gowns.

Oz has become a utopia, where nobody is ever ill or dies, where everyone works half the time and plays half the time, is prosperous and happy. But Oz is full of different kinds of people, including Wild People, who live happily removed from everyone else; this was a hopeful image of what might have been the place of Native Americans in an alternative America.

Dorothy and the Wizard (who has been taught how to do real magic by Glinda) take Em and Henry on a grand tour of Oz, to introduce them to their new home. The Gales are like European immigrants to the bright new world that America should have been. They set off in a carriage pulled by the Saw-Horse and visit many of the peculiar sights in Oz. In the land of the Cuttenclips they discover a terrifying image of the trapped author. A child, known as Miss Cuttenclip, is arrested in a permanent state of childhood and lives in her "workshop" (the term Baum used for his writing room), where she cuts paper figures out of magic paper all day, every day. "This is live paper," she explains. The strings of paper dolls come alive and live around her. She has built an entire world out of paper. The city is walled up to keep breezes from blowing in and disrupting the paper people, like a cyclone. The child is the queen of her lonely paper kingdom.

The Nome King and his accomplices, who include the shape-shifting wolf "phanfasms" who take on many truly frightening forms, fail to conquer Oz when Ozma tricks them into drinking from the fountain of forgetfulness, reducing them to a state of benign innocence. Peace is restored and Dorothy finally makes Oz her home. But then the story turns outward and faces its readers. In the real world, flight was just taking off. The Wright brothers' early efforts were being perfected into real flying machines by 1910. In Baum's story, the natives of Oz fear that flight will enable people from the outside world to visit them, believing Oz is such a desirable place that it was in danger of being overrun by hordes of enthusiastic visitors. In an antitourism and anti-immigration move, Glinda makes the Land of Oz invisible, so that if a hot air balloon or flying machine should enter its air space, the utopian world below will remain unseen.

On the final page of the story, Baum reported that the "writer of these Oz stories has received a little note" from Dorothy, written "on a broad white feather of a stork's wing." It read, "You will never hear anything more about Oz, . . . because we are now cut off from the rest of the world." Baum gave Dorothy the job of telling his readers that there would be no more Oz stories, sidestepping his role as author and refusing to take responsibility for ending the series.

Closing off the Land of Oz in order to protect it from the outside world mirrored what Baum was trying to do in his own life, shutting out tyrannical readers who were demanding that he shape and manipulate his imagination for their ends. He feared that the constant demand for more Oz stories was stifling him, threatening to break his mind.

The Emerald City of Oz had a glowing cover and numerous elaborate full-page color illustrations taken from watercolors by Neill and printed using a new metallic emerald green ink that shimmered on the page. It was the final Oz book, so the publishers really went to town. The book was a great success and flew off the shelves in the fall of 1910. Reviews were positive, but one reviewer refused to believe that this was the end of Oz, because the "children won't have it." "The only graceful way Baum can quit telling tales of Oz," it read, "is to die."

The Gales' move to Oz was paralleled by the Baums' permanent migration west in 1910 to California, to the state that had so beguiled them. Baum's finances had become so chaotic and his debt so disastrous that he and Maud decided to sell the summer cottage filled with flying geese in Macatawa Park and the apartment in central Chicago. They would move permanently to the far West, where it was cheaper to live. They certainly could no longer afford to winter in the luxury of the Hotel Del Coronado. Perhaps Baum was finally tired of living between landscapes, of being constantly on the move between Chicago, California, and Macatawa. He and Maud wanted to be close to a big city, so there would be ample opportunities for the boys to find jobs and make lives close by. They chose a small, quiet rural village surrounded by orange and lemon groves in the hills above Los Angeles. It was called Hollywood.

Baum was thrilled with the success of *The Emerald City of Oz*, and perhaps by the thought that the Oz series was finally complete. He was struggling with debt, but to celebrate, he bought Maud a gorgeous ring, a circle of diamonds with a large emerald pressed into its center.

Part V

HOLLYWOOD

1910 TO 1919

Chapter 23

aum took copious photographs of the two-story wooden frame house under construction in Hollywood, paid for with who knows what money, Maud's inheritance from her mother most likely. As usual, he entered a new landscape through a camera lens. The house was built on a large corner lot where Yucca Street met Magnolia Avenue (later renamed Cherokee Avenue), 100 yards north of Hollywood Boulevard and 550 yards north of Sunset Boulevard. He photographed the wooden shell when its roof was only half on, ladders and scaffolding puncturing the structure. He and Maud took up residence in the finished house in 1911; Baum named it Ozcot. As with the Sign of the Goose, the Macatawa cottage, Baum liked to feel he was living inside his stories. He took more photographs of the spacious interior and mounted them in albums. He was very proud of the house and must have strolled around the airy rooms, chewing a cigar, admiring the spacious living room with its large open fire. The solarium was a sun trap filled with wicker chairs and Navajo rugs. A library was lined with bookshelves heaving with some of Baum's own books no doubt, but also with leather volumes of classics, for show as much as for reading. If Baum's true reading tastes tended toward Lang's collections of old folktales and the odd potboiler, the library suggested otherwise. Above the books, a frieze of trees ran around the room. One of the four bedrooms upstairs was turned into a workshop for Baum. The house was filled with dark wooden chairs, patterned rugs thrown at odd angles over the floorboards, knickknacks, lace doilies, and basket ware. It was comfortable rather than fashionable. The heavy oak dining room furniture was set off by the sharp California light. Hanging above the dining room

table was an ornate copper and emerald green glass light that Baum had made. He cut out the intricate design from the copper with a jeweler's saw, inserted the glass, and wired it up. It must have thrown a glowing emerald light across the rich meals he enjoyed there, turning potatoes and his beloved cheese green.

Baum covered one wall of Ozcot with photographs of Maud taken throughout her life. He named it his Yard of Maud. The mutual devotion that made the marriage so happy seems to have been based on the way each embraced the other's different, almost opposing, nature. More importantly, both accepted one another's considerable flaws without attempting to change them. Baum was terrible with money, Maud had a short temper. So it was and always would be.

Along the street outside the house grew pepper trees, which blossomed with scarlet berries. The Baums bought the lot in 1910, the year Hollywood officially became part of Los Angeles, to gain access to the water from the Los Angeles aqueduct. The rural suburb of fruit groves, vines, farmer's barns, and livestock had a population of five thousand. Dirt roads wound through the village, where early automobiles chuffed and sputtered along. There were no hotels or restaurants. Behind rolled the Hollywood hills covered in fruit groves and pungent pines. The spot where the Hollywood sign would be erected in 1923 was a thickly wooded hillside overlooking the rural settlement.

In June 1911, Baum's financial problems finally overtook him and he filed for bankruptcy in the Los Angeles District Court. *The Wizard of Oz* musical had stopped touring after nine years on the road, which meant a key source of income had dried up. Baum had left Chicago with significant debt. He had signed a contract in 1910, turning over the copyrights to all his Bowen-Merrill and Bobbs-Merrill books, including *The Wonderful Wizard of Oz*, to a Chicago friend called Harrison Rowntree, who he owed at least $3,000, probably from a loan to pay for the hand-tinted films for the *Fairy-logue and Radio-Plays*. Rowntree made a contract with Baum's other creditors, to pay them off with earnings from these early books. Baum owed a total of over $12,000, the equivalent today of approximately $250,000. Baum's personal assets amounted to a couple of suits, a typewriter, and a few reference books, altogether valued at $85. Maud owned the copyright to Baum's Reilly & Britton books, so all royalties were paid to her. Baum had a small checking account that was topped up when it went into overdraft.

Maud also owned Ozcot and everything in it. She controlled the domestic finances but had no power over her husband's spending on creative projects and travel. In 1911, age fifty-five, Baum faced his later years bankrupt and with a declining income, which had dropped by now by about one-third. Baum had lost the rights to his most famous story, *The Wonderful Wizard of Oz*, and he wouldn't make another cent from this book for the rest of his life.

Humiliating newspaper stories announcing the bankruptcy appeared in Los Angeles and Chicago. "L. Frank Baum is 'Broke'" was the Los Angeles headline; "Chicago Artist Now a Bankrupt," read the *Chicago Tribune*.

While he had been arranging the move west across the country, as his debts spiraled out of control, and overseeing the sale of the Chicago apartment and the Macatawa cottage, Baum had somehow managed to put together five new books, all of which came out with Reilly & Britton in 1911. *The Boy Fortune Hunters in the South Seas* was his last potboiler adventure story for boys published under the pen name Floyd Akers, the big faker. Drawing on memories of his first automobile driving tour of the Southwest in 1904, Baum sent Aunt Jane's nieces on the same journey in *Aunt Jane's Nieces and Uncle John*. Edith Van Dyne wrote cruelly about Native Americans, threading her tale with ethnic stereotypes that are for the most part thankfully missing from Oz. Baum's imaginative fantasy worlds were far less racist than his adventure stories set in this world. There was no place for prejudice in the imagination, this suggested, but it was sadly accommodated in the fallen "real" world.

Baum also launched a new series for older girls and boys, about the adventures of the sixteen-year-old Daring Twins, Phoebe and Phil. Stories were supposed to offer escapism, but here Baum poured his worries into his writing. *The Daring Twins* was a leaden, monochrome tale of how the twins' father's "vast fortune had been swept away and he was heavily in debt." He died in a train wreck and left debts to his orphaned children; Phoebe's "days and nights had been filled with anxieties." The sleepless, anxious characters burdened with financial problems were a reflection of Baum's reality. Perhaps he vented his worries in this book because he managed to write two new fanciful stories, also published in 1911, that took his mind off in new directions. He used the move to California as an opportunity to find a new direction in his writing, to branch out into new imaginary worlds now that Oz was closed off to him. In *The Sea Fairies* he swam through the ocean and in *The Flying Girl* he soared up into the clouds.

He conjured a new child hero called Trot in *The Sea Fairies* and sent her to the bottom of the sea. She acquires a mermaid's tail and gills, and explores the seabed accompanied by the wily old sea dog Cap'n Bill, an amputee forced to retire onto land after losing his leg in an accident at sea, though he says his "hickory" stump is the better of his two legs. Heroic figures in Baum's work must be vulnerable and imperfect, either so-called powerless children or broken adults. Trot and Cap'n Bill adventure across the ocean floor, visiting coral palaces worthy of an underwater world's fair, meet a sea serpent, an aristocratic cod, a bashful octopus, and a grumpy hermit crab. They also meet Zog, a sea devil, a magician who enslaves sailors he rescues from drowning, gives gills, and forces to serve him. *The Sea Fairies* sold reasonably well, but only about half the number of the last Oz book.

There were constraints placed around Baum's imagination when he wrote as the respectable Edith Van Dyne, like a band of iron clamped around his head. Publishers liked to err on the safe side in Baum's writing for older girls, ever concerned that books for girls needed "to pass muster with their parents, teachers and librarians." Baum strained against this and tried to create exciting, perhaps "unladylike," adventures for unconventional girls. He had made it clear in a 1902 article titled "What Children Want," published in the *Chicago Evening Post*, that he didn't believe in the gender stereotypes so often applied to children. "There is little excuse," he asserted, "for giving namby-pamby books to girls." Girls want marvelous adventures as much as boys, he said, and "in many cases," he added, "the boy child is as grossly misunderstood as the girl." He thought that "conservative publishers" were too keen to print "goody-goody" books that lacked excitement for girls and aimed to please "placid parents." In 1911, he pushed the boundaries and invented a new series for girls to be published under Miss Van Dyne's name, starring a young woman who takes to the air as one of the first women to pilot an airplane. Baum attended an aviation meet as research for the book, where he witnessed a pilot crash out of the clouds and die. *The Flying Girl* starred the highly modern Orissa Kane, a working secretary with ambition. In his introduction, Baum championed both the new era of flight and the woman aviator, recognizing women's "competence to operate successfully any aircraft that a man can manage." He went on, "There are twenty women aviators in Europe; . . . in America are thousands of girls ambitious to become aviators."

Orissa navigates an awesome storm and impresses the crowd down below with her sky stunts, swoops, and spiral dips. Her piloting success fuels her ambition and by the end of the book she is determined to fly to Europe and then to Mars.

The book sold moderately well, but Reilly & Britton were anxious about Baum's championing of girls' ambitions, especially in the guise of the respectable Miss Van Dyne. In 1911, few people believed that women could pilot flying machines. In Baum's second book in the series, *The Flying Girl and Her Chum*, the book jacket blurb, written by the publishers, reassured parents that although the story was "thrilling and full of adventure," it was also of "that wholesome type parents are glad to put in the hands of their daughters." But Baum, as a rather excited Edith Van Dyne, wouldn't be censored. He has one man in the story voice the view that "Miss Kane deserves to break her venturesome, unmaidenly neck" for presuming to become an "aviatrix." Orissa declares that when she flies, she has "the most glorious sense of freedom when I'm in the air." A local newspaper in the story compares her to a witch flying on a broomstick.

Sky Island was a follow-up to *The Sea Fairies* that came out in 1912. Trot and Cap'n Bill fly by magic umbrella to an island in the clouds. The island is more vaporous and less concrete than Baum's other worlds, and the characters that inhabit it, parrots, frogs, monarchs, a blue wolf, and several snub-nosed princesses aren't particularly compelling. But the island enforces a dreadful form of punishment that is the most vivid thing about the story. Those who break the laws of Sky Island are butchered in half: "they stand you under a big knife, which drops and slices you neatly in two . . . then they match half of you to another person who has likewise been sliced." You have been "patched." "It's a terrible punishment"; the patched body doesn't know which half is their original self and which isn't. They are left divided, incoherent, working one half against the other. Baum's storytelling mind had been splintered into numerous voices, which often wrote tales against one another—the gung-ho, chauvinistic fortune-hunting stories for boys were morally at odds with the Oz books, for instance. Perhaps Baum was aware of his divided, inconsistent nature.

In *Aunt Jane's Nieces on Vacation*, the Edith Van Dyne serial book for

1912, Baum drew on memories of his years running a newspaper in Aberdeen, South Dakota. He returned once again to the desolate place and the hard years he had spent out on the Great Plains. The drought-ridden prairies were an ongoing, rich source of stories. The *Aunt Jane's Nieces* series continued to sell well, but Baum's imaginative heart was never in it. He was bitterly disappointed that his new fantasy tales published under his own name, set in the sea and the sky, weren't selling as well as the Oz books. He still earned far more than the average American, living on approximately four hundred dollars a month (the equivalent of about seven thousand dollars) but he had become accustomed to the life of a wealthy gentleman; he continued to borrow from his publishers.

He began to think the unthinkable. He would have to buckle down and return to the Land of Oz. But in order to return there, he had to think of a way to find Oz. It was, after all, invisible. In 1913, Reilly & Britton published *The Patchwork Girl of Oz*, Baum's seventh Oz novel. In his introduction, Baum announced that one of his readers had solved the problem of how to locate Oz. A child suggested contacting Dorothy Gale, now resident in Oz, by wireless telegraph. Baum told readers that he had thought this a good idea and "rigged up a high tower" in the backyard, "took lessons in wireless telegraphy and then sent messages into the air," calling out to Dorothy of Oz. Dorothy received the messages and sent back news, which Baum, a "humble writer in the United States of America," wrote up as a story.

But there's another image that shadows the technological idea of communicating with Oz by wireless telegram. Baum was like a spirit medium receiving messages from another plane. Like many authors, Baum understood his writing process, especially the Oz books, as a form of channeling. *The Wonderful Wizard of Oz*, Baum said, had simply "moved right in and took possession" of his mind. The "odd characters are a sort of inspiration," he said, "liable to strike at any time." His Oz tales were "pure inspiration." "I think that sometimes the great Author has a message to get across," he told Edwin Ryland, a friend and Methodist minister in Hollywood, "and he has to use the instrument at hand. I happened to be that medium." Baum told his eldest son that he enjoyed telling stories "because I, too, like to hear about my funny creatures. I never know what strange characters are going to pop into my head when I begin telling a story . . . these characters seem to develop a life of their own. They often surprise me by what they do." In the middle of writing a story, Baum sometimes fell into black moods. He would complain to Maud that "my characters just won't do what I want them to." He learned that in order to finish a story, he had to let go and stop trying to force his characters to obey him; if he just let them do as they pleased, they would find their story themselves. This was a tough lesson, but he came to accept it, even if he didn't fully understand it.

Baum lived and wrote in a culture preoccupied with access to the spirit world through various forms of communication. In Baum's world, spirits spelled out their stories on the alphabetized letters of Ouija boards, so popular at this time you could even buy them through the Sears catalogue. One of the main journals of the spiritualist movement was the *Spiritual Telegraph*, and the taps and raps set off by the Fox sisters in 1848 were remarkably similar to the language of dots and pauses used to send telegrams. Wireless telegraphy was a well-established analogy for communication with the spirit world at the time Baum was writing. The analogy between the writing process and spirit mediumship was at work in Baum's relationship with Oz; he made this explicit in *The Patchwork Girl of Oz* by communicating with Dorothy via wireless telegraphy.

Finding stories through a form of "second sight" or clairvoyance went right back to *The Wonderful Wizard of Oz*. Soon after Dorothy landed with a thump in Oz in that first book, squished the Wicked Witch of the East, and met the Munchkins, the Good Witch of the North sends her on a journey to the Emerald City only after consulting her magic slate:

> She took off her cap and balanced the point on the end of her nose, while she counted "one, two, three" in a solemn voice. At once the cap changed to a slate, on which was written in big, white chalk marks:
> "LET DOROTHY GO TO THE CITY OF EMERALDS."
> The little old woman took the slate from her nose, and, having read the words on it, asked,
> "Is your name Dorothy, my dear?"

The good witch knows less than her trusted spirit slate. She seems to have channeled some advising oracle, who communicates with her through slate writing. The Good Witch of the North was a mirror image of Baum as author, who saw his own story writing as a form of second sight.

The image of the writer as Royal Historian, and behind this as a medium channeling news from the higher plane of Oz, offers some insight into how Baum saw himself. This idea of author as medium served a series of important psychological functions that enabled Baum to write. He had taken so long to fully discover and unleash his storytelling talents because of a cluster of anxieties about the idea of writing for children. When Baum had begun publishing children's books with *Mother Goose* all those years ago in 1897, he had seen himself as a failure, describing his "evident inability to do anything great." He identified with Lewis Carroll in the way the famous English writer felt about his success as a children's writer. "It's said," wrote Baum, "that Dr. Dodgson . . . was so ashamed of having written a children's book that he would only allow it to be published under the penname of Lewis Carroll." This anxiety was shared by other writers Baum admired. In his preface to *The Blue Fairy Book*, Andrew Lang's first collection of tales, he described his job as the "arranging of old wives' fables." "This may not seem a taste to be proud of," Lang added.

In understanding his children's tales as written through channeling, Baum excused himself from responsibility for his stories; he was simply their vehicle, bringing them to the eager ears of children. In understanding his creativity as a form of spirit possession, Baum disowned his imagination. The paradox is that by seeing the writing process as a kind of spirit writing, Baum let his mind breathe and liberated it from overengineering his stories for children (as he so often did in his writing for adults), and created a space for his unconventional instincts, half imagined as spirits, to surface and take hold of his pen.

Andrew Lang lamented in his introduction to *The Green Fairy Book*, which was published in 1892, the lack of new folktales. "There are not many people now," he wrote, "perhaps there are none, who can write really good fairy tales, because they do not believe enough in their own stories." Baum's success was born out of the fact that he believed in Oz, as a story and also as a semi-real place. Thoughtful picked up on this. One wrote in the *Cleveland Leader* back in 1904 that Baum's Oz tales were successful "because Mr. Baum himself believes in his work." A review of *The Patchwork Girl of Oz* in the *St. Louis Times* stated that the book "has an air of earnestness—as if the author really believed in the mythical land he depicts." Baum partially believed in Oz and the characters he discovered there in the same way that he half believed in the astral plane, in his own reincarnation, and in ghosts.

The Patchwork Girl of Oz starred a new character called Scraps, a girl made out of a crazy quilt stitched together from scraps of old clothes. Her eyes are buttons, her teeth are pearls, and her tongue is a strip of scarlet velvet. She was brought to life with a Magic Powder made by a magician who had stirred a bubbling pot for six years with spoons attached to both his hands and his feet. Scraps travels across Oz to the Emerald City. By now, the capital of Oz has become a rather tedious walled city ruled by Ozma, the child ruler. The city is run according to strict laws that all must obey; it's become a wealthy estate where Ozma dresses for dinner each evening and is served by a team of obedient servants. The Emerald City has become stuffy, polite, and rather dull. Scraps, in contrast, is fueled by a joyous spirit of carnivalesque rebellion; she's full of disobedient energy and a wild, vivacious, vibrant, unchecked life force. She leaps and dances, sings and whistles, is physically loose and supple, unlike Ozma. She's naughty, clever, and full of laughter. She lacks vanity, and laughs at her own strange reflection in the mirror, calling herself with a shriek "a gaudy dame." "I'm an Original," she shouts. Scraps is a gently subversive creature directed at Baum's depiction of girls in his serial books. He disliked the tiresome, obedient, prim, and proper girls of many children's books. Girls were so often expected to be sensible and upright. He had stretched the stereotype in the *Flying Girl* books, but all his female characters, even Ozma and Dorothy to an extent, are somewhat trapped in goody-two-shoes personalities. Scraps burst through the constraints on girl characters like a clown leaping out of a cake. She's impolite, extravagant, shocking even. She's "no one's sweetheart, no one's wife / Lacking sense and loving fun." By the end of the book, she's free to "live in the palace (of the Emerald City), or wherever she pleases, and be nobody's servant but her own." One review described the Patchwork Girl as "the most unique character creation from Mr. Baum's pen," who "represents the spirit of the day and age"; she was "quite the liveliest girl ever put into a story."

Kenneth, Baum's youngest son, would marry Dorothy Duce at Ozcot in 1914. In 1916, Dorothy would give birth to Baum's first granddaughter. The proud grandfather would insist that she be called Ozma, and he would give her a locket with her name engraved on it. The child would grow up under the shadow of the name of the ruler of Oz; none of the other children could say it and she was teased and called Cosmos. In response, Ozma decided that she'd prefer to be called Scraps, after the patchwork girl. This was easier to say and to spell, but perhaps another reason the child chose it was because it was much more fun to be the leaping, dancing, humorous, and disobedient Scraps than the rather tiresome, rule-obsessed Ozma.

Scraps represents another spirit of the age outside female liberation, and embodies ideas that were preoccupying many people as the age of machines geared up. Baum created a crazy-quilt character, a homespun, vernacular folk art creature, at just the moment when the American economy was embracing mass production and assembly-line factory systems. In the very same year as Scraps leapt into readers' minds, Henry Ford unveiled the first automated moving assembly line. In 1913, Ford began making the Model T automobile in his Michigan plant through a researched, rationalized assembly-line production method. Before 1913, automobiles were custommade. One of Ford's engineers was inspired by a visit to a meatpacking factory in Chicago, where he saw dead cows butchered in a rational assemblyline process, where a carcass was chopped into recognizable joints as it moved along a conveyor. The engineer reversed the idea and envisaged building an automobile along a moving line where static workers performed the same repetitive task over and over again. The cost of a Model T fell rapidly from $575 to $240, and became affordable to middle-income households. The era of the automobile truly began in 1913.

Ford's assembly line would soon revolutionize the automobile industry, and inspire all kinds of producers to develop rationalized, moving assembly production lines, which reduced the price of many goods and spurred on the mass consumer economy of the twentieth century. But not everybody was happy to see these changes. In Britain, John Ruskin and William Morris had expressed their anxieties in the nineteenth century about what happens to skilled craftsmanship when industrial machine manufacturing takes over. Morris had been appalled by the vision of the technological, mechanized future imagined in Edward Bellamy's 1888 utopian novel, *Looking Backward*, and wrote *News from Nowhere* (1891), which put forward a future where people take pleasure in making things by hand. These ideas developed in America in the late nineteenth century into what became the Arts and Crafts movement. What happened, some asked, to workers who were forced to do repetitive, dull tasks that were unskilled and boring? Wasn't this dehumanizing? Didn't the assembly line in effect turn the human being into a machine? The Arts and Crafts movement valued skilled craftsmanship, unique handcrafted goods, and the satisfaction and meaning of skilled workmanship.

The Arts and Crafts movement had begun in upstate New York, just outside Syracuse, in the 1890s, and many of the most important artists and architects, designers and thinkers in the movement were based in and around Chicago at the time Baum lived there. The architect Frank Lloyd Wright emerged out of this movement; his sister, Maginel Wright Enright, was an artist and she illustrated Baum's *Twinkle Tales* of 1906 and *Policeman Bluejay* of 1907. William Denslow, Baum's first illustrator, had been more closely attached to the movement. He knew Elbert Hubbard well, the founder of the Roycrofters, one of the main Arts and Crafts societies in America, and had spent some time working as an illustrator at the Roycrofters printing house. Hubbard was a fan of Denslow's work, and liked *Father Goose* very much. Baum, therefore, had skirted the edges of the Arts and Crafts movement when he lived in Chicago, and he would have known about its ideas. His fascination with novel technologies and modern machinery put him at odds with the more purist Arts and Crafts supporters, but Oz is full of many of the ideas at work in the movement. In the Oz books, Baum expressed nostalgia for handmade, imperfect things, for the uniqueness of handmade scarecrows and toys, whose wonky imperfections bear the mark of the skilled but imperfect humans who made them.

Many of Baum's earlier non-Oz tales had begun with bored forest immortals that yearn to immerse themselves in the messy, demanding, and exciting business of the human world. Mischievous immortals flee the forest of Burzee for the cities of modern America in the short stories "The Dummy That Lived" and "The Enchanted Types." A bored fairy adopts a human baby she names Claus in Baum's 1902 book *The Life and Adventures of Santa Claus*, and a bored immortal is transformed into a human for one year to experience adventures in *The Enchanted Island of Yew*. The image of paradise became even more troubled in *Policeman Bluejay*, a story published in 1907 under the name Laura Bancroft. Two children are transformed into birds and fly through the forest, discovering the varied and difficult life of wild birds. They live in a nest, meet owls, orioles, jays, and eagles, and experience the horrors of being hunted and preyed upon by other creatures. But deep in the middle of the forest, the child-larks discover the bird fairy kingdom, which is superficially a gorgeous dazzling paradise. At first the children gape in amazement at the silver vines coated with jeweled blossoms and the ever-changing false lighting that makes the silver and gold trees glow. Flowers emit powerful perfumes, and bells tinkle out melodious music. But this paradise soon appears as a ghastly, bewildering, cold fantasy world inhabited by vain birds of paradise that strut and primp themselves and scream for help if a single feather is "disarranged." This is a metal, perfumed, stagey paradise where strutting multicolored creatures admire their iridescent feathers reflected in the trees' silver leaves.

In Oz, unique handmade creatures like the Saw-Horse, the Gump, Jack Pumpkinhead, the Scarecrow, and Scraps are all given life and are highly respected. It's their imperfect, handmade quality that makes these creatures special. In an era of encroaching mass production, uniformity, and machine-made perfection, Oz is nostalgic for the vernacular folk art of scarecrows, handmade toys, jack-o'-lanterns, and painstakingly hand-stitched quilts.

The Patchwork Girl sold far better than any of Baum's other books published since *The Emerald City of Oz*. The appetite for Oz had clearly not abated. Baum now knew that he was trapped in the gilded cage of Oz and that he would have to return there again and again to please his readers, to maintain his fame and keep the money rolling in.

But if he could be forced back to the Land of Oz, he could also return to the stage. The tremendous amount of money he had earned from *The Wizard of Oz* musical lured him back, and in 1912 he set about writing a new Oz show. He had joined the Los Angeles Athletic Club, a social organization for the successful men of the city from the worlds of business and the arts. Through the club he found investors for the show, as well as a composer and producer. At last he was back in show business. *The Tik-Tok Man of Oz* opened at the Majestic Theater in Los Angeles in March 1913. The production included impressive sets and effects: a Metal Monarch's jeweled cavern glowed with electric lights pushed through false gems, and a rainbow was projected onto the stage by refracting light through a glass prism. The show received good reviews and had a successful short run in San Francisco before heading east to Chicago. But when it reached the city on the lake, reviewers recognized it as a pale imitation of the original *Wizard of Oz* musical. In the

Daily News, Amie Leslie advised the people of Chicago to "put on your old gray bonnet with the wild rose on it and bask in fond recollection handsomely dolled up for 1913." It was a blatantly nostalgic imitation of the successful old show. Reviewers weren't convinced by *The Tik-Tok Man of Oz*, but it was a success at the box office.

Baum joined the production on a national tour to put in an appearance as the famous author of Oz. He wanted, no doubt, to grasp the opportunity to smell the greasepaint melting under hot spotlights once again, and see one of his stories come to life on stage before a live audience. As an author of books, especially those written secretly under pen names, Baum was remote from his audience. Here he got to see eyes light up and hear the gasps as one scene magically transformed into another. He continued to enjoy stage illusions, many of which he had designed; he claimed copyright to the transformation scenes. The show, wrote one Los Angeles review, was "such a maze of scenic effects and imagination that it pops and sizzles like a live wire."

The show closed in January 1914, having covered costs and made a moderate profit. But it was clear that, as James O'Donnell Bennett put it in the *Chicago Record-Herald*, the "old style, tinsel extravaganza is dead." The big musical children's story with "pink fairies on a pulley" had grown tired. This "form of folly" was finally worn out.

If the musical extravaganza was truly over, Baum would remake it in the new form of moving pictures, where the magic he had created in his books and onstage would be reborn. He was trapped in Oz, but he would renew his relationship with it by transforming his stories into full-length trick pictures, into amazing illusions that flickered like shadows thrown onto a screen.

Chapter 24

inematic mythmaking began to take over the little suburb of Hollywood before it had the chance to become a distinct place in its own right. The first film was shot there in 1910, the year Hollywood became part of the city of Los Angeles. *In Old California* was about the Mexican era of the state, and was filmed by D. W. Griffith, who would soon become a pioneering film director. The burgeoning eastern movie industry began to move west around 1910, attracted by the quality of the California light, the cheap real estate, good weather, and varied landscape, which could be used to create backdrops of the old Wild West, the Virginia forests where the Civil War was fought, or the Oregon Trail. As soon as cinema began, filmmakers started staging the history of America, conveniently reimagined and mythologized for the twentieth century. By 1910, when Baum moved there, some of the many farms around Hollywood were already being leased and transformed into makeshift film studios; barns were taken over. Cecil B. DeMille shared the barn of his first studio with livestock. The earliest studios in Hollywood primarily made westerns. But the filming spilled over the edges of the basic studio lots and spread out into the growing settlement, which in turn was transformed into a film set. You could turn a corner on a Saturday morning on Hollywood Boulevard to see cowboys on horseback charging down the dusty street, or a bank being held up by a group of actor-robbers. The boundary between real life and the movies was already becoming blurred in Hollywood.

Vaudeville houses and theaters across America were rapidly being transformed into venues for screening films, and nickelodeons, the first cheap cinemas, were springing up all over the country. Americans started going to the movies. Seeing the novel film industry that was growing up all around him, Baum and three friends from the Los Angeles Athletic Club decided to start their own studio to film Baum's stories and transform his famous tales into the latest storytelling medium. Having been bankrupted by his previous escapade in moving pictures, Baum sensibly (for once) didn't invest financially in the project, and he had no spare money to do so. He gave the film rights to the new Oz Film Manufacturing Company for those of his books whose film rights he owned, and agreed to write all the scenarios for the films they would shoot. Baum was the president of the studio; composer Louis F. Gottschalk was vice president. Gottschalk would write original music scores for the films, which would be silent of course, accompanied only by tinkling, pounding, melodious, jingling piano tunes that shaped the audience's emotional response to the action onscreen.

Baum believed that the magic of his modern fairy tales could be perfectly translated onto the screen, using the illusion techniques of trick films pioneered by Méliès. The marvelous effects of electricity and photography, which had fascinated Baum for many years, would now be used to conjure his stories. Baum's films would be waking mechanical daydreams, ignited by the spiritual energy of electricity, which drove the cameras and the projection. Moving pictures were an ideal medium through which Baum could renew and reenergize the Land of Oz.

The Oz Film Manufacturing Company raised $100,000 to invest, and secured a seven-acre lot on Santa Monica Boulevard, between Gower and Lodi Streets, surrounded by large trees and scrub. There was a three-story mansion on the site; the drawing room became a projection and darkroom; the dining room became the studio offices; and the upstairs floors were dressing rooms. A vast stage was built, punctured throughout with hidden trapdoors. Beneath the stage were a series of concrete tunnels. This was the stage machinery that would help create the vital illusions necessary to bring Oz to life onscreen. A low, dark brick wall surrounded the lot and had THE OZ FILM MNFG. CO in large white letters painted along the side. Baum could park his big Hudson sedan along the edge of the wall. His bankruptcy and dramatic fall in income hadn't prevented him from buying a new car.

In the summer of 1914, at age fifty-eight, Baum launched into this demanding project, and the company started filming their first movie, *The*

Patchwork Girl of Oz. Baum put in long days, working at the studios from seven thirty in the morning until eleven at night. "Probably the busiest man of the lot," read one local report on the new studio, "is Frank Baum, the energetic president and writer of the stories." He put on overalls, pulled up his sleeves, and, hat on to shade him from the sun, cigar in mouth, supervised the building of the fabulous sets. The report noted that Baum "personally designs and makes the intricate mechanisms connected with his freak animals." Reporters hadn't yet fully developed a language to describe trick photography, so "freak" was a common catchall term for anything journalists didn't understand. As usual, Baum was behind the design of the film illusions, using his considerable knowledge and experience of photography and stagecraft. A sign posted in the studio read: "The Man Who Says it Can't Be Done May Go to the Office and Get His Pay Check." The company was extremely ambitious and optimistic. They hoped to film all of Baum's fairy tales and were convinced that the movies would be a hit.

Across the Atlantic, the nations of Europe were lining up against each other that summer, and by August 1914, world war had broken out between the Central Powers of Germany and Austria-Hungary, and the Entente Powers of Britain, France, and Russia. The conflict between the groups of European countries soon spread out into their global empires. Ancient divisions erupted and it quickly became barely orchestrated chaos. In 1914, it looked as though the United States would leave the Old World to its old squabbles; this conflict was no matter for the New World, with its mixed population of European immigrants from nations on both sides.

Anxious but relatively untouched by the conflict abroad, the Oz Film Manufacturing Company made three films of Baum's fairy tales. *The Patchwork Girl of Oz* starred Pierre Couderc, a French acrobat and contortionist. The filmmakers didn't think a woman could perform as Scraps in a suitably vivacious, physically supple, and free way. The plot followed that of Baum's Oz book quite closely, but a love interest between two new characters was added to appeal to adults. The second film was *The Magic Cloak of Oz*, which was a version of Baum's 1905 non-Oz fairy tale, *Queen Zixi of Ix*. The third was *His Majesty, the Scarecrow of Oz*, which was a patchwork plot pieced together from numerous Oz books. The film featured a cast of 130 and cost the vast sum of $23,500 to make. A teenage Mildred Harris played Button Bright, a lost boy; she would soon become famous as Charlie Chap-

lin's wife and later the lover of Prince Edward, who would eventually abdi-
cate the British throne to marry the American divorcee, Wallis Simpson. A
young Harold Lloyd had a minor role in one film. The "double jointed rubber comedian" would later become a silent star famous for hanging from the
falling hands of a town clock.

The sets were elaborately painted to create, for example, a regal throne
room at the center of the Emerald City and the Tin Woodman's tin castle.
Costumes were as elaborate. The seamstresses and costumers of the studio
must have been exhausted by the army of wigs and frock coats, diaphanous
fairy gowns and jewel-encrusted crowns they had to produce. It was a dream
dressing-up box of fantasy outfits. Live animals, horses, and even bears
romped through various outdoor scenes, and poor old Fred Woodward was
squeezed into all kinds of hot, stuffy animal costumes to play a lion, a tree-
swinging monkey, a man-size crow, and a half-witted kicking mule.

Many of the scenes were filmed outdoors in the lush open countryside
around Hollywood. The unspoiled, unoccupied Hollywood hills flicker in
the background as Scraps leaps, backflips, and clowns around in the fore-
ground. The forest of Burzee, where *The Magic Cloak* opens, was California
woodland. Gottschalk had a piano wheeled out into the woods, and he
played the music he had written for the scene as thirty dancing girls kept the
beat. They filmed in fields, on riverbanks, near brooks, and in dappled
woodlands, and in so doing reimagined this part of California as Oz. This
was oddly fitting; Hollywood would take on many of the utopian and
disillusioning features of Oz and the Emerald City later in the twentieth
century.

The films were filled with startling illusions. *The Magic Cloak* directly
copied Méliès's famous man-faced moon from his 1902 film *A Trip to the
Moon*; this made explicit that these films were inspired by the pioneering
grand prankster of the cinema of the fantastic. They used techniques much
like the double exposures used to create spirit photography, where semitrans-
parent ghostly images of the dead appeared to float in ordinary drawing
rooms or above tables during a séance. In the opening scene of *The Magic
Cloak*, women in long dresses dance around a loom, spinning the magic cloak
of the title. Their bodies are as transparent as tissue paper; the dark shapes of
the trees are visible through their smiling faces.

Transformation scenes created by using stop-motion photography were a favorite. People froze into marble statues, shrunk to one foot high, and were transformed into animals. Witches appeared out of nowhere and turned into innocent young maidens. Another witch was trapped inside a large can that was then shrunk before the eye to the size of a can of beans. Objects were animated, as when furniture moved about a room of its own accord and a table laid itself—the cutlery, crockery, and glassware stalking across the table into meal position.

In *His Majesty, the Scarecrow of Oz*, an inanimate scarecrow puppet on a pole in a cornfield is suddenly surrounded by corn spirits led by a Native American woman. They chant and dance around him, filling the straw man with the spirit of life. These spirits gradually melt back into the cornfield, and the Scarecrow leaps off his pole. The Tin Woodman chops off a witch's head, which lands in her lap. The headless woman waves her arms around like a headless chicken until she finds and replaces her head, twisting it back onto her neck.

The Magic Cloak included one of the first vision sequences in a movie. A washerwoman who we are told has second sight has a premonition about her husband drowning; a blurry bubble appears near her head as she washes, in which we see her vision flickering. Moving pictures were a kind of collective vision that could portray the interior of the mind, externalizing the inner eye. The fact that the early films were silent added to their dream- or visionlike quality. The filmmakers created a highly innovative illusion scene in *His Majesty, the Scarecrow of Oz* when they filmed the Scarecrow underwater in a river. Reeds and fishes float past him, and he meets a mermaid.

Through his understanding of film technology, Baum was able to fully develop what he had begun in the *Fairylogue and Radio-Plays* debacle, and make visible the ancient magical thinking of folktales.

But the finished films were, in truth, somewhat unwieldy, with large casts and numerous long subplots that barely fitted together. The silent actors exaggerated their gestures, made their facial expressions as unsubtle and explicit as possible, and generally hammed it up to try to explain to baffled audiences what was going on and what it all meant. But Baum had every confidence in his new venture, and believed wholeheartedly that the movies would be taken up by distributors and shown across America. In a letter to Reilly, his publisher, he discussed using the forthcoming films to promote his Oz books, and stated confidently that the Scarecrow film was "a crackerjack, . . . the best trick picture ever made," and it would "probably be shown quite generally throughout the US for six or eight months."

In *The Patchwork Girl of Oz*, Scraps and her traveling companions come across a high wall that blocks their way, but it turns out the wall is an illusion that you can walk straight through if you refuse to believe it exists. This was often Baum's attitude to obstacles; he simply refused to see them and optimistically walked toward them in denial of their existence.

Frank Jr. was sent to New York City to open an office on West 42nd Street, to represent the company and secure a distributor. *The Patchwork Girl* was taken up by the Paramount Picture Company and released all over the country. In New York City it was shown at the newly opened Strand, a 3,000-seat ornate theater on Broadway. Reviews were excellent, lauding the film as "the greatest production ever shown on the screen," an "original and rich" "photo-extravaganza," full of strange "happenings that will leave the layman dumbfounded." The film was shown at the Iris Theatre in Topeka, Kansas, in Dorothy Gale's home state. The Gale homestead was said to be on the outskirts of Topeka. Audiences were thrilled by the film. "To think," wrote a local woman to the theater proprietors, "of the children of Topeka who were not taken to see it makes my heart ache." Walt Disney was thirteen years old and living in Kansas City in 1914; he was an avid reader of the Oz books as well as an eager moviegoer.

But numerous unofficial reports came in from theaters that adults had asked for their money back. They didn't want to pay to see a children's story; box office takings were very poor, despite the glowing reviews. Adults, it seemed, weren't prepared to pay to watch fairy tales. Distributors were put off. The company couldn't find distributors for *The Magic Cloak* or *His Majesty, the Scarecrow of Oz*. Paramount rejected them both. The Oz Film Manufacturing Company decided to change direction and make a film for adults. Baum and his associates set about making a film of his 1908 anonymous adult novel, *The Last Egyptian*. This melodramatic tale of ancient kings of Egypt, tombs, and treasure chambers was completed in October 1914. The Alliance Company distributed it. Reviews were reasonable and the film was moderately successful. Alliance then seems to have forced the Oz Film Manufacturing Company into an agreement in which the distributors took control of choosing which stories the studio made into films. "This will eliminate," read a report in *Moving Picture News,* "the making of productions for which there are no markets," meaning the fairy tale. The "pulse of public demand" was not beating for moving pictures of folktale magic. The Oz Film Manufacturing Company was simply ahead of its time. Baum rightly saw that cinema was the natural new medium for telling fairy tales—this modern technology was ideally suited to this most ancient of storytelling.

Baum had worked like a dog on the films. Their failure to reach an audience made him extremely distraught. By December 1914, he was no longer the president of the film company, which limped on, made a couple more films, but then began to rent the studio to other filmmakers. He wrote to Maud, expressing his discouragement while on a trip to meet eastern film distributors. She wrote a supportive letter back, to which he responded, thanking his "darling old Sweetheart," for her "heart-warming" letter that had kept "me happy for many days." "Yes, sweetheart," he wrote, "nothing can dismay us while we have each other and while the old love, which has lasted and grown stronger during all these years remains to comfort and encourage us." He signed the letter, "Always your lover, Frank."

In the summer of 1915, the company finally closed. Baum's body responded violently to the stress and overwork. He developed pains in his gall bladder, tic douloureux, and angina pectoris. Tic douloureux, also known as trigeminal neuralgia, sent stabbing, shooting pains across one side of his face like an electric shock. The awful pains were alleviated by morphine administered by a doctor who came to Ozcot. But Baum tried to minimize his intake of morphine because he knew it was highly addictive and that the more he used it, the less effective it became. Instead, he sought the help of patent medicines, mysterious potions that promised healing powers they rarely delivered. In pain, Baum was susceptible to the extravagant claims of advertisements for these quack medicines, and he would try anything. Angina pectoris gave him severe chest pain caused by a lack of blood and oxygen to the heart. He experienced burning sensations, a feeling of being crushed, of intense pressure on his chest. Both tic douloureux and angina are much exacerbated by stress. He would on occasion be bent over in pain and forced to crawl along the floor in agony, tears rolling down his cheeks.

In photographs taken at this time, Baum has clearly aged considerably. His hair and eyebrows are streaked with gray. His moustache is less bushy and is graying at the sides. He wears glasses and his cheeks are creased with fine lines. The right side of his face has fallen slightly after the effects of facial paralysis years earlier and the recent episodes of tic douloureux.

Baum's income continued to be unsatisfactory. The financial strain on him sometimes disturbed what was generally a good, cooperative relationship with his publishers. Reilly or Britton might politely suggest a few alterations to a manuscript, adding, for instance, "far be it from me to suggest any way to make a change" or "it is a shame to make a suggestion, but . . ." Baum would usually respond generously. "Sometimes, my dear Britt," he wrote in October 1912, "you are always right." He discussed book length and titles with them and usually followed their advice willingly and with characteristic humor. But his cooperative nature was shaken as financial worries and frustrations at the failure of his films and other projects closed in around him. Since the outbreak of war, book sales had generally declined. His frustration mounted after 1914, when cheap editions of Baum's books under the lost Bowen-Merrill and Bobbs-Merrill copyrights appeared. M. A. Donohue and Co. began republishing cheap editions of Baum's books without warning Reilly, Britton, and Baum. This forced the price of Baum's new titles down, to compete with a market flooded with his books. Absurdly, Baum was being forced to compete with his own work.

Reilly & Britton occasionally took on the role of cautiously censoring Baum. They objected to a short Oz story Baum wrote for a 1913 promotional series called *The Little Wizard Stories of Oz*, in which Tik-Tok seems to be killed by the Nome King and then reappears because in fact the machine can't be destroyed. But the evil king thinks he sees a ghost. "Ghosts are not for the very little tots that this story will reach," wrote Reilly. He feared that violence and apparitions would contradict "our slogan that 'no Baum story ever sent a child to bed to troubled dreams.'" Baum responded that Reilly had missed his "occult humor" in the suggestion that a metal clockwork machine could have a ghost. The publishers had deemed a chapter of *The Patchwork Girl of Oz* entitled "The Garden of Meats" too violent for an Oz book and asked that Baum cut it. The episode seems to have featured an assorted vegetable tribe who grow meat people in their gardens to be eaten. A big leafy root crop gardener circulates, shoving the spout of a watering can into the mouths of the children's human heads that jut out of the ground and wave about on the end of stalks; he force-feeds the children like foie gras geese. Reilly & Britton thought these meat-eating vegetables to be out of "harmony with your other fairy tales." Baum agreed to remove the chapter, but this showed that intuitively Baum imagined danger, threats, and violence in his stories; he knew these were essential features of the best fairy tales.

Baum's publishers continued to censor his depiction of girls. The slightly anxious publisher's blurb on the jacket of *The Flying Girl and Her Chum* showed how close to the wind the new series had sailed. It's no surprise it was discontinued. The publishers suggested in 1915 that after ten volumes, the *Aunt Jane's Nieces* series should be replaced with a new Edith Van Dyne book. Baum rapidly penned a new adventure story for girls in the fall of 1915, despite the failure of the film company and his stress-induced health problems, and he sent it off in December. He tried something new and wrote a story showing the development of a mischievous twelve-year-old girl into a thoughtful fourteen-year-old. The publishers rejected it because they thought the girl too boisterous. Baum was forced to start again, and in his new version, the main character, Mary Louise, is age fifteen and already thoughtful and sensible, almost a prig. "She possessed," wrote Edith Van Dyne, "charming manners." The whole voice of the book was priggish in fact, unlike the natural, direct style of Baum's Oz books. In the voice of Edith Van Dyne, characters "vacate" rooms rather than leave them, "converse" rather than talk, and "enact" things rather than simply doing them, like a pupil with pretensions from Aunt Kate's elocution lessons all those years ago in Syracuse. *Mary Louise* became the first in a new series of mystery detective stories for girls penned by the respectable Miss Van Dyne. Mary Louise was the opposite of Scraps, the vivacious, disobedient patchwork girl. In the subsequent Mary Louise books, however, Baum couldn't help himself, and he introduced Josie O'Gorman, who was far more adventurous, risk-taking, and disobedient.

Baum's unique fantasy films had failed to find an audience and his body was in painful decline. But his Oz books brought him renewed prestige. He pasted into his scrapbook an item announcing that the "International Fairy and Folklore Society, with headquarters at Bayreuth, Germany, has honored Mr. L. Frank Baum with its 'Medal of Distinction,' in recognition of his fairy tales of the 'Land of Oz.'" The article went on to explain that it "is but the second time in fifty years that the medal has been awarded, the last previous recipient having been Rev. Charles L. Dodgson, better known as 'Lewis Carroll.'" It must have swelled Baum's head to be placed alongside the famous author of the Alice books. From 1915, Baum retreated to Ozcot, put on his old gardening clothes, and stepped out into the crowded flower beds, a notebook and pencil in hand, to see what further stories he could find there.

Chapter 25

here were no more films or theater productions to work on, except amusing amateur productions with the Uplifters, a society Baum formed within the Los Angeles Athletic Club with a group of fellow pranksters who enjoyed putting on shows. For one production, Baum dressed up as a cowboy and danced on a table in knee-length boots, dodging invisible bullets. He also banged the big bass drum in the club's orchestra. From 1915, he established a stately rhythm of writing an Oz book annually and the odd serial story for girls as Edith Van Dyne.

His writing became inextricably linked to gardening at Ozcot, the process of tending and pruning plants mapped onto the process of telling stories. This looped back to the old idea that fairy tales were an organic outcrop of the imagination. Baum would rise at eight and head out into the garden in work clothes after a hearty breakfast and several cups of sweet coffee. The large garden at Ozcot was lined with beds, each packed with a single variety of flower: iris, poppy, aster, columbine, marigold, snapdragon, dahlia, and chrysanthemum dominated the garden, but one summer when the garden was in full bloom, Baum counted forty-six varieties of flowers. The heady scent must have been almost overwhelming. Carp swam around in the circular pond covered with lilies; a large circular aviary with a fountain at its center was filled with forty songbirds so tame that Baum could feed them seeds from his hands and even from his open mouth. A summerhouse covered with vines offered shade in the middle of the garden. There was a chicken coop to one side, a remnant from Baum's past. If he wanted to know the time, he could always wander over to the copper sundial that stood on a

stone pedestal, its face to the sun. Baum had made it himself in 1912, scoring the Roman numerals into a circle and working out exactly where to place
it in the garden so that the pin would cast a long straight shadow across the
correct time.

He would take a notebook out into the garden and find a spot to sit and
write among the rosebushes, in the summerhouse, or in a chair next to the
pond, the fishes flicking through the water like his thoughts. The garden was
edged on two sides by a six-foot-high redwood fence, and behind one length
of it was a film studio. The studio asked Baum's permission to use the rear
side of the fence as a backdrop for shooting. While Baum wrote stories set
in Oz, on the other side of the fence were filmed painted scenes of who
knows where.

When he reached a natural pause or got stuck, he would put down his
notebook and tend the garden. He took as many pains over his gardening as
he did over any other of his projects. He mixed his own fertilizer using a
secret recipe, and in the summer heat he carefully placed cheesecloth over
flowers to protect them from the harsh sun. He even entered flower compe-
titions, and won twenty-one cups in total, gaining a reputation throughout
California as an expert in growing dahlias. Digging about in the garden, hat
on and cigar in mouth, strangely mirrored Baum's writing process, in which
he dug about in the turf of his own mind. And for Baum, both writing and
gardening were an essentially intuitive process.

This life in Hollywood wasn't perfect, however. It wasn't a sparkling
luxury like all those expensive winters at the Hotel Del Coronado. In an
article published in a local magazine in 1915, Baum explained that life in
Hollywood wasn't "an Eden or a fairyland." It wasn't "utopian . . . it has its
drawbacks. . . . I can grow beautiful flowers in my garden," he said, "but I
have to fight slugs and cut-worms and aphids and their like continually."
The wealthy residents of Pasadena looked down on the humdrum folk of
Hollywood, he said, because "we haven't any gilded palaces" back East. Hollywood offered a simple life in a gorgeous climate. The winds from the
Pacific meant Baum had to sleep under blankets even at the height of summer, which was a blessing after the years of stifling Chicago summers. At last
Baum had found a home that wasn't an exotic fairyland accessible only to
the super-rich, a group to which he no longer belonged. It was a real place,
full of natural imperfections.

The success of *The Patchwork Girl of Oz* in 1913 made it clear to Baum that he had to go back to Oz. In 1914, *Tik-Tok of Oz* was published. He and the publishers decided to include in it a map not only of Oz but of the entire extensive regions of Baum's imaginative continent. This double-page map showed Oz at the center, surrounded by the wastelands of the Impassable Desert, the Deadly Desert, the Great Sandy Waste, and the Shifting Sands. Beyond these were lands from Baum's other Oz books and places from his non-Oz stories. The Kingdom of Ix was to the north of Oz, and the forest of Burzee was to the south of the Munchkin country, on the very edge of the map. This position suited the archetypal forest that hovered permanently at the edge of Baum's thinking, at the corner of his inner eye.

This map of Baum's inner worlds clarified where the different places he took his readers were positioned in relation to each other, but it also raised all kinds of problems. How could the Vegetable Kingdom and the country of the Gargoyles (from *Dorothy and the Wizard in Oz*), which were beneath the surface of the earth in California, be located alongside the Deadly Desert that backs onto Oz? Unless of course Oz was located somehow beneath the earth's crust, an underneath place below the surface of this world. Perhaps this was a good metaphorical description of the place the Land of Oz had come to occupy in people's minds, as somewhere beneath the surface of their conscious minds.

Many of the territories on the 1914 map had not yet appeared in Baum's stories. So the map also signaled the direction for the future. It was a geography of future stories as well as a map of past tales.

Some readers had noticed that many of the Oz books were inconsistent, and created contradictory ideas about the nature of Oz. But in truth, these inconsistencies contributed to the power of Oz. In its inconsistencies, Oz was shown to be like the imagination itself, liquid, more like water than rock. Once a newly discovered land has been mapped and charted by cartographers, it's somehow caught, trapped, and anchored. With this 1914 map, Oz and its surrounding story places seemed to become part of the known and tamed world. This pushed out the idea that Oz was a vast and unsettled wilderness, which was at the heart of its appeal. The one good thing about the map was that it didn't contain a measure of scale, so it was impossible to tell the size of Oz and its surrounding kingdoms; Baum could take advantage of this oversight.

In *Tik-Tok of Oz*, the United States continues to maintain contact with Oz via wireless telegraph, so there was an ongoing sense that Oz was out there but inaccessible. The only way to get to Oz, as ever, is through some kind of traumatic crisis, and in this new book, another American girl, Betsy Bobbin this time, finds herself marooned in Oz after a shipwreck. Ozma continues to rule in the tedious Emerald City, and the Wizard has now become powerful and wise. Baum knew that stories couldn't be found in such a tame and static place, so he pushed out to the lesser-known, wilder edges of Oz, where he found interesting new creatures and lands where Ozma's laws have not yet reached.

In one of these lesser-known regions of Oz, Betsy discovers trees that blossom and fruit with storybooks; if they're picked before they're ripe, the tale doesn't make sense. This was another image of Baum's sense that stories are organic.

In 1915, *The Scarecrow of Oz* was published, which Baum developed from the film *His Majesty, the Scarecrow of Oz*. Following the advice of his insistent little fans, Baum sent Trot and Cap'n Bill from *The Sea Fairies* and *Sky Island* to Oz via a whirlpool. They land on an island and discover a miserable old man called Pessim, the Observer. Pessim, the lonely worrywart on the island, was clearly a tribute of sorts to Baum's first artistic collaborator, William Wallace Denslow, the odd man who had bought an island, and fallen out so spectacularly with Baum. Denslow died in 1915 and Baum was at first misinformed that it was suicide.

Baum continued to conjure arresting new characters in *The Scarecrow of Oz*, such as the Mountain Ear, a highly sensitized man whose skin is covered in bumps that enable him to detect the tiniest of tremors on top of the mountain he guards. His job is to listen attentively for quakes and eruptions. The 1906 San Francisco earthquake and the volcanoes Baum had witnessed in Europe haunted his understanding of landscapes still; the ground was unstable, unpredictable, shifting and unreliable no matter how carefully you mapped it.

Sales of these new Oz books were initially disappointing. The publishers said they had discussed the issue with their staff at the publishing house and gently suggested that perhaps Baum's latest books were lacking in the "youthful viewpoint" of his previous stories. Uncharacteristically, Baum erupted. His financial worries and physical pains must have torn at his nerves. "I honestly believe," he wrote to Reilly in early 1916, "I am doing right now the very best work of my career." He cited the hundreds of letters he received from children clamoring for more, and remarked: "As against the judgment evidenced in these letters, the judgment of your 'staff' doesn't amount to a row of pins. You are not obliged to print my books, if you do not wish to," he went on, "but let me ask you where you could find another juvenile author as dear to the American children as Baum." The author was now referring to himself in the third person.

Looking for an explanation for his poor sales, Baum searched for someone to blame other than himself, so he wouldn't have to face the reality of his crumbling body and his still vivid but flagging imagination. It was his illustrator, Neill's fault, he decided. He wrote to Reilly asking for a new illustrator, "who could infuse new life and a spirit of fun into the Oz characters, which in Mr. Neill's hands are now perfunctory and listless." But then he retracted, admitting to Reilly that "perhaps no author is ever satisfied with his illustrator, and I see my characters and incidents so differently from the artist that I fail to appreciate his talent." He might have been projecting his fears about his own writing onto Neill's work, which was still full of energy and style.

The Oz book for 1916 was a reworking of a manuscript Baum had written in 1905 but never published. In *Rinkitink in Oz*, Baum grafted onto Oz an old story set in an island kingdom, starring a boy hero and a string of magic pearls, placing the islands on the very edge of his imaginary continent. Perhaps reworking this story gave the tired author some respite from thinking up a new one.

In 1916, Baum's income improved and he approached the next Oz book with renewed vigor. *The Lost Princess of Oz* came out in 1917 and was dedicated to his baby granddaughter, Ozma. In his introduction, he made a statement about what he saw as the importance of stories. "Imagination" he declared, "led Franklin to discover electricity. Imagination has given us the steam engine, the telephone, the talking-machine and the automobile, for these things had to be dreamed of before they became realities. So I believe that dreams—day dreams, you know, with your eyes wide open and your brain-machinery whizzing—are likely to lead to the betterment of the world. The imaginative child will become the imaginative man or woman most apt to create, to invent." He added, "A prominent educator tells me that fairy tales are of untold value in developing imagination in the young. I believe it." His stories were kinds of daydreams, not those one had when asleep. Machines had come to dominate Baum's thinking so much that thinking was now "brain-machinery whizzing."

In *The Lost Princess of Oz*, the patchwork girl was back. She climbs trees, leaps, and shouts through the book. But Oz has now become a bureaucratic Big Brother nightmare. Ozma's Magic Picture sees everything that takes place at the very moment it's happening, like a giant satellite spy system. And a magic pen writes a short summary in the Book of Records of everything that happens in Oz.

Beyond the Emerald City, Oz has become an amusement park fairground, stationary, mapped, and known but full of rip-roaring rides. Permanent amusement parks as opposed to traveling fairs had begun to appear across the United States in the early twentieth century, inspired by the Chicago World's Fair of 1893. Enabled by electricity and developments in engineering, Ferris wheels, roller coasters, and water slides sprang up everywhere. The early 1900s were the golden age of amusement parks, which were often called White City, Dreamland, or Lunar Park. The scream-machine roller coasters were usually called the Twister, the Cyclone, or the Whirlwind.

These parks and their mechanical rides enabled children to escape their hometowns momentarily, to go on a high-speed adventure that shook up their bodies and minds in ways travel was supposed to. The roller coaster was a rollicking train journey that didn't take you anywhere. It was the illusion of escape, and a miniature imitation of the road trip beginning to take place across the United States as automobiles became more affordable and roads improved. In *The Scarecrow of Oz*, the characters ride on the back of Quox the Dragon, descending through a tunnel in the earth shooting right through and out the other side. Neill drew Quox quite explicitly as a roller coaster. In *The Lost Princess of Oz*, the static mapped land is animated when Baum turns unknown mountainous regions into spinning rubber hills. Scraps and others are spun and bounced about, flung into the air to land and bounce up again, disoriented but laughing.

In *The Lost Princess of Oz*, Baum also included a favorite illusion ride of the nineteenth- and twentieth-century fairground called the Haunted Swing. Scraps, the Wizard, and their fellow traveling companions are trapped by an

evil shoemaker in a grand domed circular hall, which, to their surprise, starts
to slowly tip sideways, slanting more and more until they slide down the wall
and tumble onto the circular ceiling that has revolved to become the floor.
They bump up against the big glass chandelier that juts up from the center
of what had been the ceiling. This spinning room was based on the popular
illusion ride in which people entered what appeared to be an ordinary room,
with chairs, tables, rugs, and pictures hung upon the wall. A metal pole
stretched across the middle of the room and a large swing was suspended
from it. Visitors climbed aboard and were swung back and forth as the swing
gradually increased in height and speed. Then slowly, the room began to
revolve around the swing, increasing in speed as the swing moved higher and
higher. Eventually the room revolved right around; the pictures hung on the
wall, the rugs and the ornaments were all nailed down. The room was, in
fact, a box hanging from an external frame with a swing inside it. The people
in the swing would have the weird sensation that they were revolving right
over the bar, 360 degrees, whizzing upside down. The Haunted Swing was
a genteel way of losing grip of your senses, of taking part in a simple but
extremely effective illusion.

If Baum had inadvertently made Oz static by mapping it, he shook it
up again by reimagining it as an amusement park full of fantasy rides and
strange illusions.

In 1915, the neutral position of the United States in World War I shifted
dramatically when in May, the *Lusitania*, a vast British ocean liner, was
torpedoed by German U-boats off the coast of Ireland. It sank in eighteen
minutes, and more than a thousand people drowned, many of them American citizens, including Albert Hubbard, the founder of the Arts and Crafts
organization the Roycrofters. News that Germany was conspiring with
Mexico with the aim of returning Texas to Mexican rule further damaged
German-American relations. In April 1917, President Wilson declared war
on Germany, against the wishes of many Americans. The U.S. government
sent just over four million troops to Europe, mainly to the Western Front.
Baum's sons Frank Jr. and Rob joined up; both were officers. Frank was soon
sent to France. The decision to join the conflict had an enormous impact
on German Americans, and unleashed a cultural war against all things German. Sauerkraut was renamed "liberty cabbage." Baum reflected on this in
his Edith Van Dyne book for 1918, *Mary Louise and the Liberty Girls*. This

was a reworking of *Aunt Jane's Nieces in the Red Cross*, which had first been published in 1915. In this first version, the tone had been against American involvement in the war. But now Baum expressed his support for the American troops and also highlighted the plight of German Americans forced to defend themselves against accusations of being anti-American. Baum didn't stint from showing the brutalities of war, and included a man who has his right arm amputated. As Edith Van Dyne, he wrote in his introduction: "I wish I might have depicted more gently the scenes in hospital and on the battlefield, but it is well that my girl readers should realize something of the horrors of war."

The full horror of what was being done to men's bodies and minds on the Western Front in trench warfare had come to light by 1917, when Baum wrote the next Oz book, *The Tin Woodman of Oz*. When the book was published in 1918, *Publishers Weekly* suggested that "there is one country where no shadow has been cast by the war; it is the Land of Oz." In fact the war had penetrated Oz in Baum's preoccupation with bodily dismemberment and amputation. This story is haunted by the specter of the broken bodies of soldiers, and the psychological devastation left even after men had been stitched back together. The Tin Woodman meets his "tin twin," a soldier who was also chopped to pieces, like him, by the Wicked Witch's curse. He too was remade by the tinsmith. They discover that their dismembered body parts have been sewn together to create a new, patchwork man of flesh and blood, a kind of Frankenstein's monster. The new, unhappy man is not himself in any part, and is yet another image of a divided self, like the patched people of Sky Island.

The Tin Woodman finds his old human head in a box, and talks to it, wondering where his true self lies. He concludes that he prefers to be made of tin, because "nothing can hurt" you.

Baum's niece, Matilda Gage, now a young woman, had stayed at Ozcot for several months in 1916. The little girl who had grown up in Aberdeen, South Dakota, out on the prairie, was like a daughter to Frank and Maud. After she returned to Aberdeen, Baum kept up a lively correspondence with her, mostly about growing flowers. He sent her bulbs and extremely detailed instructions about how to plant and tend them. But the hot summer prairie wind ruined Matilda's flowers, and Baum wrote to sympathize and was reminded of the harsh plains weather, in "that God blasted country you live

in." "Why not shake South Dakota and come out here to live," he asked
Matilda. Since moving to California, he was constantly asking Maud's siblings, Clarkson, Julia, and Helen, who had all stayed on the Great Plains, to
come to join him in the far West, to leave the wind-bullied prairie. Baum
kept returning to his memories of the landscape there. In searching for
wilder regions beyond the mapped outlines of Oz, Baum imagined places
through his memories of the western Great Plains. In *The Tin Woodman of
Oz*, he discovered Mount Munch in a far-flung region of the Munchkin
country, a flat-topped mountain jutting straight up out of the plains, based
on the Devils Tower in Wyoming, near the border with South Dakota.

Baum's patent medicines and strict diet did little to heal his body. By the
beginning of 1918, he finally realized he would have to go into the hospital
for an operation to remove his gall bladder. He borrowed three hundred fifty
dollars from his publishers to pay for the treatment and aftercare. Sales of his
books were up, so considerable royalties would be forthcoming. Despite
his illness, Baum had continued to work on new Oz stories, mentally traveling to a sunny land where nobody ever ages, falls ill, or dies. His heart was
under such strain that he knew the operation was a serious risk. Before entering the hospital in February 1918, he wrote a short will, leaving everything
to Maud; because she owned Ozcot and royalties, he was worth only one
thousand dollars. He wrote to Reilly, "I want to tell you, for your complete
protection, that I have finished the second Oz book . . . which will give you
a manuscript for 1919 and 1920." These were in a "safety deposit box . . . in
case anything happens to me." He stayed in the hospital for five weeks after
the operation, before returning to Ozcot, where he was bedridden. There he
lay in his brass bed, with ornate metal flowers curling around upon themselves behind his head.

If they came to him in the night, he would scribble down ideas for stories on the pale striped wallpaper on the wall beside his bed. His stories often
surfaced in hypnagogic states. Maud slept in an identical brass bed a foot
from Baum's. The midnight scribbling must have sounded like scuttling
mice, or worse, the scratching of the deathwatch beetle.

By April, Baum was able to sit up. He chewed cigars because there was
no way now that he could smoke. He worked in bed, reading letters from
his young fans that continued to pour in. "Mamma is so glad and proud,"

wrote Paul Lawrence, "that we have at last an American writer of fairy tales." Betty Hungerford wrote she "liked the Patchwork Girl best of all." "I wish you will write some more Oz books," wrote Belle Palmer from New Orleans, "I can't ever get tired of them." "I love your Oz books so," wrote Bobbie Rodge, "(age 11) (I'm a girl)," "I can read them over and over." "I think they are the bestest best kind of best books," wrote Florence.

Baum was particularly moved by a letter from a woman whose son had recently died. He was rescued from drowning but became gravely ill; he lived for a few days before tragically passing away; he was a fan of the Oz books and his last words were "princess of Oz."

Baum's fans continued to make demands. "Won't you please write another book about Oz? . . . you will, won't you?" pleaded Bobbie; Jean Burritt from Los Angeles wrote to Baum "to ask you if you will write another about Betsy Bobbin in time for my birthday which is on January 11th." Many little girls named Dorothy wrote to him. "My name is Dorothy, too," wrote one; "I would like very much to have you write another story about Dorothy. You don't have to make it very long and, of course, you don't have to do it if you don't want to." "We had a cyclone here once," she added, "but I wasn't born." Fans made story suggestions, asking Baum, for instance, to "tell more about" Dorothy, to "please write more about the Scarecrow and the Tin Woodman," to "please ask Ozma to let Trot and Cap'n Bill come to Oz." "I think you ought to have Dorothy go fishing and fall in the water and go down down and in some way reach the land of Oz," wrote Elizabeth Fowler from Minneapolis. The fans inundated Baum with questions such as "could you tell me which has the most power—Ozma or Glinda?," and they pleaded with him to reply. William Beard from New Jersey wrote asking Baum to "make arrangements with Glinda the Good Or Ozma to let the family and me make a visit to the Land of Oz." "And if there isn't any Land of Oz, let me know," he added. William explained that he wanted "to go to the Land of Oz," "to get courage." He signed off, adding, "I will pay for the wireless message."

Baum tried to answer as many letters as he could, writing short notes on personal notepaper headed "Oz." He also wrote to Frank Jr. out fighting in France, and said, "I continually pray for a speedy end to this terrible war and your safe return." So many fathers were losing their sons in the brutal conflict; Baum must have feared the worse.

He managed to sit up and work on his manuscripts in bed, redrafting the two Oz tales he had kept in a safety deposit box when he was in the hospital. His breathing difficult, his body broken, he returned to Oz and to the wild regions of Mount Munch, the remote stone hill based on the Devils Tower in Wyoming, and he found there a mischievous Munchkin boy who knows the magic word that will transform one thing into anything else. This Oz book is filled with so many transformed creatures that it's hard to remember who's who or what's what. The idea of being able to reach out beyond the body and be transformed into something else must have deeply appealed to Baum, who had now become, at only age sixty-two, a still-vivacious spirit trapped inside a dying animal.

Despite his health, he finished the manuscript of what would be titled *The Magic of Oz* in October 1918. He immediately set about revising the second Oz manuscript. War now reached even the land of Oz. Glinda, Ozma, Dorothy, and all the familiar characters from Oz travel to a remote corner of the land to try to broker peace between the Flatheads (the name of a western Native American tribe), a mountain-dwelling "tribe" who carry their brains in cans in their pockets, and the Skeezers, who live under a giant glass dome on an island in the middle of a lake. The Skeezers' glass dome can sink beneath the surface of the lake, and they travel about under water in submarines, like German U-boats. Baum managed to secure peace in Oz by defeating the vain and ruthless rulers of the Flatheads and the Skeezers, and restoring order. Ozma is established as the rightful ruler of the whole of Oz, a benevolent dictator or mother ruler.

In November 1918, Germany was defeated. The male population of Europe was devastated. Millions were dead, millions more were physically and mentally maimed by a conflict fought with advanced technological weaponry never seen or experienced before, such as tanks, machine guns, and fighter planes. America lost 116,000 men, a small number compared to the scale of other nations' losses, but the impact of the involvement of the United States was considerable. America emerged as a major power on the world stage.

Baum's health rapidly declined at the end of 1918 and in early 1919; he remained bedridden. On May 5, 1919, he lapsed into unconsciousness. On May 6, he resurfaced. He and Maud talked quietly together as the palm fronds of the big tree that Baum had planted waved back and forth outside the window. Baum told Maud that she was the only woman he had ever loved, and he asked that she never leave Ozcot; it reassured him to think that she would live on in the house after his death. He whispered something into her ear about crossing shifting sands, and then he died.

Maud was inconsolable. She wrote to her sister Helen: "he told me many times I was the only one he ever loved," she wrote. "He hated to die, did not want to leave me, said he was never happy without me, but it was better he should go first if it had to be, for I doubt if he could have got along without me." "It is all so sad," she went on, "and I am so forlorn and alone. For nearly thirty-seven years we had been everything to each other, we were happy, and now I am alone, to face the world alone."

Baum was buried in Forest Lawn Cemetery in Glendale, not far from Hollywood, in a plot he had chosen. This was a fashionable new cemetery called a memorial park, opened in 1906, with the aim of creating a multidenominational, ideal landscape, "dedicated to a joyous life after death." The three-hundred-acre park was a vast manicured lawn dotted with reproductions of European Renaissance sculptures, a "sunshine place, . . . filled with towering trees, sweeping lawns, splashing fountains, beautiful statuary," as one of its founders put it. Forest Lawn sounded remarkably like the grounds of the Emerald City. The dedicated children's area was called Slumberland.

Edwin Ryland, the Methodist minister and friend of Baum's, officiated at the funeral, which was attended by family and Baum's fellow Uplifters. A friend, possibly Ryland, wrote a eulogy for Baum that was published in a Los Angeles magazine soon after the funeral. Baum had given, it read, "wings to the imagination and flame to thought." "He was not a churchman," it went on, "but he lived the religion of delight . . . He had no creed, but possessed abundant spirituality; with him the spiritual was a living experience."

Baum was born in the same year as Sigmund Freud, 1856, and he died on Freud's sixty-third birthday, the birthday of the man who was making dreams the key to the twentieth-century mind. On the 1914 map of Oz, Baum had included a small country on the edge of the Deadly Desert that borders Oz called the Kingdom of Dreams. But he had never mentioned such a place in any of his stories. He had made efforts to show his readers that his modern folktales weren't simply dreams. Perhaps this small region of the continent of his imagination was a distinct area where dreams were cordoned off, kept in their place so that it was clear that the rest of Baum's interior landscape was something more than a patchwork of dreamscapes; stories should be freed, this seemed to say, and allowed out beyond the captivity of dreams.

The map also showed a lake on the edge of the Emerald City. This too never appeared in any of Baum's books. His imagination had first come to life on the edge of the Finger Lakes; Lake Michigan had irrigated it and helped Baum discover the Land of Oz. Perhaps it was only right that Oz should have a lake at its center; it was the circle of water at the heart of things that didn't need to be mentioned. Looking down at the map, the lake looks both like an eye staring out at the strange countries that surround it, and like a well, a deep and bottomless source of sustenance.

The Afterlife

rom 1919 until her death in 1953, Maud lived alone in Ozcot. Perhaps she wasn't too lonely at first because, for a while after Baum died, she occasionally saw him sitting in his favorite chair, smoking a cigar; she found this to be a great comfort. For a year after Baum's death, letters from his child fans continued to flood in, but Maud couldn't bring herself to write back and inform them that he was dead, so she pretended to be him and replied on his headed notepaper, signing off with a good forgery of her husband's signature. She soon had a rubber stamp of Baum's signature made so she could continue to pen replies to children, posing as the creator of Oz. Perhaps she imagined Baum's spirit moving her pen.

A month after Baum died, *The Magic of Oz* was published and no mention was made in the book of the author's death. Baum had written an introduction to the story just before he died, in which he mentioned a "long and confining illness" that had prevented him from answering his fan mail. But reviewers knew he had gone. "L. Frank Baum has left a host of sincere mourners in the children who have traveled with him . . . through that marvelous land of Oz," wrote *Publishers Weekly.* "The wonderful land will yield no more of its magical secrets," read a review in the New York *Sun*, "this is the end of the trail." In 1920, *Glinda of Oz* was published, the final Oz novel that Baum had completed in his brass bed toward the very end of his life. The author hadn't written an introduction, so the publishers decided to tell the truth in their own. "Mr. Baum did his best to answer all the letters from his small earth-friends before he had to leave them," it read. "In May,

1919," it continued, "he went away to take his stories to the little child-souls who had lived here too long ago to read the Oz stories for themselves."

That summer of 1920, Maud was given the one thing her mother (and husband) had fought so hard for: the right to vote. In August 1920, the Nineteenth Amendment was signed, which gave women the right to vote in all elections at both the federal and state levels.

Baum's publishers, now Reilly & Lee, knew that he had made the Land of Oz so believable that it lived on beyond its initial creator; the series was so successful that if someone else were to pen more stories from Oz, they could surely sell them. They contacted a young and lively children's author named Ruth Plumly Thompson and, with Maud's approval, asked her to continue the series. Thompson had grown up reading the Oz books, and she felt familiar enough with the Land of Oz to take on the grand appointment of Royal Historian. But having taken on the job, she admitted she felt she was "clumping around in another man's boots." *The Royal Book of Oz*, her first Oz novel, was published in 1921, and she would keep alive the world that Baum had first discovered in 1898, by writing an Oz book every year until 1939.

The year 1920 marked the beginning of a decade of rapid transformation in Hollywood. When Frank and Maud had moved there in 1910, the population of the little rural town was five thousand; by 1920 it had mushroomed to thirty-six thousand and was continuing to grow. And by 1920, forty million Americans were going to the movies every week. Hundreds of small studios had sprung up in the suburbs of Los Angeles, pumping out movie after movie to meet the mounting demand for electric dreams. In the twenties, Universal, Warner Brothers, MGM, and Fox emerged as the major studios, and grew into little kingdoms ruled by powerful producer-kings. And the movie star came into being. These were earthbound humans, but their faces and bodies appeared the size of giants on screens across the country, and people began to dream about them. They soon became glamorous commercial gods who earned unimaginable salaries, far more than the the nation's president. Streams of hopeful budding actors flooded to Hollywood in the 1920s, their heads full of fantasies of stardom. The town was becoming so overrun with out-of-work actors that the chamber of commerce took out advertisements in newspapers, warning others to stay away. "Don't try to break into the movies in Hollywood," one announced. Only five in every one hundred thousand people who came to town, the notice explained, made it big in the industry. Hollywood had become a dream factory full of disillusionment, a twentieth-century Emerald City.

The Hollywood landscape was totally transformed in the 1920s from a quiet, undeveloped rural suburb of fields, woodlands, and fruit groves into an urban center of high-rise apartment buildings, hotels, stores, restaurants, and offices. In 1923, real estate investors put up a huge advertisement in the hills above Hollywood for a newly built housing development called Hollywoodland. Fifty-foot-high gleaming white letters studded with four thousand lightbulbs rose above the hills, like names in lights on Broadway. This advertising stunt cost the developers the vast amount of twenty-one thousand dollars, and it was meant to stay up for only a year or so. As the twenties progressed, the letters remained standing and people began to like them. The sign was changed simply to HOLLYWOOD and the bulbs were all stolen. The letters announced the small town to the heavens and expressed the growing sense that, as the center of filmland, this was a place of real importance. The town seemed to shout its name from the hilltops.

Hollywood roared drunkenly through the twenties, despite Prohibition. The town's numerous speakeasies and nightclubs were all-night stages where film stars showed off their wealth, glamour, and power and exercised the psychological ghouls that often accompanied stardom. The gossip rags were full of news of partying and scandal.

Grand palaces for showing the products of the moviemaking frenzy opened in Hollywood in the twenties. Sid Grauman built the Egyptian Theater in 1922, an extravagant building of sphinxes and hieroglyphics. In 1927, Grauman's Chinese Theater opened on Hollywood Boulevard. This exotic, flamboyant movie house featured an imported pagoda and authentic Chinese artifacts. Passing between the huge orange pillars with giant faces staring down, visitors entered a palatial interior in jade, red, and gold, with hanging orange Chinese lanterns and walls covered with clawed dragons engulfed in marble flames. Grauman's popular Egyptian and Chinese theaters had the exotic glamour of the movie industry written into their architecture, and suggested that cinemas were emporiums of otherworldly treasures. Films promised to take people out of themselves.

Maud continued to live alone at Ozcot, not a mile from Grauman's Chinese Theater, as multistory buildings went up all around her. She existed in a pocket of the late nineteenth century, surrounded by photographs, books, clothes, and objects from an era that was fast disappearing. She continued to do her ironing with the old flatiron heated on the stove, even though electric irons were available. She drove her heavy sedan downtown often, passing through a place transformed. Change whirled around Ozcot but the house remained roughly the same as it had been when Baum was alive. Maud did occasionally have a clear-out. She found a trunk full of Baum's handwritten manuscripts of Oz novels, and thinking nobody would ever want them, she took them out into the garden in which many of them had been written, and burned them. The notepaper covered in Baum's neat, black, spidery handwriting must have crackled as it was consumed by the flames.

Moving pictures began to speak in 1927 when Warner Brothers released *The Jazz Singer*, the first full-length sound feature film. The film industry made the painful transition to sound over the next few years; silent film stars, including Charlie Chaplin, found it difficult to make the change. Many stars were foreign-born and their accents didn't translate well onto the quintessentially American screen. Greta Garbo had elocution lessons, and Chaplin, if he did have to speak, preferred to do so in nonsense, made-up languages. If film could talk, then it could surely sing; Hollywood soon began to make musicals, and scores of all-singing, all-dancing movies followed.

The 1929 Wall Street crash brought some of the partying in Hollywood to an end. A devastating economic depression swept across America in the 1930s and early 40s. The film industry didn't completely collapse; jobs were lost and salaries cut, but people continued to go to the movies. For a relatively low price, a film offered a brief respite from the brutal realities of many people's lives.

In the early 1930s, when America was in the grip of the Great Depression, film producer Samuel Goldwyn approached Maud for the film rights to *The Wonderful Wizard of Oz*. She explained that the copyright had been lost in 1910 to pay off debts. Goldwyn's lawyers investigated and discovered that the royalties to Baum's Bowen-Merrill and Bobbs-Merrill books were likely to have paid off all his debt years previously, possibly as early as 1916. Baum obviously hadn't inquired about the royalty payments to his creditors. The lawyers retrieved the copyright for Maud, and Goldwyn bought the film rights to *The Wonderful Wizard of Oz* from her.

But nothing further happened until Walt Disney released *Snow White and the Seven Dwarfs* in 1937, the first full-length animated feature. Naysayers, including Walt's wife, had tried to stop Disney from pushing ahead with the project, dubbed "Disney's Folly." "No one's gonna pay a dime to see a dwarf picture," Lillian Disney had told her husband. It cost 1.5 million dollars to make, a vast sum; Disney was even forced to mortgage his house to fund it. The film took three years to complete, in part because it was made with the new, astounding, glowing colors produced by a filming process called Technicolor. When *Snow White* was released in 1938, reviewers and audiences went wild for it. The film made millions in profit and remains one of the top ten box office hits of all time. Disney had proved that it was possible to make a feature-length fairy tale if you made it with enough pizzazz.

In 1938, the vast MGM Studios was completing a film on average every nine days. Producers decided the time was right to make *The Wizard of Oz* as their big-budget status movie of the year and bought the rights from Goldwyn, who wasn't, despite his name, part of the studio. MGM was inspired to make the film by some of the very same things that had influenced Baum when he first wrote the story back in 1898. Disney's *Snow White* was taken from the Grimms' collection of old folktales, which Baum had read, loved, and feared as a child.

Importantly, the plot of Baum's story had space to acknowledge the economic situation of the 1930s. The Depression had been deepened for rural midwesterners by drought and dust storms. If the Great Plains had been reduced to a cracked desert that seared into Baum's memory in the 1890s, in the thirties it became a dust bowl. After decades of extensive farming, deep plowing, and then drought, the grasses that held the topsoil in place had died. Gigantic dust storms gathered up the soil into giant clouds of earth that roared across the plains and buried homesteads; acres and acres of farmland became useless. Thousands abandoned the land and migrated west to California to look for work; these were not Hollywood hopefuls but starving "Okies." *The Wizard of Oz* would reflect the realities of the thirties in the opening Kansas scenes, and then whisk audiences away with Dorothy to a lush, colorful wonderland where they would be entertained by the highly skilled vaudeville antics of Ray Bolger as the Scarecrow, Jack Haley as the Tin Man, and Bert Lahr as the Cowardly Lion. The Land of Oz was a colorful escape from reality, and a mirror of cinema itself.

In 1938, MGM Studios was a miniature city containing the most highly skilled and dedicated set designers and builders, costume designers and makers, special effects artists and makeup artists in Hollywood. The studio hired the top composers, the biggest orchestra, and the best screen writers, directors, and actors. This enormous and intricate machine set to work on Baum's story.

Baum's original book was at the center of the production from the start. Gilbert Adrian, the talented costume designer, took Denslow's drawings from the first edition of *The Wonderful Wizard of Oz* as his model. The studio searched for a dog to play Toto that looked just like the one in Denslow's drawings, and the costumes for the Scarecrow and the Tin Man were based directly on Denslow's originals. Baum had described Dorothy's dress as blue-and-white gingham and so it would be. Taking a cue from Baum's descriptions of gray Kansas, and Denslow's illustrations in the first edition, which were gray in the Kansas section and moved into color in Oz, the studio had the idea to film the Kansas scenes in black-and-white and Oz in the glowing hues of Technicolor.

The film looked back to Baum's world in other ways too. It took the plot of the 1902 musical and had the travelers escape from the poisoned poppy field with a cooling snowstorm conjured by Glinda the Good Witch. Ray Bolger, who played the Scarecrow in the movie, admitted that his vaudeville hero was Fred Stone, who had played the Scarecrow in Baum's musical extravaganza.

The special effects experts set to work on many of the magical scenes that would be needed to create an amazing but believable fairy tale. They invented some new and unique effects, such as the spinning Kansas twister, designed by an ex-pilot, but they also used many established film tricks that went all the way back to Baum's stage illusions and trick films.

Far from being a separate world, the magnificent studio that set about making production "1060," as *The Wizard of Oz* was labeled, was deeply connected to the world in which Baum had written the original story. Many of the actors who were cast in the picture had grown up reading the book; Margaret Hamilton, who was cast as the Wicked Witch of the West, had loved the book since she first read it at age four. The story was already inside most of the people who set about the monumental task of turning it into a movie in 1938.

After at least ten screenwriters had worked on the script, filming began in October 1938. Maud "became engulfed in that magical world" of movie-making and she visited the set. She might have toured the many vast stages in which different parts of Kansas and Oz were being painstakingly put together. The entire film would be shot on-site. Huge canvas backdrops of the yellow brick road disappearing into the distance, the gates of the Emerald City, and the witch's castle were being painted. Some of these sets had miniature doubles; there was a tiny Gale Kansas homestead, for instance, behind which a thirty-five-foot tapered muslin funnel was dragged as powerful wind machines blew powdery earth up inside it, to create the frighteningly realistic tornado.

Who knows if Maud saw Ray Bolger, made up in his Scarecrow costume, studying the racing form between takes and sending a stagehand out each day to place his bets on the horses; or if she noticed that Frank Morgan, who played Professor Marvel and the humbug Wizard, carried an old suitcase around with him; it was filled with the ingredients to make martinis.

Putting this vibrant fairy tale together over the next five months was extremely hard work. In fact, it was a pretty tortuous process. It wasn't easy to make ordinary humans appear believable as fantastic characters in a fantastic world. Toto was played by a fearful, shy terrier called Terry; she and Carl Spitz, her trainer, were pushed to their limits as scenes were filmed over and over again. Terry particularly hated the ferocious wind machines that blew gales across the Kansas set, and she hid behind the legs of her costars. Lahr, Bolger, Haley, and Hamilton were subjected to the daily ordeal of getting into their costumes and makeup. Margaret Hamilton arrived at the crack of dawn each morning to be coated in a copper-based green makeup that stained her skin for months after shooting was complete. Haley was covered in an aluminium paste that prevented his skin from breathing, and he couldn't sit down once he was encased in his silver papier-mâché Tin Man costume. But Lahr surely had it the worst. His costume was two real lion skins sewn together and lined with mattress padding. The Technicolor filming process required very strong lighting, and the sets were lit with thousands of lamps that beamed burning hot light onto the actors. MGM even had to borrow more lights from other studios, and an extra generator was added to boost the local grid to produce sufficient electricity for this super-powered, luminescent production. Poor Bert Lahr sweated and almost suffocated in the heat. Between takes, stagehands unpeeled his costume to reveal him dripping in sweat beneath. He'd be dried and cooled before being stuffed back into the skins. Lahr couldn't eat in his costume except through a straw, so at lunch he sucked up soups and milk shakes. Some people fainted in the unbearable heat on set, so the studio occasionally opened the back doors wide to let in some air. Actors in otherworldly costumes and wigs would gather outside to cool off.

In November, 124 little people arrived at MGM to play the Munchkins. They were all measured for costumes and plastered in all kinds of elaborate wigs and makeup. Towering above these middle-aged men and women was sixteen-year-old Judy Garland, squeezed into a gingham dress, her breasts bound beneath her shirt. She sat on the yellow brick road with the little actors during the Christmas season of 1938 and shared a huge box of chocolates with them. The Munchkin actors had been brought in from across America and they all lived together during filming, at the Culver City Hotel. Some were seasoned actors and vaudeville players, but others had never been on stage or even seen another little person before, and had left small hometowns to find themselves suddenly at the center of Hollywood.

Actors weren't the only ones to be coated in colors by the frantic makeup artists and set dressers at MGM; a number of ducks were accidentally dyed blue by the dye in the water of the stream in Munchkin City, and the Emerald City cab horse of a different color was in fact three different horses sponged all over in colored Jell-O powder.

There were a few on-set accidents. Two Los Angeles jockeys buckled into flying monkey suits fell crashing to the stage floor when the piano wires that flew them through the Haunted Forest snapped, as the recorded and then reversed sounds of thousands of singing birds echoed around them. Margaret Hamilton was severely burned when she disappeared from Munchkin City in plumes of red smoke and orange flames, and Betty Danko, her stand-in, was blown off her broomstick and badly hurt while filming the skywriting sequence.

Shooting was finally complete in March 1939, and editors and sound specialists took over. At a screening in June, several terrified children had to be removed from the auditorium because the Wicked Witch of the West frightened them so much. Hamilton was just too good, and MGM decided to cut many of her scenes and lines. In the first cut of *The Wizard of Oz*, the cackling green witch who would come to haunt so many children's nightmares in years to come was even more prominent than in the final version.

MGM pumped out extravagant publicity lies worthy of P. T. Barnum. "A total of 9,200 actors faced the camera in *The Wizard of Oz*," claimed one press release; "3,210 costumes were designed and made, 8,428 separate make-ups were . . . applied to faces," it went on. This was all nonsense; there were six hundred actors in the film and just under one thousand costumes were made. The studio also claimed that one of the few costumes that wasn't made on-site was Professor Marvel's long black velvet-collared coat, which was bought in a secondhand store. Wearing the coat, so the story went, Morgan put his hand in a pocket and pulled out a label with the name "L. Frank Baum" written on it. The studio claimed that further investigation confirmed that the coat had belonged to Baum. This story had the whiff of publicity about it, but it showed that the studio wanted to connect the production to the original creator of Oz, and include him in the film in some way.

In a publicity photo taken at MGM, Maud and Judy Garland were photographed reading a first edition of *The Wonderful Wizard of Oz* together and having tea. Maud wore a black-and-white polka-dot dress that tied in a ruffle at the neck.

The Wizard of Oz had its Hollywood premiere at Grauman's Chinese Theater on August 15, 1939. On the other side of the world, war was raging in the Pacific after Japan had invaded China. In September, France and Britain would declare war on Nazi Germany after Hitler's troops invaded Poland. Winston Churchill, the British prime minister, would later vividly recall that Australian troops sang "We're off to see the Wizard" as they marched into battle. The entrance of *The Wizard of Oz* into the world in the summer and fall of 1939 became entangled in many people's memories with the outbreak of World War II.

Maud attended the premiere alone. She wore a fluffy fur coat with a big metal brooch of a flower on her shoulder, and strolled up the red carpet outside Grauman's. She stood on a podium and was interviewed by the teeming hordes of press, and was so overwhelmed by the experience that she didn't notice the numerous members of her own family waving and shouting to her from the crowd. She then walked between the orange pillars of the pagoda and took her red velvet seat among movie executives, actors, and press. The lights went down and a giant sepia circle appeared on the screen framing the head of Leo, the MGM lion, who roared in a most uncowardly way. Then the title *The Wizard of Oz* spread across the screen, and a choir of female voices sang in a haunting howl, like a gathering storm. The opening scene on the Kansas prairie at the Gale homestead must have taken Maud back, not only to her husband's original story but to her sister's homestead in North Dakota, which had inspired Baum.

But when Judy Garland sang "Somewhere Over the Rainbow," the song that had come into composer Harold Arlen's mind out of the blue as he drove past Grauman's Chinese Theater a year earlier, everyone was surely astounded. Judy sang the song with such a deep longing and yearning for some place where she wouldn't "get into any trouble," somewhere "beyond the moon, beyond the rain." Maud had known that feeling back in drought-ridden South Dakota in the 1880s. The ferocious, twisting tornado that ripped Dorothy from Kansas was so convincing, it must have also reminded Maud of the tornado strikes back in the Dakotas all those years ago.

Everyone that hot summer night would have been amazed when Dorothy stepped out of her gray wooden house into the Technicolor Land of Oz. The reds, jades, and oranges of the "Chinese" auditorium glowed in the Technicolor hues. The bright yellows, greens, blues, and reds of the film leapt off the screen and bored into people's retinas. The magic Ruby Slippers were an amazing transformation of Baum's original silver shoes. They glinted and glowed on screen, pulsating like the blood of something alive. The thousands of sequins stitched by hand onto silk caught the light and sparkled as Dorothy skipped along the yellow brick road. They were the brightest things on screen and looked like two hot embers about to burst into flame.

Maud was reunited with the characters she had lived with for forty years, the Scarecrow, the Tin Man, and the Cowardly Lion, but she might have looked askance at the two witches of Oz. In her baby-pink princess frock, Glinda was far more soppy than Baum's more earthy good witch clairvoyant. The Wicked Witch of the West in the movie was a terrifying character from the oldest folklore, unlike the less frightening witch in Baum's original book. Here the green-faced, cackling witch was a powerful force of impotent evil, a dark energy that pulsates just below the surface throughout the film.

Maud was used to seeing Baum's story chopped about, as in the 1902 musical, so it probably didn't surprise her that much of the original story was cut from the film. Gone were the Hammerheads and the Dainty China Country. The film also made much more of Dorothy's desire to return home to Kansas than Baum's book did. This aspect of the story hadn't quite made sense in the original book and here too it didn't ring true. Why does Dorothy want so badly to return to monochrome Kansas, to the family that doesn't listen to her and the vicious schoolteacher (Miss Gulch) who threatens to destroy Toto? Baum had of course sent Dorothy back to live permanently in Oz in subsequent books because it had become impossible for her to live in America; the depression of the 1930s must have made this seem true in the hot summer of 1939, which made Dorothy's keening for Kansas even less convincing.

The one enormous and unforgivable difference between Baum's original story and the movie was the film's ending. In Baum's book, Dorothy clicked the heels of her magic shoes together three times, flew through a mysterious space somewhere above America, and physically returned with a bump to the grassy plains on the homestead, where Uncle Henry had built a new wooden farmhouse. The old house had, after all, flown with her to Oz in the tornado and landed on the Wicked Witch of the East. In contrast, the film made the Land of Oz into the product of a delirium, of illness brought on by a bump to the head. This connected obliquely to Baum's original story in that Oz was in part inspired by the deaths of many children and the need to imagine their souls traveling about in a joyous heaven specially designed for children. But in other ways, this ending was a gross betrayal of the story. Baum hadn't created the Land of Oz as a child's delirious vision, a vaporous place imagined by a broken mind. He had conjured Oz in a moment of absolute clarity. The land was a vital and living place for Baum and all those who read his books.

"There's no place like home," chimed Dorothy before the words "The End" appeared on the screen and the credits began to roll. The lights came up, and Maud, along with everyone else in the audience, must have blinked as the sepia colors of Kansas slowly faded from their minds. She returned to a movie theater in which Baum was absent (or present only as a ghost). But the theater had been filled with the inner workings of Baum's imagination, reincarnated in this magical moving picture, in the cinematic form he had seen back in 1914 as the story's natural destiny. Baum's imagination had been reborn in the film, as it would be over and over again in the later twentieth century and beyond.

The End

Acknowledgments

I couldn't have completed the extensive research and travel for this book without the generous financial support of The Leverhulme Trust and The British Academy. I thank them heartily. Thanks to David Bradshaw, Laura Marcus, Ellen Hughes, and Dominic Pisano for their kind support for my grant applications. A summer researching and writing in New York City wouldn't have been possible without the hospitality of Suzanne Tremblay at the Gershwin Hotel, where I was writer-in-residence for one summer. A big thanks to Suzanne for making me so welcome. Thanks also to Joel Oury, the hotel manager, for making my stay so enjoyable and productive. Todd Thorn kindly let me tag along on his storm-chasing tour through Tornado Alley.

For their expertise and help, I would like to thank the archivists and librarians at The New York Public Library; The Special Collections Research Center, Syracuse University; The Matilda Joslyn Gage Foundation; The Onondaga Historical Association, Syracuse; The Butler Library, Columbia University; The Beinecke Rare Book and Manuscript Library, Yale University; The New York State Library; The Bodleian Library, Oxford University; and The Library of Congress.

Many people in the places where Baum lived gave me their time and knowledge generously during my visits. Thanks to Mike Quirk and Terry Ross at the L. Frank Baum Museum in Chittenango, and to Clara Houck for tea in Baum's home village. Thomas Howard and Robert Henry were unbelievably generous with their extensive research into all kinds of important details about the Baums of Syracuse. Their ongoing commitment to preserving the oak groves of Baum's childhood is inspiring.

Thanks to Mr. Augustowski at the Peekskill Military Academy Alumni

Society for showing me around Peekskill and sharing his collection of academy memorabilia with me. Thanks also to John J. Curran at The Peekskill Museum. Judy English kindly accompanied me on a tour of Oakwood Cemetery in Syracuse and helped me find the Baum family plot. I fondly recall how moved we were that hot summer afternoon to see the graves of Baum's many siblings who died in infancy. Thanks to Peter Hanff, Peter Glassman, Gita Dorothy Morena, and Justin G. Schiller for sharing their Oz and Baum expertise. Thanks to John and Pat Fowler for their help in researching Baum and Oz in the United States. Thanks to Olivia Plender for taking me to a séance at the Spiritualist Church in London, and accompanying me to a Magic Lantern show. A big thanks to friends for their hospitality during research trips to America: to Tanio McCallum for letting me stay with her in Nyack, to Jon Fasman and Alissa Krimsky for putting me up in Brooklyn, and to Yasmin Khan for the room and company in Washington, DC.

A massive thanks to those hospitable friends who offered me space to write: Peter Howitt and Elizabeth Pink for letting me stay with them during the early stages of the writing at La Pena, Tarifa, surrounded by strong ocean winds, tinkling cowbells, and mischievous pigs. Thanks to John and Vicki Brice for letting me write in their lovely house in France. Thanks to Steve and Della Moran for the Cornwall cottage, and to Abigail Reynolds and Andy Harper for their hospitality at Assembly in Cornwall.

A giant thanks to James Gill and Zoe Pagnamenta, my agents, for believing in this project and in me. Many thanks to William Shinker at Gotham for taking this book on. Thanks to Erin Moore, my first editor at Gotham, for her fantastic help getting the book up and running; and to my subsequent editor, Jessica Sindler, for her patience, support, and insightful reading of the manuscript as it emerged. Thanks to everyone at Gotham and Penguin USA for their hard work on this project. Emma Tinker couldn't have been a more efficient and reliable typist, and I'm extremely grateful to her for her help.

Thanks to Yasmin Khan and Tanio McCallum for reading drafts and offering such honest and generous feedback. Thanks to Floyd Skloot for the writing advice. A million thanks for the support and humor of those many friends who patiently listened to my persistent ideas about Oz and Baum, and accompanied me to many Oz-related films and shows of varying quality: Joe Luscombe, Harriet Bell, Andrew Marsham, Farrhat Arshad, Harriet

Jaine, Leon Wilson, Abigail Reynolds, Brontë Flecker, Ant Bale, Tim Phillips, Mina Gorgi, Louise K. Wilson, Olivia Plender, Daria Martin, Zillah Eagles, Oliver and Betina Brice, Helen Carr, Richard Caplan, Luisa Cale, Carolyn Cowey, Jane, Maddy, and Mercedes White, Roger Sweet, Christine Schick, and Joe Griffiths.

Thanks to my extended family, the Lindesays and the Loncraines, for their love and support over the years, especially my grandmothers, Lena Shanley and Elizabeth Lindesay. My love and all the thanks in the world must go to my Mum and Dad, Trisha and Tony Loncraine. I thank them for their love, and for nurturing and encouraging my imagination throughout my childhood, for taking stories seriously, and for giving me a copy of Baum's *The Wonderful Wizard of Oz* and a VHS of the MGM movie when I was very young. I thank them also for their unflinching support throughout the research and writing of this book.

Finally, I want to thank Ben Brice, for his love and encouragement, for accompanying me on my travels in America, for reading this book at all its stages, and offering such thoughtful and honest advice. I dedicate this book to him with my real love.

Notes on Sources

General Remarks

The family tree at the beginning of this book is designed to help the reader understand who is who in Baum's story, and how they are all related. It cites only those people I mention in the book and isn't a comprehensive family tree. Where I haven't been able to find birth or death dates, I have marked a "?"

I have created this portrait of L. Frank Baum and his world through meticulous research. This research has taken many forms. In the bibliography, the reader will find a list of Baum's major works and the secondary reading I consulted, with full bibliographical references for all the citations mentioned here. The enormously helpful books containing material on Baum's life that I used throughout this portrait are: Baum and Macfall's *To Please a Child: A Biography of L. Frank Baum, Royal Historian of Oz*; Hearn's *The Annotated Wizard of Oz*; Rogers's *L. Frank Baum, Creator of Oz: A Biography*; Carpenter and Shirley's *L. Frank Baum, Royal Historian of Oz*; Gardener's "The Royal Historian of Oz" in *The Wizard of Oz and Who He Was*; Morena's *The Wisdom of Oz: Reflections of a Jungian Sandplay Therapist*; and Riley's *Oz and Beyond: The Fantasy World of L. Frank Baum*.

The vast majority of my research material on Baum's life, his family, publishing history, and early writing came from *The Baum Bugle*, a journal of Oz and Baum matters published since 1957 by the International Wizard of Oz Club. The enthusiasts and editors at *The Baum Bugle* worked tirelessly to bring into print lost works by Baum, and extremely valuable interviews and memoirs by Baum family members who knew Frank. There is a collection of *Bugles* in the New York Public Library.

I consulted various archives containing material on Oz, Baum, and his times: The Special Collections Research Center, Syracuse University; The Onondaga Historical Association, Syracuse; The New York Public Library; The Butler Library, Columbia University; The Beinecke Rare Book and Manuscript Library, Yale University Library; The Alexander Mitchell Library, Aberdeen, South Dakota; The New York State Library; the Matilda Joslyn Gage Foundation in Fayetteville, New York; and the Library of Congress.

Visits to the places where Baum lived, worked, and wrote were very useful; pounding the streets of Syracuse, looking up at buildings Baum would have known well, provided physical details of his world. I was extremely moved by the Baum plot in Oakwood Cemetery, where the stone markers of Baum's four siblings who died in infancy emerged from out of the clover. Walking through Matilda Gage's house in Fayetteville, owned by The Matilda Joslyn Gage Foundation, was extremely helpful. Aberdeen, South Dakota, has changed much since the 1890s, but the vast grass prairies that surround it have continued to depopulate. I was privileged to visit the site of the Wounded Knee Massacre on Pine Ridge Reservation, a simple, stark cemetery in the midst of rolling grassland. The lack of resolution over the treatment of the Lakota people is still palpable.

Purkiss's *At the Bottom of the Garden: A Dark History of Fairies, Hobgoblins, and Other Troublesome Things* and Briggs's *The Fairies in Tradition and Literature* provided useful histories of folklore and fairies.

PART I

Weisberg's *Talking to the Dead: Kate and Maggie Fox and the Rise of Spiritualism* gives a full account of the lives of the Fox sisters. Dye and Smith offer a helpful context for understanding the importance of infant mortality in the era in "Mother Love and Infant Death, 1750–1920." Ferrara's *The Family of the Wizard: The Baums of Syracuse* is a history of the Baum extended family in central New York State. Material on the Baums and the oak groves near Rose Lawn was generously provided by Thomas Howard and Robert Henry. I am grateful to Tom and Bob for walking me through the oak woodlands of Baum's childhood, now known as "The Wizard of Oz Oak Grove." I found further material on life in Syracuse in Baum's day in the Onondaga Historical Association in Syracuse, an extraordinary archive of different aspects of life in the region. A tour of Chittenango with Mike Quirk was very fruitful, particularly when we pulled over to sniff the pungent air from what used to be the Salt Springs. The L. Frank Baum Museum in Chittenango provided the letters by Benjamin Baum Sr. and family photographs. A tour of Peekskill with Mr. Augustowski of the Peekskill Military Academy Alumni Society was helpful, as was Curran's *Peekskill*. Adam Clarke Baum's Civil War letters are housed in the archives of The New York State Library.

PART II

The Baum papers in the Alexander Mitchell Library in Aberdeen, South Dakota, provided much essential research for Part II. Copies of the *Aberdeen Saturday Pioneer* are housed in the library, along with the private collection of letters, photographs, and Baum-related documents donated to the library by Baum's niece, Matilda Jewell Gage. This collection contains Baum's marriage certificate and Clarkson Gage's enormous scrapbook of Aberdeen history. The library also has an excellent collection of books on local history. The Dakota Prairie Museum, Aberdeen, provided further useful details about the area. For essential material on Baum's time in South Dakota, I relied heavily on *Our Landlady*, edited by Tystad Koupal, and *Baum's Road to Oz: The Dakota Years*, also edited by Koupal. Readers will find Baum's "Our Landlady" and "Editor's Musings" columns in these collections. Memoir essays by Matilda Jewel Gage, published in *The Baum Bugle*, provided useful family details. Driving around Aberdeen and through South and North Dakota, the Badlands, Pine Ridge, and the Black Hills provided me with essential landscape details. On the extraordinary western weather, I used Laskin's *Braving the Elements* and *The Children's Blizzard*, and also Norris's *Dakota: A Spiritual Geography*. I also went storm chasing across the vast midwestern plains, and was caught in an epic storm while crossing Pine Ridge Reservation. I was terrified out of my wits; thanks to Ben for getting us out of there safely. On the Native Americans of Dakota I relied on Utley's *The Lance and the Shield: The Life and Times of Sitting Bull*, Fowler's *The Columbia Guide to the American Indians of the Great Plains*, Frazier's *Great Plains* and *On the Rez*, Black Elk and Neihardt's *Black Elk Speaks: Being the Life Story of a Holy Man of the Oglala Sioux*, Lear's *Radical Hope: Ethics in the Face of Cultural Devastation*, Nabokov's *Native American Testimony: A Chron-*

icle of Indian-White Relations from Prophecy to the Present, 1492–2000 and
Where the Lightning Strikes: The Lives of American Indian Sacred Places, and
Mooney's *The Ghost-Dance Religion and Wounded Knee*. Butler and Lansing's
The American West is a good history of the region.

PART III

In this part, Baum's writing finally appears and it is this that offers the best
insight into his mind from here on in. You can find everything you want to
know about the history of American hot air ballooning in Couch's *The Eagle
Aloft: Two Centuries of the Balloon in America*. Wagner's *Sisters in Spirit:
Haudenosaunee (Iroquois) Influence on Early American Feminists* offers an ac-
count of the role of the Iroquois in Matilda Joslyn Gage's thinking. On the
history of Chicago and the World's Fair, I consulted Appelbaum's *The
Chicago World's Fair of 1893: A Photographic Record*, Gilbert's *Perfect Cities:
Chicago's Utopias of 1893*, Larson's *The Devil in the White City*, Platt's *The
Electric City: Energy and the Growth of the Chicago Area, 1880–1930*, Rydell's
*All the World's a Fair: Visions of Empire at American International Expositions,
1876–1916*, and Mayer and Wade's *Chicago: Growth of a Metropolis*. For
histories of electricity and its social impact, I used Nye's *Electrifying America:
Social Meanings of a New Technology, 1880–1940* and *American Technological
Sublime*, and Davis's *TechGnosis: Myth, Magic and Mysticism in the Age of
Information*. Copies of *The Show Window* are held in the Beinecke Rare
Book and Manuscript Library, Yale University Library. An edition of *The Art
of Decorating Dry Goods Windows and Interiors* is held in The Butler Library,
Columbia University. Swartz's *Oz Before the Rainbow: L. Frank Baum's The
Wonderful Wizard of Oz on Stage and Screen to 1939* has a detailed account
of the 1902 musical extravaganza *The Wizard of Oz*.

PART IV

Zitkala-Ša's *American Indian Stories, Legends, and Other Writings* contains
many of the Native American stories that would have been available to
Baum. Maud Baum's letters provide all the details about her and Frank's trip
to Europe and North Africa, and they were published privately as *In Other
Lands than Ours* in 1907. Winchester's *A Crack in the Edge of the World: The
Great American Earthquake of 1906* is a full account of the San Francisco

earthquake. Swartz's *Oz Before the Rainbow: L. Frank Baum's The Wonderful Wizard of Oz on Stage and Screen to 1939* has a detailed description of the *Fairylogue and Radio-Plays*. Ted Hughes's poem "Shire Horses" from *What Is the Truth?* best expresses the emotional loss felt by some people after the disappearance of horses.

Part V

Swartz's *Oz Before the Rainbow* has details about The Oz Film Manufacturing Company. *The Baum Bugle* has numerous articles on Baum's films. Prints of the films are held in the Library of Congress film archive, but some have been included as DVD extras accompanying new editions of the MGM movie.

Afterlife

For the behind-the-scenes story of the making of the 1939 MGM movie, see Harmetz's *The Making of the Wizard of Oz*, Cox's *The Munchkins of Oz*, Thomas's *The Ruby Slippers of Oz*, Carroll's *I, Toto: The Autobiography of Terry, the Dog Who Was Toto*, and Salman Rushdie's essay for the British Film Institute, *The Wizard of Oz*.

A Selected Bibliography
of Works by L. Frank Baum

Baum's Oz Novels

The Wonderful Wizard of Oz (George M. Hill, Chicago 1900)

The Marvelous Land of Oz (Reilly & Britton, Chicago, 1904)

Ozma of Oz (Reilly & Britton, Chicago, 1907)

Dorothy and the Wizard in Oz (Reilly & Britton, Chicago, 1908)

The Road to Oz (Reilly & Britton, Chicago, 1909)

The Emerald City of Oz (Reilly & Britton, Chicago, 1910)

The Patchwork Girl of Oz (Reilly & Britton, Chicago, 1913)

Tik-Tok of Oz (Reilly & Britton, Chicago, 1914)

The Scarecrow of Oz (Reilly & Britton, Chicago, 1915)

Rinkitink in Oz (Reilly & Britton, Chicago, 1916)

The Lost Princess of Oz (Reilly & Britton, Chicago, 1917)

The Tin Woodman of Oz (Reilly & Britton, Chicago, 1918)

The Magic of Oz (Reilly & Britton, Chicago, 1919)

Glinda of Oz (Reilly & Lee, Chicago, 1920)

Other books published under the name L. Frank Baum

Baum's Complete Stamp Dealers Directory (1873): Norris & Co.

The Book of the Hamburgs (1886): H. H. Stoddard

Mother Goose in Prose (1897): Way and Williams

By the Candelabra's Glare (1898): Privately printed by Baum

Father Goose, His Book (1899): George M. Hill

The Songs of Father Goose (1900): George M. Hill

The Art of Decorating Dry Goods Windows and Interiors (1900): Show Window Publishing Company

The Army Alphabet (1900): George M. Hill

The Navy Alphabet (1900): George M. Hill

A New Wonderland (1900): R. H. Russell

American Fairy Tales (1901): George M. Hill

Dot and Tot of Merryland (1901): George M. Hill

The Master Key (1901): Bowen-Merrill

The Life and Adventures of Santa Claus (1902): Bobbs-Merrill

The Enchanted Island of Yew (1903): Bowen-Merrill

The Surprising Adventures of the Magical Monarch of Mo and His People (1903): Bobbs-Merrill

Queen Zixi of Ix (1905): Century

The Woggle-bug Book (1905): Reilly & Britton

John Dough and the Cherub (1906): Reilly & Britton

Father Goose's Year Book (1907): Reilly & Britton

Baum's American Fairy Tales (1908): Bobbs-Merrill

Juvenile Speaker (1910): Reilly & Britton

The Sea Fairies (1911): Reilly & Britton

The Daring Twins (1911): Reilly & Britton

Baum's Own Book for Children (1911): Reilly & Britton

Phoebe Daring (1912): Reilly & Britton

Sky Island (1912): Reilly & Britton

The Little Wizard Series (six volumes) (1913): Reilly & Britton

The Little Wizard Stories of Oz (1914): Reilly & Britton

The Snuggle Tales—"Little Bun Rabbit," "Once Upon a Time," "The

Yellow Hen," "The Magic Cloak" (1916): Reilly & Britton (reissued as the *Oz-Man Tales*)

The Snuggle Tales (six volumes) (1917): Reilly & Britton

Babes in Birdland (1917): Reilly & Britton

Books by Baum published anonymously or under pen names

Schuyler Staunton
The Fate of a Crown (1905): Reilly & Britton

Daughters of Destiny (1906): Reilly & Britton

Laura Bancroft
The Twinkle Tales (six volumes) (1906): Reilly & Britton

Policeman Bluejay (1907): Reilly & Britton

Twinkle and Chubbins (1911): Reilly & Britton

Capt. Hugh Fitzgerald
Sam Steele's Adventures on Land and Sea (1906): Reilly & Britton

Sam Steele's Adventures in Panama (1907): Reilly & Britton

Suzanne Metcalf
Annabel, A Novel for Young Folks (1906): Reilly & Britton

Edith Van Dyne
Aunt Jane's Nieces (1906): Reilly & Britton

Aunt Jane's Nieces Abroad (1907): Reilly & Britton

Aunt Jane's Nieces at Millville (1908): Reilly & Britton

Aunt Jane's Nieces at Work (1909): Reilly & Britton

Aunt Jane's Nieces in Society (1910): Reilly & Britton

Aunt Jane's Nieces and Uncle John (1911): Reilly & Britton

The Flying Girl (1911): Reilly & Britton

Aunt Jane's Nieces on Vacation (1912): Reilly & Britton

The Flying Girl and Her Chum (1912): Reilly & Britton

Aunt Jane's Nieces on the Ranch (1913): Reilly & Britton

Aunt Jane's Nieces Out West (1914): Reilly & Britton

Aunt Jane's Nieces in the Red Cross (1915): Reilly & Britton

Mary Louise (1916): Reilly & Britton

Mary Louise in the Country (1916): Reilly & Britton

Mary Louise Solves a Mystery (1917): Reilly & Britton

Aunt Jane's Nieces in the Red Cross (1918): Reilly & Britton

Mary Louise and the Liberty Girls (1918): Reilly & Britton

John Estes Cooke
Tamawaca Folks (1907): Tamawaca Press

Anonymous
*The Last Egyptian; a Romance of the Nile (*1908): Edward Stern

Floyd Akers
The Boy Fortune Hunters in Alaska (1908): Reilly & Britton

The Boy Fortune Hunters in Panama (1908): Reilly & Britton

The Boy Fortune Hunters in Egypt (1908): Reilly & Britton

The Boy Fortune Hunters in China (1909): Reilly & Britton

The Boy Fortune Hunters in Yucatan (1910): Reilly & Britton

The Boy Fortune Hunters in the South Seas (1911): Reilly & Britton

Plays I mention
The Mackrummies, 1882

The Maid of Arran, 1882

Matches, 1882

The Wizard of Oz, 1902

Prince Silverwings, 1903

The Woggle-Bug, 1905

Fairylogue and Radio-Plays, 1908

The Tik-Tok Man of Oz, 1913

Short stories I mention

"A Cold Day on the Railroad," *Chicago Sunday Times-Herald*, May 26, 1895

"My Ruby Wedding Ring," copyrighted 1896

"Yesterday at the Exposition," *Chicago Sunday Times-Herald*, February 2, 1896

"The Return of Dick Weemins," *The National Magazine*, July 1897

"The Suicide of Kiaros," *The White Elephant*, September 1897

"The Loveridge Burglary," *Short Stories*, January 1900

"American Fairy Tales," *Chicago Chronicle* and other newspapers, March 3 to May 19, 1901

"Queer Visitors from the Marvelous Land of Oz," syndicated by the *Philadelphia North American*, August 28, 1904, to February 26, 1905

"Animal Fairy Tales," *The Delineator*, January to September 1905

"Nelebel's Fairyland," *The Russ*, June 1905

Journalism I mention

"A Russian Wedding," *Aberdeen Daily News*, July 24, 1889

Editor and contributor, *The Aberdeen Saturday Pioneer*, January 1890 to April 1891

Editor, *The Western Investor*, August to November, 1890

Editor, *The Show Window*, November 1897 to October 1900

"What Children Want," *Chicago Evening Post*, November 29, 1902

"Modern Fairy Tales," *The Advance*, August 19, 1909

"Our Hollywood," *Hollywood Citizen*, December 31, 1915

Poems I mention

"The Latest in Magic," *Chicago Sunday Times-Herald*, May 31, 1896

"Coronado: The Queen of Fairyland," *San Diego Union* and *Daily Bee*, March 5, 1905

"To Macatawa, a Rhapsody," *Grand Rapids Sunday Herald*, September 1, 1907

Exhaustive Bibliographies of Baum's total published output can be found in Michael Patrick Hearn, *The Annotated Wizard of Oz*, and Michael O. Riley, *Oz and Beyond: The Fantasy World of L. Frank Baum*.

Selected Bibliography

Ackroyd, Peter. *Dickens*. (London: Vintage, 2002)

Appelbaum, Stanley. *The Chicago World's Fair of 1893: A Photographic Record*. (New York: Dover Publications, 1980)

Adams, Rachel. *Sideshow USA: Freaks and the American Cultural Imagination*. (Chicago: University of Chicago Press, 2001)

Andersen, Hans Christian. Trans. Tina Nunnally. *Fairy Tales*. (New York: Penguin, 2004)

Armstrong, Isobel. *Victorian Glassworlds*. (Oxford: Oxford University Press, 2008)

Armstrong, Karen. *A Short History of Myth*. (Edinburgh: Canongate, 2005)

Armstrong, Tim. *Modernism, Technology and the Body*. (Cambridge: Cambridge University Press, 1998)

Bachelard, Gaston. Trans. Maria Jolas. *The Poetics of Space*. (Boston, Massachusetts: Beacon, 1994)

Baudrillard, Jean. Trans. Chris Turner. *America*. (London and New York: Verso, 1988)

The Baum Bugle, 1957–present. Journal of the International Wizard of Oz Club.

Baum, Frank Joslyn, and Macfall, Russell P. *To Please a Child: A Biography of L. Frank Baum, Royal Historian of Oz*. (Chicago: Reilly & Lee, 1961)

Baum, Maud Gage. *In Other Lands than Ours*. (Chicago: Privately printed, 1907)

Bellamy, Edward. *Looking Backward*. (1897) (Oxford: Oxford University Press, 2007)

Benjamin, Walter. Trans. Harry Zohn. *Illuminations*. (London: Fontana, 1992)

Besant, Annie. *The Ancient Wisdom: An Outline of Theosophical Teachings*. (London: Theosophical Publishing Society, 1897)

Bettelheim, Bruno. *The Uses of Enchantment: The Meaning and Importance of Fairy Tales*. (London: Thames and Hudson, 1976)

Black Elk and Neihardt, John G. *Black Elk Speaks: Being the Life Story of a Holy Man of the Oglala Sioux*. (1932) (Lincoln: University of Nebraska Press, 1988)

Madame Blavatsky. *Isis Unveiled: A Master-Key to the Mysteries of Ancient and Modern Science and Theology*. 2 Vols. (London: The Theosophical Publishing House, 1877)

Blum, Deborah. *Ghost Hunters: William James and the Search for Scientific Proof of Life After Death*. (New York: The Penguin Press, 2006)

Bodanis, David. *Electric Universe: How Electricity Switched on the Modern World*. (London: Abacus, 2006)

Bogdan, Robert. *Freak Show: Presenting Human Oddities for Amusement and Profit*. (Chicago: University of Chicago Press, 1988)

Bowlby, Rachel. *Carried Away: The Invention of Modern Shopping*. (London: Faber and Faber, 2000)

Boyt, Susie. *My Judy Garland Life*. (London: Virago, 2008)

Brammer, Leila R. *Excluded from Suffrage History: Matilda Joslyn Gage, Nineteenth Century American Feminist*. (Westpoint, Connecticut: Greenwood Press, 2000)

Brands, H. W. *The Age of Gold*. (London: Arrow, 2006)

Briggs, Asa. *Victorian Things*. (Stroud, UK: Sutton Publishing, 2003)

Briggs, Katharine. *The Fairies in Tradition and Literature*. (London: Routledge, 1967)

Brogan, Hugh. *The Penguin History of the USA*. (London: Penguin, 2001)

Brown, Dee. *The American West*. (London: Pocket Books, 1994)

Butler, Anne M., and Lansing, Michael J. *The American West.* (Oxford: Blackwell, 2008)

Calvino, Italo. Trans. William Weaver. *Invisible Cities.* (San Diego: Harcourt Brace, 1972)

Capote, Truman. *In Cold Blood.* (1966) (London: Penguin, 2000)

Carpenter, Angelica Shirley, and Shirley, Jean. *L. Frank Baum, Royal Historian of Oz.* (Minneapolis: Lerner Publications, 1992)

Carroll, Lewis. *Alice's Adventures in Wonderland* and *Through the Looking Glass.* (1865 and 1871) (London: Penguin, 1998)

Carroll, Willard. *I, Toto: The Autobiography of Terry, the Dog Who Was Toto.* (New York: Stewart, Tabori & Chang, 2001)

Carter, Angela (ed.) *The Virago Book of Fairy Tales.* (London: Virago, 1990)

———. (ed.) *The Second Virago Book of Fairy Tales.* (London: Virago, 1993)

Cather, Willa. *My Antonia.* (1918) (London: Virago, 1980)

Christie, Ian. *The Last Machine: Early Cinema and the Birth of the Modern World.* (London: British Film Institute, 1994)

Clarke, William. *The Boy's Own Book.* (Bedford, Massachusetts: Applewood, 1829)

Clarke, Graham. *The Photograph.* (Oxford: Oxford University Press, 1997)

Collier, G., Hasselstrom, L., and Curtis, N. (eds.). *Leaning into the Wind: Women Write from the Heart of the West.* (New York: Houghton Mifflin, 1997)

Cottom, Daniel. "On the Dignity of Tables," *Critical Inquiry*, Vol. 14, No.4 (Summer, 1988)

Cox, Stephen. *The Munchkins of Oz.* (Nashville, Tennessee: Cumberland House, 1989)

Couch, T. *The Eagle Aloft: Two Centuries of the Balloon in America.* (Washington, DC: Smithsonian Books, 1983)

Crichton, Judy. *America 1900: The Sweeping Story of a Pivotal Year in the Life of the Nation.* (New York: Henry Holt, 1998)

Culver, Stuart. "Growing up in Oz," *American Literary History* (Winter 1992)

————. "What Manikins Want: The Wonderful Wizard of Oz and The Art of Decorating Dry Goods Windows," *Representations* 21 (Winter, 1988)

Cunningham, Michael. *Specimen Days.* (London: Harper Perennial, 2005)

Curran, John J. *Peekskill.* (Charleston, South Carolina: Arcadia, 2005)

Davis, Erik. *TechGnosis: Myth, Magic and Mysticism in the Age of Information.* (London: Serpent's Tail, 1999)

Donaghy, Michael (ed.). *101 Poems about Childhood.* (London: Faber and Faber, 2002)

Donald, James, Friedberg, Anne, and Marcus, Laura (eds.). *Close up 1927–1933: Cinema and Modernism.* (London: Cassell, 1998)

Dearborn, R. F. *Saratoga and How to See It.* (1872)

Dye, Nancy Schrom, and Smith, Daniel Blake. "Mother Love and Infant Death, 1750–1920," *The Journal of American History*, Vol. 73, No. 2 (September, 1986)

Earle, Neil. *The Wonderful Wizard of Oz in American Popular Culture: Uneasy in Eden.* (Lewiston: Edwin Mellen Press, 1994)

Erlich, Gretel. *The Solace of Open Spaces.* (London: Penguin, 1985)

————. *A Match to the Heart.* (New York: Pantheon, 1994)

Ekirch, A. Roger. *At Day's Close: A History of Nighttime.* (London: Phoenix, 2006)

Erdoes, Richard, and Ortiz, Alfonso (eds.). *American Myths and Legends.* (New York: Pantheon, 1984)

————. (eds*.) American Indian Trickster Tales.* (London: Penguin, 1999)

Eyles, Allen. *The World of Oz.* (Tuscon: HP Books, 1985)

Ferrara, Susan. *The Family of the Wizard: The Baums of Syracuse.* (Xlibris Corporation, 2000)

Ford, Alla T., and Martin, Dick. *The Musical Fantasies of L. Frank Baum.* (Chicago: Wizard Press, 1958)

Fowler, Loretta. *The Columbia Guide to the American Indians of the Great Plains.* (New York: Columbia University Press, 2003)

Frazier, Ian. *Great Plains.* (1989) (London: Granta, 2006)

————. *Family.* (New York: Picador, 1994)

————. *On the Rez.* (New York: Picador, 2000)

Freud, Sigmund. Translated from the German under the general editorship of James Strachey, in collaboration with Anna Freud. *The Standard Edition of the Complete Psychological Works of Sigmund Freud: Volume 4. The Interpretation of Dreams (First Part).* (1900) (London: Vintage, 2001)

Fricke, John. *100 Years of Oz.* (New York: Stewart, Tabori and Chang, 1999)

Gage, Helen Leslie. "L. Frank Baum: An Inside Introduction to the Public," *The Dakotan*, 1903

Gage, Matilda Joslyn. "Woman as an Inventor," *North American Review*, 1883. (The Matilda Joslyn Gage Reader Series, published by the Matilda Joslyn Gage Foundation, 2006)

————. *Woman, Church and State.* (1893) (Aberdeen, South Dakota: Sky Carrier Press, 1998)

Garber, Marjorie. *Symptoms of Culture.* (London: Penguin, 1999)

Gardener, Martin. "The Royal Historian of Oz," in *The Wizard of Oz and Who He Was.* (East Lansing, Michigan: Michigan State University Press, 1957)

Gilbert, James. *Perfect Cities: Chicago's Utopias of 1893.* (Chicago: University of Chicago Press, 1991)

Goldsmith, Barbara. *Other Powers.* (London: Granta, 1998)

Grimm, J. L. C. and W. C., Maria Tatar (ed.), *The Annotated Brothers Grimm.* (New York: Norton, 2004)

Harmetz, Aljean. *The Making of the Wizard of Oz.* (New York: Dell, 1977)

Hearn, Michael Patrick (ed.) *The Annotated Wizard of Oz.* (New York: Norton, 1973, 2000)

————. (ed.) *The Victorian Fairy Tale Book.* (New York: Pantheon, 1988)

————. "Discovering Oz (the Great and Terrible) at the Library of Congress," *The Quarterly Journal of the Library of Congress*, Vol. 39. No. 2 (Spring 1982)

Hendrickson, Robert. *The Grand Emporiums: The Illustrated History of America's Great Department Stores.* (New York: Stein and Day, 1979)

Hopkins, Albert A. *Magic: Stage Illusions and Scientific Diversions, including Trick Photography.* (London: Low 1897)

Houck, Clara M. *Journey to Oz: The History of L. Frank Baum.* (Chittenango: Privately printed, 1983)

Hyde, Lewis. *The Gift.* (Edinburgh: Canongate, 2006)

———. *Trickster Makes This World.* (Edinburgh: Canongate, 2008)

Jacobs, Joseph. *English Fairy Tales.* (1890 and 1894) (London: Frederick Muller, 1942)

Jenkins, Philip. *A History of the United States.* (Basingstoke: Palgrave Macmillan, 2003)

Jolly, Martyn. *Faces of the Living Dead.* (London: The British Library, 2006.)

Koolhaas, Rem. *Delirious New York.* (London: Thames and Hudson, 1978)

Koupal, Nancy Tystad (ed.). *Baum's Road to Oz: The Dakota Years* (Pierre: South Dakota State Historical Society Press, 2000)

———. (ed.) *Our Landlady.* (Lincoln: University of Nebraska Press, 1996)

Lahr, John. *Notes on a Cowardly Lion: The Biography of Bert Lahr* (1969). (London: Bloomsbury, 1992)

Lang, Andrew (ed.). *The Blue Fairy Book*, 1889

———. (ed.). *The Red Fairy Book*, 1890

———. (ed.). *The Green Fairy Book*, 1892

———. (ed.). *The Yellow Fairy Book*, 1894

———. (ed.). *The Pink Fairy Book*, 1897

———. (ed.). *A Book of Dreams and Ghosts*, 1897

Larson, Erik. *The Devil in the White City.* (London: Doubleday, 2003)

Laskin, David. *Braving the Elements.* (New York: Doubleday, 1969)

———. *The Children's Blizzard.* (New York: Harper Perennial, 2004)

Leach, William. *Land of Desire: Merchants, Power, and the Rise of a New American Culture.* (New York: Pantheon Books, 1993)

Leadbeater, C. W. *The Astral Plane: It's Scenery, Inhabitants and Phenomena.* (London: Theosophical Publishing Society, 1895)

Lear, Jonathan. *Radical Hope: Ethics in the Face of Cultural Devastation.* (Cambridge, Massachusetts: Harvard University Press, 2006)

Lesy, Michael. *Wisconsin Death Trip.* (New York: Doubleday, 1973)

Littlefield, Henry M. "The Wizard of Oz: Parable on Populism," *American Quarterly*, Vol. 16, No.1 (Spring, 1964)

Mannguel, Alberto, and Guadalupi, Gianni. *The Dictionary of Imaginary Places.* (London, Bloomsbury, 1999)

Marshall, Joseph M III. *The Journey of Crazy Horse: A Lakota History.* (London: Penguin, 2004)

Mayer, Harold M., and Wade, Richard C. *Chicago: Growth of a Metropolis.* (Chicago: University of Chicago Press, 1969)

McManus, Chris. *Right Hand, Left Hand: The Origins of Asymmetry in Brains, Bodies, Atoms and Cultures.* (London: Pheonix, 2002)

Mooney, James. *The Ghost-Dance Religion and Wounded Knee.* (New York: Dover, 1991)

Morena, Gita Dorothy. *The Wisdom of Oz: Reflections of a Jungian Sandplay Therapist.* (Berkeley: Frog, 1998)

Murch, Walter. *In the Blink of an Eye.* (Los Angeles: Silman-James, 2001)

Nabokov, Peter (ed.). Native *American Testimony: A Chronicle of Indian-White Relations from Prophecy to the Present, 1492–2000.* (London: Penguin, 1999)

———. *Where the Lightning Strikes: The Lives of American Indian Sacred Places.* (London: Viking, 2006)

Norris, Kathleen. *Dakota: A Spiritual Geography.* (Boston and New York: Houghton Mifflin, 1993)

Nye, David E. *Electrifying America: Social Meanings of a New Technology, 1880–1940.* (Cambridge, Massachusetts: MIT Press, 1992)

———. *American Technological Sublime.* (Cambridge, Massachusetts: MIT Press, 1994)

Phillips, Adam. *Houdini's Box: On the Arts of Escape.* (London: Faber and Faber, 2001)

Picker, John M. *Victorian Soundscapes*. (Oxford: Oxford University Press, 2003)

Pilbeam, Pamela. *Madame Tussaud and the History of the Waxworks*. (London: Hambledon and London, 2003)

Platt, Harold L. *The Electric City: Energy and the Growth of the Chicago Area, 1880–1930*. (Chicago: University of Chicago Press, 1991)

Preston, Richard. *The Wild Trees: A Story of Passion and Daring*. (New York: Random House, 2007)

Purkiss, Diane. *At the Bottom of the Garden: A Dark History of Fairies, Hobgoblins, and Other Troublesome Things*. (New York: New York University Press, 2003)

Rabinovitz, Lauren. *For the Love of Pleasure: Women, Movies, and Culture in Turn-of-the-Century Chicago*. (New Brunswick, New Jersey: Rutgers University Press, 1998)

Riley, Michael O. *Oz and Beyond: The Fantasy World of L. Frank Baum*. (Lawrence, Kansas: University Press of Kansas, 1997)

Robinson, David. *From Peep Show to Palace: The Birth of American Film*. (New York: Columbia University Press, 1996).

Rodgers, Daniel T. "Socializing Middle-Class Children: Institutions, Fables, and Work Values in Nineteenth-Century America," *Journal of Social History*, Vol.13, No. 3 (Spring 1980)

Rodley, Chris (ed.). *Lynch on Lynch*. (London: Faber and Faber, 2005)

Rogers, Katharine M. *L. Frank Baum, Creator of Oz: A Biography*. (New York: St Martin's Press, 2002)

Roterberg, A. *The Modern Wizard*. (Chicago, 1896)

Rushdie, Salman. *The Wizard of Oz*. (London: British Film Institute, 1992)

Ruskin, John. *On Art and Life*. (London: Penguin Books, 2004)

Rydell, Robert W. *All the World's a Fair: Visions of Empire at American International Expositions, 1876-1916*. (Chicago: University of Chicago Press, 1984)

Sante, Luc. *Low Life: Lures and Snares of Old New York*. (London: Granta, 1991)

Scarry, Elaine. *Dreaming by the Book.* (Princeton, New Jersey: Princeton University Press, 1999)

Solnit, Rebecca. *River of Shadows: Eadweard Muybridge and the Technological Wild West.* (Harmondsworth, UK: Viking, 2003)

———. *A Field Guide to Getting Lost.* (Edinburgh: Canongate, 2006)

Stacey, Jackie. *Star Gazing: Hollywood Cinema and Female Spectatorship.* (London: Routledge, 1994)

Stannard, David E. *American Holocaust: The Conquest of the New World.* (Oxford: Oxford University Press, 1992)

Stearns, Peter N., and Haggerty, Timothy. "The Role of Fear: Transitions in American Emotional Standards for Children," *The American Historical Review*, Vol. 96, No. 1 (February 1991)

Steele, Valerie. *The Corset: A Cultural History.* (New Haven: Yale University Press, 2001)

Stratton, Joanna L. *Pioneer Women: Voices from the Kansas Frontier.* (New York: Simon and Schuster, 1981)

Swartz, Mark Evan. *Oz Before the Rainbow: L. Frank Baum's The Wonderful Wizard of Oz on Stage and Screen to 1939.* (Baltimore, Maryland: Johns Hopkins University Press, 2000)

Thomas, Rhys. *The Ruby Slippers of Oz.* (Los Angeles: Tale Weaver Publishing, 1989)

Updike, John. "Oz Is Us," *The New Yorker* (September 2, 2000)

Usai, Cherchi. Trans. Emma Sansone Rittle. *Burning Passions: An Introduction to the Study of Silent Cinema.* (London: British Film Institute, 1994)

Utley, Robert M. *The Lance and the Shield: The Life and Times of Sitting Bull.* (London: Pimlico, 1993)

Vendler, Helen (ed.). *The Anthology of Contemporary American Poetry.* (London: I. B. Tauris, 2003)

Vidal, Gore. "The Wizard of the 'Wizard,'" *The New York Review of Books*, 24:15 (September 29, 1977), and "On Rereading the Oz Books," *The New York Review of Books*, 24:16 (October 13, 1977)

Volpe, Tod M., and Cathers, Beth. *Treasures of the American Arts and Crafts Movement, 1890–1920* (London: Thames and Hudson, 1988).

Wagner, Sally Roesch. *Sisters in Spirit: Haudenosaunee (Iroquois) Influence on Early American Feminists.* (Summertown, Tennessee: Native Voices, 2001)

Waller, Gregory A. (ed.). *Moviegoing in America* (Oxford: Blackwell, 2002).

Warner, Marina. *From the Beast to the Blonde.* (London: Vintage, 1995)

———. *Phantasmagoria.* (Oxford: Oxford University Press, 2006)

Weisberg, Barbara. *Talking to the Dead: Kate and Maggie Fox and the Rise of Spiritualism.* (San Francisco: HarperCollins, 2004).

Welsh, Irvine, and Cavanagh, Dean. *Babylon Heights.* (London: Vintage, 2006)

Wheeler, Marjorie Spruill (ed.). *One Woman, One Vote: Rediscovering the Woman Suffrage Movement.* (Troutdale, Oregon: NewSage Press, 1995)

Winchester, Simon. *A Crack in the Edge of the World: The Great American Earthquake of 1906.* (London: Penguin, 2006)

Wood, Gaby. *Living Dolls: A Magical History of the Quest for Mechanical Life.* (London: Faber and Faber, 2002)

Workers of the Federal Writer's Project Works Program, South Dakota. *Unfinished Histories: Tales of Aberdeen and Brown County.* (Mitchell: South Dakota Writer's League, 1938)

Wullschlager, Jackie. *Hans Christian Andersen: The Life of a Storyteller.* (London: Penguin, 2000)

Zipes, Jack. *When Dreams Came True: Classical Fairy Tales and Their Tradition.* (London: Routledge, 1998)

———. (ed.). *The Oxford Companion to Fairy Tales.* (Oxford: Oxford University Press, 2000)

Zitkala-Ša. *American Indian Stories, Legends, and Other Writings.* (1901) (London: Penguin, 2003)

Index

About the Author

Rebecca Loncraine was born in England and grew up on a hill farm in the Black Mountains of Wales, and as a child was immersed in folktales and the Land of Oz. Rebecca has a doctorate in literature from Oxford University. She is a freelance writer and writes regularly for national UK publications, including the *Independent*, the *Guardian*, and the *Times Literary Supplement*, and she teaches creative writing workshops in Oxford and London.